# LIVES OF VICTORIAN LITERARY FIGURES IV

SERIES EDITOR: RALPH PITE
VOLUME EDITORS: JANET BEER
SARAH ANNES BROWN
ELIZABETH NOLAN
JANE SPIRIT

# LIVES OF VICTORIAN LITERARY FIGURES IV

VOLUME 1: OSCAR WILDE
VOLUME 2: HENRY JAMES
VOLUME 3: EDITH WHARTON

LIVES OF VICTORIAN LITERARY FIGURES IV

OSCAR WILDE, HENRY JAMES AND EDITH WHARTON
BY THEIR CONTEMPORARIES

VOLUME
2

# HENRY JAMES

EDITED BY
SARAH ANNES BROWN

LONDON
PICKERING & CHATTO
2006

Published by Pickering & Chatto (Publishers) Limited
21 Bloomsbury Way, London WC1A 2TH

2252 Ridge Road, Brookfield, Vermont 05036-9704, USA
www.pickeringchatto.com

All rights reserved.
No part of this publication may be reproduced,
stored in a retrieval system, or transmitted in any form or by any means,
electronic, mechanical, photocopying, recording, or otherwise
without prior permission of the publisher.

© Pickering & Chatto (Publishers) Limited 2006

BRITISH LIBRARY CATALOGUING IN PUBLICATION DATA

Lives of Victorian literary figures
   Part 4: Henry James, Edith Wharton and Oscar Wilde by their contemporaries
   1. Authors, English – 19th century – Biography   2. Great Britain – History –
Victoria, 1837–1901 – Biography
   I. Pite, Ralph   II. Mullan, John   III. Beer, Janet, 1956–   IV. Brown, Sarah
Annes   V. Spirit, Jane
820.9'008

ISBN-10: 1851968148

∞

This publication is printed on acid-free paper that conforms to the
American National Standard for the Permanence of Paper for Printed Library
Materials

*New material typeset by P&C*

*Printed and bound in Great Britain by*
*CPI Bath, Bath*

# CONTENTS

| | |
|---|---|
| Acknowledgements | vii |
| Introduction | ix |
| Bibliography | xxv |
| Chronology | xxix |
| Copy Texts | xxxiii |
| Abbreviations | xxxv |

| | | |
|---|---|---|
| 1. | W. D. Howells, 'Henry James, Jr.', *Century Magazine* | 1 |
| 2. | London Society | 11 |
| | a) E. S. Nadal, 'Personal Recollections of Henry James', *Scribner's Magazine* | 15 |
| | b) Justin McCarthy, *Reminiscences* | 24 |
| 3. | Edmund Gosse, *Aspects and Impressions* | 25 |
| 4. | Jacques-Emile Blanche, *Portrait of a Lifetime* | 65 |
| 5. | Henry James and Scandal | 75 |
| | a) Violet Hunt, 'The Last Days of Henry James', *Daily Mail* | 79 |
| | b) Violet Hunt, *The Flurried Years* | 81 |
| | c) Vincent O'Sullivan, *Aspects of Wilde* | 98 |
| 6. | A. C. Benson, *Memories and Friends* | 99 |
| 7. | Detachment and Morality | 117 |
| | a) Desmond MacCarthy, *Portraits* | 119 |
| | b) F. M. Colby, 'The Queerness of Henry James', *Bookman* | 140 |
| 8. | Mrs Humphrey Ward, *A Writer's Recollections* | 143 |
| 9. | Compton Mackenzie, 'Henry James', *Life and Letters Today* | 159 |
| 10. | Henry James and the Theatre | 173 |
| | a) W. Graham Robertson, *Time Was* | 175 |
| | b) Henry Mackinnon Walbrook, 'Henry James and the English Theatre', *Nineteenth Century* | 180 |
| 11. | Hamlin Garland, *Roadside Meetings* | 185 |
| 12. | Ford Madox Ford, *Mightier than the Sword* | 201 |

13. Henry James in Rye ... 229
    a) A.G. Bradley, 'Henry James As I Knew Him: The Human
       Side of a Great Novelist', *John O' London's Weekly* ... 231
    b) Ella Hepworth Dixon, *As I Knew Them* ... 235
    c) Matilda Betham-Edwards, *Mid-Victorian Memories* ... 239
    d) Anon., 'General Gossip of Authors and Writers',
       *Current Literature* ... 248
14. Henry James's Photographers ... 249
    a) Alice Boughton, 'A Note by his Photographer',
       *Hound and Horn* ... 251
    b) Alvin Coburn, *Men of Mark* ... 254
15. Hugh Walpole, 'Henry James; A Reminiscence', *Horizon* ... 259
16. Muriel Draper, *Music at Midnight* ... 269
17. Interviews ... 283
    a) Witter Bynner, 'A Word or Two with Henry James', *Critic* ... 285
    b) Preston Lockwood, 'Henry James's First Interview',
       *New York Times* ... 288
18. Obituaries (29 February 1916) ... 293
    a) *Daily Telegraph* ... 295
    b) *The Times* ... 299
    c) *Daily Mail* ... 301

Notes ... 303

# ACKNOWLEDGEMENTS

I would like to thank several people for their helpful suggestions and support. It was particularly useful to receive advice from Simon Grimble (editor of the Ruskin volume in *Lives of Victorian Literary Figures III*) at the early stages of the project. Tamara Follini suggested some very helpful lines of enquiry when I was selecting extracts for inclusion. Several members of VICTORIA: The Electronic Conference for Victorian Studies answered queries relating to the endnotes: Andrea Broomfield, Jennifer Foster, James Gregory, Linda Hunt Beckman, Paul Lewis, Kirsten MacLeod, Patricia Rigby and Beth Sutton-Rampseck. Thanks also to Julie Dashwood, who checked my translations from French, German and Italian. I am grateful to Pat Brown of Bookbox, Stow-on-the-Wold, for lending me several volumes of writings by and about James, and to Catherine Reid, the Lucy Cavendish College librarian, for her help in tracking down other material. I would like to thank both Alex Brown and Ralph Pite for their helpful comments on the introduction. I am particularly grateful to Marian Olney at Pickering & Chatto for her patient and informed support at all stages of the project.

# INTRODUCTION

> Harry is as nice and simple and amiable as he can be. He has covered himself, like some marine crustacean, with all sorts of material growths, rich sea-weeds and rigid barnacles and things, and lives hidden in the midst of his strange heavy alien manners and customs; but these are all but 'protective resemblances,' under which the same dear old, good, innocent and at bottom very powerless-feeling Harry remains, caring for little but his writing, and full of dutifulness and affection for all gentle things.[1]

The works of Henry James (in particular the short stories) reveal a fascination with issues of reading, interpretation and biography. The best known examples are perhaps 'The Figure in the Carpet' (1896) – in which the novelist Hugh Vereker tantalises the critic narrator by hinting at a secret pattern in all his works – and *The Aspern Papers* (1888), the tale of an American editor's campaign to acquire the love letters of a fictional poet, Jeffrey Aspern. Given these, and many other tales with similarly reflexive themes, it is scarcely surprising that the afterlife of Henry James (both creative and critical) is marked by a succession of interpenetrations of various kinds between art and reality. The boundaries between fact and fiction become blurred, as hard to police as the membrane between truth and delusion in *The Turn of the Screw* (1898). Historical accounts and fictional responses overlap, and different voices – those of James, his fictional creations, his biographers and critics – mysteriously elide. Fiction reflects but also anticipates and even appears to create reality.

Although biography and fiction are usually perceived as clearly distinct genres, even the most straightforward biographies draw on some of fiction's techniques to bring pattern and order to the lives of their subjects. And fictional works – such as Shakespeare's *Richard III* – have had a huge impact on the later biographical record of historical characters. Fiction's mediation of Henry James began in his own lifetime – H. G. Wells criticised and parodied his style in *Boon* (1915) and Ford Madox Ford claimed to have used

---

[1] Henry James Jr, (ed.), *The Letters of William James*, 2 vols (London: Longman, Green, and Co., 1920), vol. i, p. 288).

him as the model for Henry VIII in *The Fifth Queen* (1907–8). More recently Henry James has been the inspiration for several novels. The central character of Alan Hollinghurst's *The Line of Beauty* (2004) is writing a thesis on James; Dan Simmons's *A Winter Haunting* (2002) is a rewriting of 'The Jolly Corner' (1908); while James himself is the central character of David Lodge's *Author, Author* (2004), Emma Tennant's *Felony* (2003) and Colm Tòibìn's *The Master* (2004). However some of the most intriguing fictional responses to Henry James can be found, not in the comparatively realistic novelisations of Lodge or Tòibìn, but in earlier ostensibly biographical accounts of his life and works. Many exponents of such creative biography are represented in this volume. Ford Madox Ford, for example, blends fiction with fact as beguilingly as he incorporated events and situations from his own life into his best known novel, *The Good Soldier*. Two further examples, not included here but widely available elsewhere, similarly reflect the literary and creative flair of their authors, Rebecca West and Gertrude Stein.

Rebecca West is best known for her novels – including *The Return of the Soldier* (1918) and *The Fountain Overflows* (1957) – as well as for her journalism, in particular her reports on the Nuremberg Trials. But at the very beginning of her long career, in 1916 when she was just twenty-four, West wrote an exuberant brief biography of James. This is a witty, whimsical and opinionated piece. She remarks tartly of the younger James that he only judged women according to 'their failures and successes as sexual beings; which is like judging a cutlet not by its flavour, but by the condition of its pink-paper frill' (West, p. 85). West also departs from convention when she gives her subject a voice. Here she imagines James's reflections on the Aesthetic movement:

> It seems to me that the cry of 'Art for Art's sake,' which is being raised by those young men, and which certainly isn't true for *them*, may be true for *me*. What if henceforth I release the winged steed of my recording art from the obligation of dragging up the steep hill of my inaptitude the dray filled with the heavy goods which I have amassed in my perhaps so mistaken desire for a respectably weighty subject, and let the poor thing just beautifully soar? (West, p. 84)

This self-conscious transgression of the boundary between biography and fiction is a move associated more readily with later biographers such as Peter Ackroyd.

But the most unusual 'biography' of James is surely Gertrude Stein's essay 'Henry James', written in 1933–4, and later included in a larger work, *Four in America* (1947). Readers hoping for information about James's works, family or friends will be disappointed. Gertrude Stein is a notoriously impenetrable writer and *Four in America* is a characteristically opaque piece which reinvents each of its four protagonists, turning George Washington into a novelist, Ulysses S. Grant into a religious leader, Wilbur Wright into a painter and James himself into a military general. It suggests a sense of competing possibilities and alternate universes, thus inviting the reader to explore multiple truths rather than insist on a single version of reality.

> Think how you can change your mind concerning this matter.
> Think how carefully you can say this.
> If you can say this carefully, you can either not change your mind concerning this matter, or you can act entirely differently, that is, you can change your mind concerning this matter.
> Remember how Henry James was or was not a general.[2]

She moves far away from the quest for the 'real' Henry James, offering instead a deconstruction of the biographical subject. John Ashbery describes Stein's works as an attempt to 'create a counterfeit of reality more real than reality'[3] and although *Four in America* presses the limits of biography, it can be read suggestively as a metabiography, which uses its four Americans to construct an account of the biographical project more generally. Through its alertness to the processes of biography, *Four in America* operates as commentary on the way iconic figures such as James become elusive through their very familiarity and as a reminder of the limitations inherent in any textual representation of a life.

Typical of Stein's movement away from any effect of mimesis is her claim that there were in fact three Jameses. Caramello[4] suggests this may be a reference to James's memoirs in which 'Henry James' is simultaneously the youthful subject, the self-conscious persona, and the elderly writer himself. In other ways too, James's autobiographical project anticipates Stein's more radically unmimetic portrait. Like Proust, James communicates a sense of the multiple selves which might be said to exist within a single individual, determined either by one's different roles (the second volume of James's autobiography was tellingly entitled *Notes of a Son and Brother*) or by the changes effected by time. Although less startling than Stein, James's novelistic manipulation of facts (his merging of two European trips into a single journey for example) and his revisions to the letters he quotes from members of his family – his nephew was shocked by the way he changed William James's words – indicate his willingness to ignore the conventional boundaries between fact and fiction (Edel, v, pp. 460–1).

---

[2] Gertrude Stein, *Four in America* (Freeport: Books for Libraries Press, 1967; 1st edn 1947), p. 128.

[3] John Ashbery, 'The Impossible', *Poetry* (July 1957), 250–4.

[4] Charles Caramello, *Henry James, Gertrude Stein, and the Biographical Act* (Chapel Hill: University of North Carolina Press, 1996), p. 178.

Stein's fractured portrayal of her subject is consistent with her overturning of normal biographical convention, and its usual tacit premise that factual accuracy should be sought as a means of recovering and reconstituting the biographical subject. Thus Stein's description of multiple Jameses may be false in the literal sense but has some validity as a description of 'Henry James', as constructed by the many writings (critical, (auto)biographical and creative) generated over the years. Individuals may only live once but, if they are celebrated, may generate any number of different 'lives':

> Epistemological or moral changes generate new concerns, stimulated by developments in science that revise our sense of time and space, or in morals that alter our notions of sexual freedom. As a genre, biography continually unsettles the past, maintaining its vitality through its continual correction, revision and interpretation of individual lives.[5]

Conforming to the developmental pattern Nadel identifies, 'Henry James' can be seen as a text which is subject to revision and reinterpretation. The same might be said of course of any prominent figure, but the process of biographical revision in this case acquires a special resonance because James himself was such a celebrated self-reviser who continued to alter his works long after their first publication, a trait which is shared by one of his many fictional alter egos, Dencombe, in the 1893 tale 'The Middle Years'. James's more general sense of the potential for one's life or works to change direction, for the choice to be made of one version of oneself over another, can be seen in one of his best known short stories 'The Jolly Corner'. Here he anticipates Stein's invocation of another James in a kind of alternate universe. The central character, Spencer Brydon, an American expatriate who is returning to New York for a short visit following an absence of thirty-three years, is clearly in part modelled on Henry James. As he revisits his property, his house on the 'jolly corner', he becomes aware of a haunting presence who is eventually revealed to be the man he would have become if he had never left America.

James anticipated Stein's 'biography' more precisely – and more strangely – in a series of curious texts dictated after he had suffered a stroke in 1915. His experiences of World War I had merged in his mind with his reading of Napoleonic memoirs, and his own persona and that of Napoleon are bizarrely fused together. In one letter (signed 'Napoléone') he addresses his dead brother and sister, telling them that he is enclosing plans for apartments in the Louvre and the Tuileries (*Notebooks*, p. 583). James's projection onto Napoleon is unlikely to have influenced Stein as the letters were not made available until after the chapter on James had been written (*Notebooks*, p. 581).

---

[5] Ira Bruce Nadel, *Biography: Fiction, Fact and Form* (London: Macmillan, 1984), p. 103.

As well as this odd apparent prefiguration of Stein's portrait of himself as a military leader, Henry James can also be seen to anticipate some of the broader shifts and developments within his biographical record in his own self-revisions. Both James (in his changes to the earlier novels) and his later biographers exaggerate his 'Jamesian' qualities and accentuate the homoerotic.

When he prepared his works for reissue in the New York Edition James made many alterations to his earlier works: 'Not only could he correct his old texts, but he could apply the varnish of his late style' (Edel, v, p. 333). This tendency can be seen at work if we compare two versions of a short passage from *The American*, the first from the 1883 edition, the second from the revised New York Edition.

> 'If I thought they talked ill of me to you, I should come down upon them.'
>
> 'They have let me alone, as you say. They have not talked ill of you.'
>
> 'In that case,' cried Newman, 'I declare they are only too good for this world!'
>
> 'If I thought they talked against me to you at all badly' – and he just paused – 'why I'd have to come in somewhere on *that*.'
>
> She reassured him. 'They've let me alone, as you say. They haven't talked against you to me at all badly.'
>
> It gave him, and for the first time, the exquisite pleasure of her apparently liking to use and adopt his words. 'Well then, I'm ready to declare them only too good for this world!'[6]

A similar self-revision is at work in section 5 of this volume, although here James himself is being tweaked. If we look at the two pieces by Violet Hunt, the first published in 1916, the second ten years later, it becomes clear that Hunt revised James's reported speech in order (rather in the manner of James's own self-revisions) to make it more characteristically, perhaps comically, 'Jamesian'. Thus:

> 'My dear Purple Patch,' he answered, 'because I wanted to be able to say "We" when I talked about an advance.' (p. 79)

becomes:

> He answered, 'My dear Purple Patch, chiefly because I wanted to be able to say *We* – with a capital – when I talked about an Advance.' (p. 93)

It seems as though Hunt, like James himself, thought the original words would be still more effective with the addition of a more characteristically Jamesian patina.

---

[6] This change is discussed by Philip Horne in *Henry James and Revision: the New York Edition* (Oxford: Clarendon Press, 1990), p. 181.

Violet Hunt's preference for truth of mood over fact was shared by her lover Ford Madox Ford. His comically baroque description of James's servant problems (see section 12), is in fact pure fantasy. However, as Simon Nowell Smith remarks in *The Legend of the Master*: 'Hueffers' imaginative inventions are often more plausible than the conscientious efforts at recollection of more sober historians.'[7] Nowell Smith's comment irresistibly recalls James's famous tale 'The Real Thing' (1892). Major and Mrs Monarch are an elegant and sympathetic couple whose reduced circumstances force them to seek work as artists' models. Although their employer is illustrating a novel dealing with high society he finds his authentic models curiously unsatisfactory compared with two 'fakes' who are working-class professionals. 'The Real Thing' is far less convincing than the specious imitation.

The same paradoxical achievement of authenticity through invention makes *The Master*, Tòibìn's portrait of Henry James, more vivid than that of David Lodge in *Author, Author*. The comparative colourlessness of the latter novel resonates with Carlyle's strictures on the limitations of facts: 'What are your historical Facts; still more your biographical? Wilt thou know a Man, above all a Mankind, by stringing-together beadrolls of what thou namest Facts?'[8] Whereas nearly every detail in Lodge is derived from printed records – indeed *Author, Author* often reads more like a biography than a novel – *The Master* presents an internalised Henry James many of whose thoughts and actions are Tòibìn's invention. Thus the effect of an inner life is produced – we know that James couldn't have left textual traces of all his ideas and that if we could read the mind of Henry James we would find something new and surprising. Tòibìn's speculations may all be factually wide of the mark, but the novel's blend of the familiar and the new, the sense of a secret door being opened on some of James's hidden thoughts and actions (however inauthentic) creates an effect of verisimilitude and revelation. The impression of bringing us closer to James even while departing from fact can be compared to the way a translation of a work in another language can bring (or seem to bring) us closer to the original by using anachronism or interpolation. *The Master* works better than *Author, Author* in the same way a wayward translation can convey the impact of the original more compellingly than a more linguistically faithful version.

One aspect of James which Tòibìn seeks to reconstitute in *The Master* is his sexuality. The same topic has increasingly been the focus of much research and speculation. Whatever he 'really' felt or did, homosexuality is clearly an important presence in recent biographical and critical studies of

---

[7] *The Legend of the Master* (London: Constable, 1947), p. xxix.
[8] Thomas Carlyle, *Sartor Resartus*, ed. by C. F. Harrold (New York: Odyssey Press, 1937; 1st edn 1833), p. 203.

Henry James. And it is certainly possible to trace hints at homosexuality in earlier biographical writings too. The numerous references to his special affinity with women (in sections 2a and 7a for example) perhaps operate in a similar coded way to phrases such as 'confirmed bachelor' in early twentieth-century obituaries. By contrast with such possible covert references is the apparently more unselfconscious, and thus more explicit, testimony of Mrs Humphrey Ward, who describes in some detail James's responsiveness to the beauty of a young Italian guide, Aristodemo, in section 8 of this volume. An altogether slyer and more arch allusion to James's supposed tastes is, I think, embedded in a fanciful narrative penned by Max Beerbohm in 1909. Here the ostensible subject is the unrequited passion of a Rye woman, Miss Peploe, for James but the subtext is rather more queer than this explicitly heterosexual outline would suggest. Miss Peploe is a writer of sonnets, explicitly modelled on Shakespeare's to Mr W. H., and her ardent expressions of love cast James in an improbably feminine role. After praising his lips like 'rose-leaves' she entreats him not to be 'damsel-coy' (Beerbohm, p. 23).

Homosexuality is invoked not just by the presence of Shakespeare's sonnets but also by a covert reference to Sappho. Beerbohm refers to another local poet who has been inspired by Miss Peploe's passion to write:

> The town of Rye, the town of Rye,
> Where burning Peploe loves and sings. (Beerbohm, p. 22)

This is a parody of Byron's lines on Sappho – 'The isles of Greece! The isles of Greece! / Where burning Sappho loved and sung' – and by framing Peploe between two writers strongly (if not exclusively) associated with homosexuality, Shakespeare and Sappho, Beerbohm seems to hint at James's own ambiguous sexuality.

James himself may have been offering a similarly oblique hint about his own feelings when he confided his sense of a charged symbolic moment in his life, a poignant glimpse of a lamp in a window, to two of his closest friends, Gosse and Walpole (see sections 3 and 15 below). The narrative has the dreamlike quality of Freud's account, included in his essay on the uncanny, of becoming lost in Florence and repeatedly finding himself in the same street, full of 'painted ladies', despite his efforts to get away from the quarter.[9] It is indicative of the gradual movement towards openness in discussions of sexuality in general, and James's sexuality in particular, that Walpole, a writer from a younger and franker generation than that of James and Gosse, encourages the reader (albeit equivocally) to connect the anecdote with unrequited sexual feelings.

Such apparent hints have now given way to a far more explicit probing of James's sexuality. Some apparently have a personal investment in the topic –

---

[9] See Sigmund Freud, *Penguin Freud Library*, 16 vols (London: Penguin, 1990), vol. xiv.

Tòibìn's project in *The Master*, for example, chimes with his more general contention that gay and lesbian history has been hidden in the past.[10] Some degree of interpenetration between biographer or novelist and subject is perhaps inevitable. Certainly Henry James responded similarly when writing his own study of Nathaniel Hawthorne, *Hawthorne* (1879), merging his portrait of the artist whom he admired with one of himself, anticipating Stein's own self-conscious sense of James as her precursor. Eric Haralson argues that Stein, like Tòibìn, experienced a specifically queer solidarity with James.[11]

A telling example of a (fictional) Jamesian whose own personality contaminates his sense of his Master is the hero of Alan Hollinghurst's *The Line of Beauty*, Nick Guest. Henry James apparently confided to Desmond McCarthy as they sat together in a particularly splendid drawing room, 'I can stand a great deal of gold' (See 7a, p. 123 below). In *The Line of Beauty*, Nick quotes this line to suggest his own sense of sympathy with James's views. However he gets it wrong, and says instead 'I can stand a great deal of gilt'.[12] The mistake suggests perhaps that Nick's aesthetic sensibility is less refined, more superficial, than James's, and also implies (through the pun on 'guilt') that Nick is being corrupted by his hedonistic lifestyle.

But again we might want to locate the most exuberantly creative evocation of James's sexuality in a work of non-fiction. Tòibìn's descriptions of James's sexual feelings and encounters (usually non-encounters) seem cautious and restrained when compared to the literary critical conjectures of Eve Kosofsky Sedgwick. Sedgwick is well known for her inventive and sometimes counterintuitive responses to well known texts, and her exploration of homoeroticism in James's works controversially detects a number of veiled allusions to anal eroticism. She writes of a passage in the *Notebooks*:

> A greater self-knowledge and a greater acceptance and *specificity* of homosexual desire transform this half-conscious enforcing rhetoric of anality, numbness and silence into a much richer, pregnant address to James's male muse, an invocation of fisting-as-*écriture*. (Sedgwick, p. 208)

Although many readers have responded with alarm and derision to the arguments of Sedgwick and others who find double entrendres in James's writings, the drive to 'out' James can be traced back to the writer himself. A parallel, though considerably less dramatic, movement away from obfuscation towards explicitness can be identified in James's own self-revisions. If we compare a real text, *Roderick Hudson*, with the virtual text which is

---

[10] See, for example, Tòibìn's collection of essays *Love in a Dark Time: Gay Lives from Wilde to Almodovar* (London: Picador, 2001)

[11] 'Rereading Gertrude Stein Rereading Henry James (After a Fashion)', *The Henry James Review*, 25:3 (2004), 239–45.

[12] Allan Hollinghurst, *The Line of Beauty* (London: Picador, 2004), p. 6.

'Henry James' we can see a rather similar dynamic at work. The novel's central characters are Roderick himself, a talented young sculptor, his fiancée Mary Garland and his friend and patron, Rowland Mallet, who is also in love with Mary. Michèle Mendelssohn asserts in recent article about *Roderick Hudson* that 'Mary's role is to create a diversion from the novel's same sex relationship'.[13] This theory is borne out far more clearly in the later New York Edition of the novel than in the original version. A good example is the moment of revelation, when Roderick discovers that his friend is in love with Mary. In the first edition Mary's name is mentioned earlier in the conversation.

> 'And all this time,' Roderick continued, 'you have been in love? Tell me the woman?'
> Rowland felt an immense desire to give him a visible palpable pang.
> 'Her name is Mary Garland,' he said.[14]

But in the New York Edition Mary's name is delayed, as is the assumption that the loved one must be a woman, allowing the possibility of another revelation (that Rowland is in love with Roderick) to intervene. This hidden alternative meaning is all the more convincing because earlier in the novel it seems that Roderick knows very well that Rowland is in love with Mary.

> 'And all this time', Roderick continued, 'you've been in love? Tell me then, please – if you don't mind – with whom?'
> Rowland felt the temptation to give him a palpable pang.
> 'With whom but the nearest – ?'
> 'The nearest – ?' Roderick maintained his cold, large stare, which seemed so to neglect and overshoot the near. But then he brought it down. 'You mean with poor Mary?'[15]

Our initial interpretation of 'the nearest' could well be Roderick himself. And this revelation might more easily account for Roderick's shock – he leaves Rowland, gets caught in a storm, and is later discovered dead in a crevasse. As it stands, Roderick seems to be over reacting, but when we register the equivocation, or sense that James is teasing the reader by hinting at homosexual revelation, Roderick's shock becomes far more realistic.

Many have noted that James seemed to become more receptive to homosexual possibilities in his later life, which is when he carried out these revisions. But a further curious coincidence may have helped encourage this reinflection of the relationship between Roderick and Rowland. In

---

[13] Michèle Mendelssohn, 'Homosociality and the Aesthetic in Henry James's *Roderick Hudson*', *Nineteenth-Century Literature*, 57:4 (2003), p. 537.

[14] Henry James, *Novels 1871–1880*, ed. by William T. Stafford (New York: Library of America, 1983), p. 500.

[15] Henry James, *Roderick Hudson* (Oxford: Oxford University Press, 1980), p. 376.

1899 James met a young American sculptor of Norwegian descent, Hendrik Andersen, whose talent and good looks might well have put James in mind of his own Roderick Hudson. Andersen stayed with James in Rye and James wrote him passionately tactile letters (see headnote to section 8). Tòibìn gives a convincing account of James's recognition that his early novel was being played out in real life:

> Both Hudson and Andersen made clear to anyone who knew them their ambitions and dreams. Both of them were doted on by a worried mother back at home, and both, once installed in Rome, were watched over by an older man, a lone visitor, who appreciated beauty and took an interest in human behaviour and kept passion firmly in check. As Henry saw Andersen and tried to make sense of him, it was as though one of his own characters had come alive, ready to intrigue him and puzzle him and hold his affections, forcing him to suspend judgement, subtly refusing to allow him to control what might now unfold.[16]

This is not the only occasion on which James's fiction strangely anticipates events in his life or afterlife. For example his story 'The Author of Beltraffio' (1884), the tale of a writer whose works are considered immoral (by implication because they deal with homosexuality) and whose wife is desperate to prevent their young son from being corrupted, was based loosely on the experiences of John Addington Symonds but for today's readers is far more likely to recall the much better known figure of Oscar Wilde. And in Tòibìn's *The Master* the Wilde trial puts James in mind of 'Beltraffio', and in a sense becomes a retrospective influence upon it. Another tale, 'The Birthplace' (1903), also gains a new resonance for later readers not available at the time of its publication. The title refers to the house in which an unnamed writer lived long ago and which has now become a museum, its history and contents fetishised by tourists. Although the most obvious parallel is with Stratford-on-Avon, reading the tale today we may reflect on the way in which Lamb House has in turn become a similar shrine for literary pilgrims. And James would associate himself with Shakespeare again, two years before his death, when he wrote to his nephew Harry about his horror of biography:

> My sole wish is to frustrate as utterly as possible the post mortem exploiter – which, I know, is but so imperfectly possible. Still one can do something, and I have long thought of launching, by a provision in my will, a curse no less explicit than Shakespeare's own on any such as try to move my bones. (Edel, v, p. 145)

Of course by making a writer (as he does so often) his subject, James might be said to consciously anticipate his afterlife. He may not have foreseen the

---

[16] Colm Tòibìn, *The Master* (London: Picador, 2004), p. 290.

Wilde trial (and its impact on the reception of 'Beltraffio') but he did know that he would one day die. And certainly there seems some consciousness of, perhaps contrivance of, a felicitous foreshadowing of life in art in James's preface to the New York edition of *The Golden Bowl* (1904). In the novel the Prince and Charlotte spend a long time searching for precisely the right present for Maggie Verver. After rejecting many shops they find one which seems more promising. Yet again, nothing at first seems appropriate until the owner produces the golden bowl itself, the perfect present despite its hidden flaw. This fictional process was apparently repeated when James and the photographer Alvin Coburn embarked on a hunt for precisely the right shop to represent the fictional establishment in *The Golden Bowl*. James's account of the search for the shop communicates the same blend of mystery and serendipity:

> The problem thus was thrilling, for though the small shop was but a shop of the mind ... our need (since the picture was, as I have said, also completely to speak for itself) prescribed a concrete, independent, vivid instance, the instance that should oblige us by the marvel of an accidental rightness ... It of course on these terms long evaded us, but all the while really without prejudice to our fond confidence that, as London ends by giving one absolutely everything one asks, so it awaited us somewhere. It awaited us in fact – but I check myself; nothing, I find now, would induce me to say where.[17]

Alvin Coburn himself contributed to the mystique of the shop's discovery. Leon Edel records that he claimed years later 'that by a curious coincidence they had found it to be almost exactly where James had placed it in his book' (Edel, v, p. 345).

If Henry James, in the preface to *The Golden Bowl*, was trying to make his life seem more like one of his novels, he was not alone. Muriel Draper's account of her acquaintance with James may well be entirely accurate but there are some odd little Jamesian details in her memoir which invite a more cautious approach. At the beginning of the extract reproduced here (in section 16) she describes how she first encountered James when she heard a friend of her mother reading from *What Maisie Knew*. Muriel at first listens unnoticed, but when her mother remembers she is there a pretext is found to send her from the room. There is a reflexivity here – a child listens inappropriately to the story of a child who is similarly exposed to overly adult influences. And Muriel is like Henry as well as Maisie, for James relates in his memoirs how he similarly hid to hear *David Copperfield* (another tale of a sensitive vulnerable child) read aloud before being sent to bed because he was crying. The impression that Draper is trying to inscribe

---

[17] Henry James, *The Golden Bowl* (Oxford: Oxford University Press, 1989), p. xlviii.

herself as James/Maisie is enhanced by the reported conversation between her mother and the friend. The mother exclaims:

> 'How does he manage to bring about such a thing!' and Elizabeth Cummings answered, 'He doesn't manage, my dear Susan; he is a genius.' (p. 271)

These lines have something of the gnomic, portentous quality of some of James's own dialogue. A further odd link between the extract and James's own early life is suggested by Draper's account of James's particular interest in her small son's buttons. In his first volume of autobiography, *A Small Boy and Others*, James describes how Thackeray was similarly struck by his own large buttons. Both he and Draper's son are intimidated by being singled out for this attention.

> 'Come here, little boy, and show me your extraordinary jacket!' My sense of the jacket became from that hour a heavy one – further enriched as my vision is by my shyness of posture before the seated, the celebrated visitor, who struck me, in the sunny light of the animated room, as enormously big and who, though he laid on my shoulder the hand of benevolence, bent on my native costume the spectacles of wonder. I was to know later on why he had been so amused and why, after asking me if this were the common uniform of my age and class, he remarked that in England, were I to go there, I should be addressed as 'Buttons'.[18]

It is perhaps unduly suspicious to accuse Draper of touching up her memories to make them more Jamesian. Perhaps (in the case of the buttons) it is rather James who was, possibly unconsciously, imitating himself, wanting to repeat the incident of 'famous novelist teases young boy about his buttons', but with himself in the senior role.

James was certainly acutely aware of his self-image, and the need to control it, and on another occasion – the interview with Preston Lockwood included here in section 17 – can be caught in the act of 'touching up'. (James disapproved of the first draft and dictated a revised version to Lockwood.) In a move which typifies the elisions between fiction and reality in James's afterlife Cynthia Ozick nicely reverses this pattern in her own 'interview' with Henry James. Here she accosts James in 'the Other World' and alarms him with a series of searching questions about what exactly he got up to with Hugh Walpole and Hendrik Andersen. While James maintained control over both participants in the Lockwood interview, Ozick supplies all of James's contributions in her own humorous piece. Whereas in the Lockwood interview James affected to let slip some remarks inadvertently, even though he had the final say over what was printed, Ozick

---

[18] Henry James, *A Small Boy and Others* (London: Macmillan, 1913), pp. 93–4.

creates a parallel fiction of an obdurate James even though she can of course make him say exactly what she pleases:

> Interviewer: I gather that you intend to inhibit my line of questioning.
> James: Madam, I do not inhibit. I merely decline to exhibit.[19]

Another encounter with a revenant James is described in Hugh Stevens's 'The Resistance to Queory: John Addington Symonds and "The Real Right Thing"'.[20] Like Ozick, Stevens effects a playful and self-conscious interpenetration between James's fiction and the real world . He also problematises generic boundaries, for 'The Resistance to Queory' is ostensibly a conventional critical essay – an analysis of James's short story 'The Real Right Thing' (1899) – published in a mainstream academic journal, *The Henry James Review*.

The central character in 'The Real Right Thing' is George Withermore, who is attempting to write a biography of a writer he greatly admired, and whom he calls his 'master', Ashton Doyne. With the permission of Doyne's widow, Withermore carries out his research in the dead writer's former home. Here he becomes increasingly aware of Doyne's presence near him, and James describes this haunting in a passage which invites a sexual reading – a fact which gains significance because Withermore is trying to find out the dead Doyne's best kept secrets.

> He was learning many things that he had not suspected, drawing many curtains, forcing many doors, reading many riddles, going, in general, as they said, behind almost everything. It was at an occasional sharp turn of some of the duskier of these wanderings 'behind' that he really of a sudden, most felt himself, in the intimate, sensible way, face to face with his friend; so that he could scarcely have told, for the instant, if their meeting occurred in the narrow passage and tight squeeze of the past, or at the hour and in the place that actually held him. [21]

Although the story ends by describing how Withermore becomes convinced that Doyne's shade doesn't want him to continue with the biography, the modern reader may, in the light of such a suggestive passage (which, I think, supports Eve Kosofsky Sedgwick's observation that 'anal erotics function especially saliently at the level of sentence structure' (Sedgwick, p. 102)), feel that James is encouraging speculation from beyond the grave. Hugh Stevens concludes his analysis of the tale with a comic fantasy of his own uncanny sense of being haunted, like Withermore, by the shade

---

[19] Cynthia Ozick, 'An (Unfortunate) Interview with Henry James', *The Threepenny Review* (Winter 2005), http://www.threepennyreview.com.
[20] Hugh Stevens, 'The Resistance to Queory: John Addington Symonds and "The Real Right Thing"', *The Henry James Review*, 20:1 (1999), pp. 255–64.
[21] Henry James, *Complete Stories 1898–1910* (New York: Library of America, 1996), p. 127.

of his favourite writer. The deceased James is a good deal more forthcoming with Stevens than with Ozick:

> And by the way ... there is another ground for my argument. I'm unsure whether I should mention this. If my hypothesizing might be regarded as unscholarly, invoking the supernatural must be less scholarly still, even if the supernatural might remove all doubt. Some might think it a porky if I said Henry James has been helping me in my research, making nightly visitations to my study and my bedroom, bringing recollections, ghosts of documents burnt, and more physical kinds of encouragement. The visitations have given me an unfair advantage, a privileged insight, that I don't want to show off about. Even so, I wonder: is Henry James coming out too beautifully – better than such a partisan as myself could have supposed? (Stevens, p. 263)

In 'The Real Right Thing', as in 'The Birthplace', James writes a story which, in a sense, can only acquire its fullest resonance after his death. To read a tale about a dead writer by a writer who is equally dead creates a bond between the two which cannot exist in quite the same way while the author is still alive. In *Shakespeare's Ghost Writers*, Marjorie Garber argues that the ghost in Hamlet becomes identified with Shakespeare for a modern audience now that the play's author, like its hero's father, is dead.

> The Ghost is Shakespeare. He is the one who comes as a revenant, belatedly instated, regarded as originally authoritative, rather than retrospectively and retroactively canonized, and deriving increased authority from this very instatement of authority backward, over time.[22]

James's ghosts similarly acquire some additional posthumous authorial significance. And (if we remember James's invocation of Shakespeare's curse on those who disturbed his bones) we might reflect that, although James's distaste is undoubtedly real, he might be said to be asking for trouble by associating himself, in this context, with Shakespeare, who has attracted so many volumes of biographical and critical speculation. Certainly, whatever Henry James wanted, 'Henry James' has burst his cerements, like the ghost of Hamlet's father, to cry 'Remember me'.

The texts chosen for this volume include pieces written by James's closest friends (such as Gosse and Walpole) and chance acquaintances (such as Blanche and O'Sullivan). The volume opens with recollections of a youthful 'Henry James, Jr.', whose career was still uncertain, and ends with recollections of the final days of the elderly 'master'. Read as a collection they return us to Stein's bafflingly multiplied 'Jameses' and indeed to William James's curious account (quoted at the beginning of the introduction) of 'Harry' turning into something rich and strange in England. This vol-

---

[22] Marjorie Garber, *Shakespeare's Ghost Writers: Literature as Uncanny Causality* (London: Methuen, 1987), p. 176.

ume invites us to excavate beneath the surface of these very different texts, to search for the elusive 'reality' of Henry James, scraping off the distracting or distorting effects of his biographers' patriotism, prudery, self-indulgence or self-promotion, laying bare the processes which turned a life into a legend.

# BIBLIOGRAPHY

**Primary Texts**

Anon., 'General Gossip of Authors and Writers', *Current Literature*, 27 (January 1900), 22

Anon., 'Death of Mr. Henry James', *Daily Telegraph* (29 February 1916)

Anon., 'Henry James, O. M.: The Man and the Artist', *The Times* (29 February 1916)

Anon., 'Death of Mr. Henry James: Novelist for the Few', *Daily Mail* (29 February 1916)

Beerbohm, Max, *Max in Verse: Rhymes and Parodies*, ed. by J. G. Riewald (London: Heinemann, 1964)

Benson, A. C., *Memories and Friends* (London: John Murray, 1923)

—, *The Diary of Arthur Christopher Benson*, ed. by Percy Lubbock (London: Hutchinson & Co., 1926)

Betham-Edwards, Matilda, *Mid-Victorian Memories* (London: J. Murray, 1919)

Blanche, Jacques-Emile, *Portrait of a Lifetime* (London: Dent, 1937)

Bosanquet, Theodora, *Henry James at Work* (London: Hogarth Press, 1924)

—, 'As I Remember – Henry James', *Time and Tide* (3 July 1954), 875–6

Boughton, Alice, 'A Note by his Photographer', *Hound and Horn*, 7:19 (1934), 471–9

Bradley, A. G., 'Henry James As I Knew Him: The Human Side of a Great Novelist', *John O' London's Weekly* (18 December 1936), 505–6

Bynner, Witter, 'A Word or Two with Henry James', *Critic* (1905), 146–8

Carlyle, Thomas, *Sartor Resartus*, ed. by C. F. Harrold (New York: Odyssey Press, 1937; 1st edn 1833)

Coburn, Alvin, *Men of Mark* (London: Duckworth & Co., 1913)

Colby, F. M., 'The Queerness of Henry James', *Bookman*, 15 (1902), 396–7

Dixon, Ella Hepworth, *As I Knew Them* (London: Hutchinson & Co. Ltd, 1930)

Draper, Muriel, *Music at Midnight* (London: Heinemann, 1929)

Ford, Ford Madox, *Thus to Revisit* (London: Chapman & Hall, 1921)

—, *Return to Yesterday* (London: Victor Gollancz, 1931)

—, *Mightier than the Sword* (London: Allen & Unwin, 1938)
Freud, Sigmund, *Penguin Freud Library*, 16 vols (London: Penguin, 1990), vol. xiv
Garland, Hamlin, *Roadside Meetings* (London: John Lane, 1931)
Gosse, Sir Edmund, *Aspects and Impressions* (London: Cassell & Co. Ltd, 1922)
Howells, W. D., 'Henry James, Jr.', *Century Magazine* (1882–3), 25–9
Hunt, Violet, 'The Last Days of Henry James', *Daily Mail* (1 March 1916)
—, *The Flurried Years* (London: Hurst & Blackett Ltd, 1926)
James, Henry, *A Small Boy and Others* (London: Macmillan, 1913)
—, *Roderick Hudson* (Oxford: Oxford University Press, 1980)
—, *Novels 1871–1880* (New York: Library of America, 1983)
—, *The Golden Bowl* (Oxford: Oxford University Press, 1989)
—, *Complete Stories 1898–1910* (New York: Library of America, 1996)
James, Henry Jr, (ed.), *The Letters of William James*, 2 vols (London: Longman, Green, and Co., 1920)
Jordan, Elizabeth, *Three Rousing Cheers* (New York: D. Appleton-Century Company, 1938)
Lockwood, Preston, 'Henry James's First Interview', *New York Times* (1915), 3–4
MacCarthy, Desmond, *Portraits* (London: Putnam, 1931)
Marsh, Edward, *A Number of People* (London: William Heinemann, 1939)
Mackenzie, Compton, 'Henry James', *Life and Letters Today* (1943), 147–55
McCarthy, Justin, *Reminiscences*, 2 vols (London: Chatto & Windus, 1899)
Moore, George, *Avowals* (London: Cumann Sean-eolais na h-Eireann, 1919)
Nadal, E. S., 'Personal Recollections of Henry James', *Scribner's Magazine* (1920), 89–97
O'Sullivan, Vincent, *Aspects of Wilde* (London: Constable & Co, 1936)
Robertson, W. Graham, *Time Was* (London: Hamish Hamilton, 1931)
Robins, Elizabeth, *Theatre and Friendship: Some Henry James Letters with a Commentary* (London: Jonathan Cape, 1932)
Stein, Gertrude, *Four in America* (Freeport: Books for Libraries Press, 1967; 1st edn 1947)
Walbrook, Henry Mackinnon, 'Henry James and the English Theatre', *Nineteenth Century*, 80 (1916), 141–5
Walpole, Hugh, 'Henry James; A Reminiscence', *Horizon*, 1:2 (February 1940), 74–81
Ward, Mrs Humphrey, *A Writer's Recollections* (London: W Collins & Co Ltd, 1918)
Wells, H. G., *Experiment in Autobiography*, 2 vols (London: Faber & Faber, 1934)
West, Rebecca, *Henry James* (London: Nisbet, 1916)

Wharton, Edith, *A Backward Glance* (London: Century, 1987; 1st edn 1934)

**Secondary Texts**

Anesko, Michael, *Letters, Fictions, Lives: Henry James and William Dean Howells* (Oxford: Oxford University Press, 1997)

Antsyferova, Olga, 'Three Interviews of Henry James: Mastering the Language of Publicity', *The Henry James Review*, 22:1 (2001), 81–92

Ashbery, John, 'The Impossible', *Poetry* (July 1957), 250–54

Booth, Alison, 'The Real Right Place of Henry James: Homes and Haunts', *The Henry James Review*, 25:3 (2004), 216–27

Caramello, Charles, *Henry James, Gertrude Stein, and the Biographical Act* (Chapel Hill: University of North Carolina Press, 1996)

Garber, Marjorie, *Shakespeare's Ghost Writers: Literature as Uncanny Causality* (London: Methuen, 1987)

Haralson, Eric, 'Rereading Gertrude Stein Rereading Henry James (After a Fashion)', *The Henry James Review*, 25:3 (2004), 239–45

Hardwick, Joan, *An Immodest Violet: The Life of Violet Hunt* (London: André Deutsch, 1990)

Hart-Davis, Rupert, *Hugh Walpole: A Biography* (London: Hamilton, 1985)

Hollinghurst, Alan, *The Line of Beauty* (London: Picador, 2004)

Horne, Philip, *Henry James and Revision: the New York Edition* (Oxford: Clarendon Press, 1990)

Hyde, H. Montgomery, *Henry James at Home* (London: Methuen & Co. Ltd, 1969)

Le Clair, Robert C., *Young Henry James 1843–1870* (New York: Brookman Associates, 1955)

Linklater, Andro, *Compton Mackenzie: A Life* (London: Chatto & Windus, 1987)

Mendelssohn, Michèle, 'Homosociality and the Aesthetic in Henry James's *Roderick Hudson*', *Nineteenth-Century Literature*, 57:4 (2003), 512–41

Murtaugh, Daniel J., 'An Emotional Reflection: Sexual Realization in Henry James's Revision to *Roderick Hudson*', *The Henry James Review*, 17:2 (1996), 182–203

Nadel, Ira Bruce, *Biography: Fiction, Fact and Form* (London: Macmillan, 1984)

Nowell-Smith, Simon, *The Legend of the Master* (London: Constable, 1947)

Ozick, Cynthia, 'An (Unfortunate) Interview with Henry James', *The Threepenny Review* (Winter 2005), http://www.threepennyreview.com

Salmon, Richard, *Henry James and the Culture of Publicity* (Cambridge: Cambridge University Press, 1997)

Sedgwick, Eve Kosofsky, *Epistemology of the Closet* (Berkeley: University of California Press, 1990)

Seymour, Miranda, *Henry James and his Literary Circle 1895–1915* (Boston: Houghton Mifflin Company, 1989)
Stevens, Hugh, *Henry James and Sexuality* (Cambridge: Cambridge University Press, 1998)
—, 'The Resistance to Queory: John Addington Symonds and "The Real Right Thing"', *The Henry James Review*, 20:1 (1999), 255–64
Tòibìn, Colm, *Love in a Dark Time: Gay Lives from Wilde to Almodovar* (London: Picador, 2001)
—, *The Master* (London: Picador, 2004)
Walbrook, H. M., *Nights at the Play* (London, W. J. Ham-Smith, 1911)

# CHRONOLOGY

| | |
|---|---|
| 1843 | (15 April) HJ born at 21 Washington Place, New York City, second child of Henry James Sr and Mary Walsh James. |
| 1843–4 | The Jameses travel abroad to France and England. |
| 1845 | Garth Wilkinson, HJ's brother, born. |
| 1846 | Robertson, HJ's second brother, born. |
| 1845–55 | HJ spends his childhood in Albany and New York where he attends a series of schools. He reads widely, including the novels of Dickens, and is an avid theatre-goer. |
| 1848 | Alice, HJ's sister, born.<br>The Jameses return to Europe where HJ attends schools in Geneva, London, Paris and Boulogne-sur-mer.<br>The family returns to settle in Newport, Rhode Island. HJ's companions include Thomas Sargeant Perry and the painter John La Farge. |
| 1859 | The family returns to Geneva where HJ attends scientific school and then studies German in Bonn.<br>They return to Newport. HJ briefly studies art with the well-known American painter William Morris Hunt. HJ becomes increasingly close to his Temple cousins, in particular Minny. He also begins to write more seriously, attempting both short stories and translations from French. |
| 1861 | HJ receives a back injury while serving as a volunteer fireman. |
| 1862–3 | HJ joins his brother William at Harvard where he studies law. |
| 1863 | HJ's brothers Wilkinson and Robertson fight in the Civil War.<br>The family moves to Boston. HJ's first published short story 'A Tragedy of Error' appears anonymously in the *Continental Monthly* and the *North American Review* publishes his first review. |

| | |
|---|---|
| 1865 | 'The Story of a Year' published in the *Atlantic Monthly*. |
| 1869 | HJ travels in England, Switzerland, France and Italy. |
| 1870 | Minny Temple dies. HJ returns to the US.<br>Serialisation of HJ's first full length novel, *Watch and Ward*, in the *Atlantic*. |
| 1872 | HJ returns to Europe with his sister Alice and Aunt Kate. |
| 1875–6 | HJ spends time in Paris and becomes acquainted with a number of French writers, including Flaubert. |
| 1875 | *Roderick Hudson* serialised in the *Atlantic*.<br>*The American* serialised in the *Atlantic*. |
| 1876–7 | HJ moves to England and becomes involved in London society. |
| 1878 | 'Daisy Miller' published to great success. Macmillan publishes *The Europeans* and HJ's first collection of essays, *French Poets and Novelists*. |
| 1879 | *Hawthorne*, a study of the novelist, published.<br>*Washington Square* published. HJ travels in Italy where he meets the American novelist Constance Fenimore Woolson. |
| 1881 | *The Portrait of a Lady* serialised in the *Atlantic*. HJ returns to the US, where he enjoys seeing old friends such as Henry and Clover Adams. |
| 1882 | HJ's mother dies in January. HJ goes back to Europe but returns to Boston after the death of his father in December. |
| 1883 | HJ visits Washington and New York before returning to London. (November) HJ's brother Wilkinson dies. |
| 1884 | Alice James comes to England with her companion Katherine Loring.<br>*The Bostonians* serialised in the *Century*. Serialisation of *The Princess Casamassima* begins in the *Atlantic Monthly*. |
| 1886 | HJ moves to a new flat in De Vere Gardens.<br>HJ travels in Italy where he spends time with Constance Fenimore Woolson. |
| 1888 | *The Aspern Papers* published in the *Atlantic Monthly*. Edward Compton suggests he write a stage version of *The American*. |
| 1889 | Serialisation of *The Tragic Muse* begins in the *Atlantic Monthly*. Death of HJ's Aunt Kate. |

1890  *The American* first performed in Southport.

1891  The London premiere of *The American*.

1892  Alice James dies.

1894  Constance Fenimore Woolson commits suicide in Venice.

1895  HJ's play *Guy Domville* is a failure. 'The Figure in the Carpet' published in a new magazine, *Cosmopolis*.

1896  *The Spoils of Poynton* serialised in the *Atlantic Monthly*. HJ visits Rye for the first time.

1897  *What Maisie Knew* serialised in the *Chap-Book*. HJ employs his first secretary, William MacAlpine. He signs a long lease on Lamb House in Rye.

1898  *The Turn of the Screw* serialised in *Collier's Weekly*. HJ moves into Lamb House in the summer. While living in Rye HJ makes a number of important literary friends including Joseph Conrad and Ford Madox Ford. Serialisation begins of *The Awkward Age* in *Harper's Weekly*. 'In the Cage' published.

1899  HJ visits Italy where he stays with Mrs Humphrey Ward. HJ meets Hendrik Andersen.

1902  *The Wings of the Dove* published.

1903  *The Ambassadors* serialised in the *North American Review*. HJ meets Jocelyn Persse and Edith Wharton.

1904  HJ sails to the US. *The Golden Bowl* published by Charles Scribner's Sons.

1905  HJ gives a series of lectures in the US and meets the President, Theodore Roosevelt. He begins work on the twenty-four-volume 'New York Edition' of his works.

1907  Theodora Bosanquet becomes HJ's secretary.

1908  *The High Bid* produced by Johnston Forbes-Robertson.

1909  HJ meets Hugh Walpole.

1910  Robertson James dies. William James dies soon after travelling back to the US with HJ.

1911  HJ returns to England. *The Saloon* produced at the Little Theatre.

1913  HJ's portrait is painted by Sargent. *A Small Boy and Others* published.

1914  *Notes of a Son and Brother* and *Notes on Novelists* published.

1915 HJ becomes a British subject.

1916 HJ receives the Order of Merit. (28 February) HJ dies in Chelsea. His funeral takes place in Chelsea Old Church and his ashes are buried in the family plot is Cambridge, Massachusetts.

# COPY TEXTS

The following extracts are reproduced in facsimile. Breaks between excerpts (which may cover paragraphs or whole volumes) are indicated by five asterisks:

★ ★ ★ ★ ★

In order to fit texts comfortably to the pages of this edition certain liberties have been taken with the format of the original: occasionally right-hand pages have become left-hand pages (and vice versa) and text from consecutive pages has been fitted onto a single page. Endnotes in this edition refer to Pickering & Chatto page and line numbers. Readers wishing to consult the passages in the original are referred to the table below where all the available conversions are given.

| TEXT NO. | ORIGINAL PAGE NUMBERS | P&C page no. ff |
|---|---|---|
| 1. | 24–9 | 4 |
| 2. a. | 89–97 | 5 |
| b. | II: 74–5 | 24 |
| 3. | 17–53 | 27 |
| 4. | 159–66 | 67 |
| 5. b. | 38–97 | 81 |
| c. | 224 | 98 |
| 6. | 192–204 | 103 |
| 7. a. | 149–69 | 119 |
| b. | 396–7 | 140 |
| 8. | 323–336 | 145 |
| 9. | 147–55 | 163 |

| TEXT NO. | ORIGINAL PAGE NUMBERS | P&C page no. ff |
|---|---|---|
| 10. a. | 268–9 | 175 |
| b. | 238–41 | 177 |
| c. | 141–5 | 180 |
| 11. | 454–65 | 189 |
| 12. | 13–27 | 203 |
| 13. b. | 67–70 | 235 |
| c. | 101–9 | 239 |
| d. | 222 | 248 |
| 14. a. | 478–9 | 251 |
| b. | 18–21 | 254 |
| 15. | 74–81 | 261 |
| 16. | 84–94 | 271 |
| 17. a. | 146–8 | 285 |

Every effort has been made to trace copyright holders of the texts reproduced in this edition. Please see the Permissions page at the end of Volume 3 for textual sources.

# ABBREVIATIONS

| | |
|---|---|
| Beerbohm | Max Beerbohm, *Max in Verse: Rhymes and Parodies*, ed. by J. G. Riewald (London: Heinemann, 1964) |
| Edel | Leon Edel, *Henry James*, 5 vols (London: Rupert Hart-Davis, 1953–71) |
| Hardwick | Hardwick, Joan, *An Immodest Violet: The Life of Violet Hunt* (London: André Deutsch, 1990) |
| HJ | Henry James |
| Horne | Philip Horne, *Henry James: A Life in Letters* (London: Allen Lane, 1999) |
| Hyde | H. Montgomery Hyde, *Henry James at Home* (London: Methuen & Co. Ltd, 1969) |
| Kaplan | Fred Kaplan, *Henry James: The Imagination of Genius* (London: Hodder & Stoughton, 1992) |
| *Letters* | *Henry James Letters*, ed. by Leon Edel, 4 vols (Cambridge, MA: Harvard University Press, 1974–84) |
| *Notebooks* | *The Complete Notebooks of Henry James*, ed. by Leon Edel and Lyall H. Powers (Oxford: Oxford University Press, 1987) |
| Nowell-Smith | Simon Nowell-Smith, *The Legend of the Master* (London: Constable, 1947) |
| Robins | Elizabeth Robins, *Theatre and Friendship: Some Henry James Letters with a Commentary* (London: Jonathan Cape, 1932) |
| Sedgwick | Eve Kosofsky Sedgwick, *Epistemology of the Closet* (Berkeley: University of California Press, 1990) |
| Stevens | Hugh Stevens, 'The Resistance to Queory: John Addington Symonds and "The Real Right Thing"', *The Henry James Review*, 20:1 (1999), 255–64 |

West     Rebecca West, *Henry James* (London: Nisbet, 1916)

Wharton  Edith Wharton, *A Backward Glance* (London: Century, 1987; 1st edn 1934)

# W. D. Howells, 'Henry James, Jr.', *Century Magazine* (1882–3)

Most records of James were written during his later years or after his death, but this piece was published when James was still 'Henry James, Jr.' rather than the 'Master', an up and coming figure rather than a fixture in the canon. William Dean Howells (1837–1920), the well-known American novelist and editor, was the son of a printer and newspaper editor from Ohio, William Cooper Howells. The elder Howells, like Henry James's own father, was an enthusiastic follower of Swedenborg. The two young writers first met in Cambridge soon after Howells's appointment as assistant editor of the *Atlantic Monthly* magazine in 1866. As he testifies in 'Henry James, Jr.', Howells was an early admirer of James's stories and played an important role in bringing his works to public attention. Howells was responsible for publishing several of James's works, including serialisations of *Roderick Hudson* (1876) and *The American* (1877). *The American* caused its editor some unease for he knew that his readers would resent James's refusal to give the novel a happy ending. James wrote to Howells in March 1877 explaining his decision:

> These are matters which one feels about as one may, or as one can. I quite understand that as an editor you should go in for 'cheerful endings'; but I am sorry that as a private reader you are not struck with the inevitability of the American dénoûement ... I don't think that 'tragedies' have the presumption against them as much as you appear to; and I see no logical reason why they shouldn't be as *long* as comedies. In the drama they are usually allowed to be longer – *non è vero?* (*Letters*, ii, pp. 104–5)

However James relented when he came to adapt the novel for the stage in 1890, allowing Christopher Newman to marry Claire de Cintré.

Howells's own novels, by contrast with those of James, are conspicuously American – typical is *The Rise of Silas Lapham* (1885), the tale of a self-made Boston millionaire. (Hamlin Garland offers a useful account of the contrasting approaches of the two novelists in

'Henry James at Rye', reprinted below in section 11.) James was a warm though not uncritical reader of Howells's works. In 1901 he wrote praising his friend's latest volume of short stories. 'I read your book with joy and found in it recalls from far far away – stray echoes and scents as from another, the American, the prehistoric existence' (*Letters*, iv, p. 198). One wonders what Howells, who baulked at James's description of Hawthorne as 'exquisitely provincial' (Edel, ii, p. 392) thought about that 'prehistoric'. Even when James is at his most enthusiastic there is something patronising in his praise of Howells's works. He wrote of *A Hazard of New Fortunes* (1890) in 1890: 'I congratulate you, my dear Howells unrestrictedly, and give you my assurance – whatever the vain thing is worth – that, for me, you have never yet done anything so roundly and totally good' (*Letters*, iii, p. 281).

The two novelists freely reviewed each other's works despite their close friendship. 'Henry James, Jr.' was written by Howells soon after the publication of *Portrait of a Lady* (1881) and helped confirm James's reputation as an important novelist. Although there are occasional hints here that Howells finds some aspects of James's work less than completely congenial, on the whole this is a sensitive, detailed and warmly appreciative tribute. In fact it was a little too enthusiastic for many readers' tastes and Howells was accused in some quarters of 'puffing' the work of a personal friend. James wrote to reassure Howells:

> You are accused of having sacrificed – in your patriotic passion for the works of H. J. Jr. – *Vanity Fair* and *Henry Esmond* to *Daisy Miller* and *Poor Richard*! The indictment is rubbish – all your text says is that the 'confidential' manner of Thackeray would not be tolerable today in a younger school, which should attempt to reproduce it. Such at least is all I see in it and all you ever meant to put. When I say 'you are accused' all I mean to allude to is a nasty little paragraph in the *World* which accuses Warner, you and me of being linked in the most drivelling mutual admiration, and which accuses me individually of a 'tepid, invertebrate, captain's-biscuit' style! (*Letters*, ii, p. 392)

Yet the criticisms perhaps hit home harder than he claimed, for when James wrote a profile of Howells for *Harper's Weekly* in 1886 he apparently felt obliged to force himself to be more critical than he actually felt about his friend's works in order to avoid similar accusations (Michael Anesko, *Letters, Fictions, Lives: Henry James and William Dean Howells* (Oxford: OUP, 1997), p. 169). The two novelists remained good friends until James's death, although, as Howells continued to reside in the United States, their meetings were infrequent. Howells has an additional significance for readers of James: he gave him the 'germ' of *The Ambassadors* (1903), providing inspiration for that novel's middle-aged protagonist, Lambert Strether.

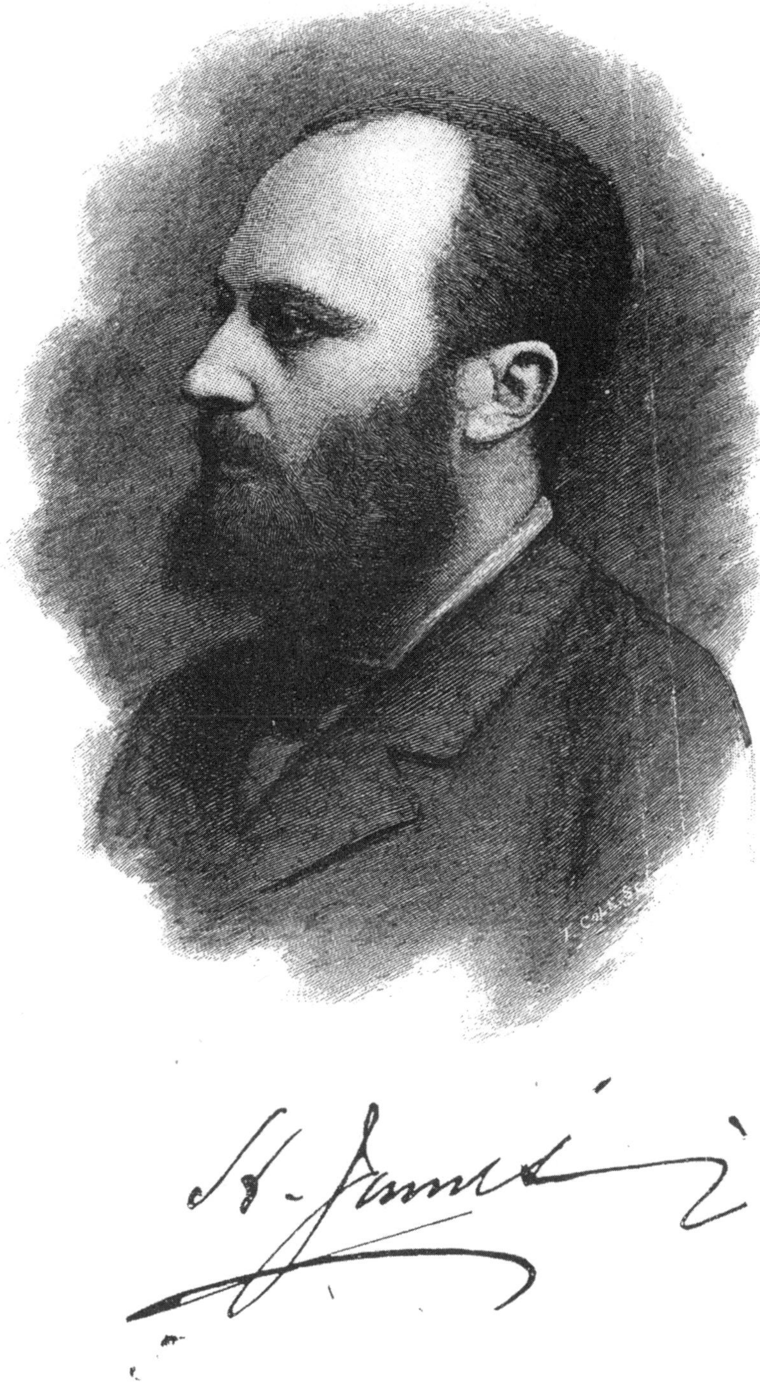

## HENRY JAMES, JR.

The events of Mr. James's life—as we agree to understand events—may be told in a very few words. His race is Irish on his father's side and Scotch on his mother's, to which mingled strains the generalizer may attribute, if he likes, that union of vivid expression and dispassionate analysis which has characterized his work from the first. There are none of those early struggles with poverty, which render the lives of so many distinguished Americans monotonous reading, to record in his case: the cabin hearth-fire did not light him to the youthful pursuit of literature; he had from the start all those advantages which, when they go too far, become limitations.

He was born in New York city in the year 1843, and his first lessons in life and letters were the best which the metropolis—so small in the perspective diminishing to that date—could afford. In his twelfth year his family went abroad, and after some stay in England made a long sojourn in France and Switzerland. They returned to America in 1860, placing themselves at Newport, and for a year or two Mr. James was at the Harvard Law School, where, perhaps, he did not study a great deal of law. His father removed from Newport to Cambridge in 1866, and there Mr. James remained till he went abroad, three years later, for the residence in England and Italy which, with infrequent visits home, has continued ever since.

It was during these three years of his Cambridge life that I became acquainted with his work. He had already printed a tale—"The Story of a Year"—in the "Atlantic Monthly," when I was asked to be Mr. Fields's assistant in the management, and it was my fortune to read Mr. James's second contribution in manuscript. "Would you take it?" asked my chief. "Yes, and all the stories you can get from the writer." One is much securer of one's judgment at twenty-nine than, say, at forty-five; but if this was a mistake of mine I am not yet old enough to regret it. The story was called "Poor Richard," and it dealt with the conscience of a man very much in love with a woman who loved his rival. He told this rival a lie, which sent him away to his death on the field,—in that day nearly every fictitious personage had something to do with the war,—but Poor Richard's lie did not win him his love. It still seems to me that the situation was strongly and finely felt. One's pity went, as it should, with the liar; but the whole story had a pathos which lingers in my mind equally with a sense of the new literary qualities which gave me such delight in it. I admired, as we must in all that Mr. James has written, the finished workmanship in which there is no loss of vigor; the luminous and uncommon use of words, the originality of phrase, the whole clear and beautiful style, which I confess I weakly liked the better for the occasional gallicisms remaining from an inveterate habit of French. Those who know the writings of Mr. Henry James will recognize the inherited felicity of diction which is so striking in the writings of Mr. Henry James, Jr. The son's diction is not so racy as the father's; it lacks its daring, but it is as fortunate and graphic; and I cannot give it greater praise than this, though it has, when he will, a splendor and state which is wholly its own.

Mr. James is now so universally recognized that I shall seem to be making an unwarrantable claim when I express my belief that the popularity of his stories was once largely confined to Mr. Fields's assistant. They had characteristics which forbade any editor to refuse them; and there are no anecdotes of thrice-rejected manuscripts finally printed to tell of him; his work was at once successful with all the magazines. But with the readers of "The Atlantic," of "Harper's," of "Lippincott's," of "The Galaxy," of "The Century," it was another affair. The flavor was so strange, that, with rare exceptions, they had to "learn to like" it. Probably few writers have in the same degree compelled the liking of their readers. He was reluctantly accepted, partly through a mistake as to his attitude—through the confusion of his point of view with his private opinion—in the reader's mind. This confusion caused the tears of rage which bedewed our continent in behalf of the "average American girl" supposed to be satirized in Daisy Miller, and prevented the perception of the fact that, so far as the average American girl was studied at all in Daisy Miller, her indestructible innocence, her invulnerable new-worldliness, had never been so delicately appreciated. It was so plain that Mr. James disliked her vulgar conditions, that the very people to whom he revealed her essential sweetness and light were furious that he should have seemed not to see what existed through him. In other words, they would have liked him better if he had been a worse artist—if he had been a little more confidential.

But that artistic impartiality which puzzled so many in the treatment of Daisy Miller is one of the qualities most valuable in the eyes of those who care how things are done, and I am not sure that it is not Mr. James's most characteristic quality. As "frost performs the effect of fire," this impartiality comes at last to the same result as sympathy. We may be quite sure that Mr. James does not like the peculiar phase of our civilization typified in Henrietta Stackpole; but he treats her with such exquisite justice that he lets *us* like her. It is an extreme case, but I confidently allege it in proof.

His impartiality is part of the reserve with which he works in most respects, and which at first glance makes us say that he is wanting in humor. But I feel pretty certain that Mr. James has not been able to disinherit himself to this degree. We Americans are terribly in earnest about making ourselves, individually and collectively; but I fancy that our prevailing mood in the face of all problems is that of an abiding faith which can afford to be funny. He has himself indicated that we have, as a nation, as a people, our joke, and every one of us is in the joke more or less. We may, some of us, dislike it extremely, disapprove it wholly, and even abhor it, but we are in the joke all the same, and no one of us is safe from becoming the great American humorist at any given moment. The danger is not apparent in Mr. James's case, and I confess that I read him with a relief in the comparative immunity that he affords from the national facetiousness. Many of his people are humorously imagined, or rather humorously *seen*, like Daisy Miller's mother, but these do not give a dominant color; the business in hand is commonly serious, and the droll people are subordinated. They abound, nevertheless, and many of them are perfectly new finds, like Mr. Tristram in "The American," the bill-paying father in the "Pension Beaurepas," the anxiously Europeanizing mother in the same story, the amusing little Madame de Belgarde, Henrietta Stackpole, and even Newman himself. But though Mr. James portrays the humorous in character, he is decidedly not on humorous terms with his reader; he ignores rather than recognizes the fact that they are both in the joke.

If we take him at all we must take him on his own ground, for clearly he will not come to ours. We must make concessions to him, not in this respect only, but in several others, chief among which is the motive for reading fiction. By example, at least, he teaches that it is the pursuit and not the end which should give us pleasure; for he often prefers to leave us to our own conjectures in regard to the fate of the people in whom he has interested us. There is no question, of course, but he could tell the story of Isabel in "The Portrait of a Lady" to the end, yet he does not tell it. We must agree, then, to take what seems a fragment instead of a whole, and to find, when we can, a name for this new kind in fiction. Evidently it is the character, not the fate, of his people which occupies him; when he has fully developed their character he leaves them to what destiny the reader pleases.

The analytic tendency seems to have increased with him as his work has gone on. Some of the earlier tales were very dramatic: "A Passionate Pilgrim," which I should rank above all his other short stories, and for certain rich poetical qualities, above everything else that he has done, is eminently dramatic. But I do not find much that I should call dramatic in "The Portrait of a Lady," while I do find in it an amount of analysis which I should call superabundance if it were not all such good literature. The novelist's main business is to possess his reader with a due conception of his characters and the situations in which they find themselves. If he does more or less than this he equally fails. I have sometimes thought that Mr. James's danger was to do more, but when I have been ready to declare this excess an error of his method I have hesitated. Could anything be superfluous that had given me so much pleasure as I read? Certainly from only one point of view, and this a rather narrow, technical one. It seems to me that an enlightened criticism will recognize in Mr. James's fiction a metaphysical genius working to æsthetic results, and will not be disposed to deny it any method it chooses to employ. No other novelist, except George Eliot, has dealt so largely in analysis of motive, has so fully explained and commented upon the springs of action in the persons of the drama, both before and after the facts. These novelists are more alike than any others in their processes, but with George Eliot an ethical purpose is dominant, and with Mr. James an artistic purpose. I do not know just how it should be stated of two such noble and generous types of character as Dorothea and Isabel Archer, but I think that we sympathize with the former in grand aims that chiefly concern others, and with the latter in beautiful dreams that primarily concern herself. Both are unselfish and devoted women, sublimely true to a mistaken ideal in their marriages; but, though they come to this common martyrdom, the original difference in them remains. Isabel has her great weaknesses, as Dorothea had, but these seem to me, on the whole, the most nobly imagined and the most nobly intentioned women in modern fiction; and I think Isabel is the more subtly divined of the two. If we speak of mere characterization, we must not fail to acknowledge the perfection of Gilbert Osmond. It was a profound stroke to make him an American by birth. No European could realize so fully in his own life the ideal of a European *dilettante* in all the meaning of that cheapened word; as no European could so deeply and tenderly feel the sweetness and loveliness of the English past as the sick American, Searle, in "The Passionate Pilgrim."

What is called the international novel is popularly dated from the publication of "Daisy Miller," though "Roderick Hudson" and "The American" had gone before; but it really began in the beautiful story which I have just named. Mr. James, who invented this species in fiction, first contrasted in the "Passionate Pilgrim" the New World and Old World moods, ideals, and prejudices, and he did it there with a richness of poetic effect which he has since never equalled. I own that I regret the loss of the poetry, but you cannot ask a man to keep on being a poet for you; it is hardly for him to choose; yet I compare rather discontentedly in my own mind such impassioned creations as Searle and the painter in "The Madonna of the Future" with "Daisy Miller," of whose slight, thin personality I also feel the indefinable charm, and of the tragedy of whose innocence I recognize the delicate pathos. Looking back to those early stories, where Mr. James stood at the dividing ways of the novel and the romance, I am sometimes sorry that he declared even superficially for the former. His best efforts seem to me those of romance; his best types have an ideal development, like Isabel and Claire Belgarde and Bessy Alden and poor Daisy and even Newman. But, doubtless, he has chosen wisely; perhaps the romance is an outworn form, and would not lend itself to the reproduction of even the ideality of modern life. I myself waver somewhat in my preference—if it is a preference—when I think of such people as Lord Warburton and the Touchetts, whom I take to be all decidedly of this world. The first of these especially interested me as a probable type of the English nobleman, who amiably accepts the existing situation with all its possibilities of political and social change, and insists not at all upon the surviving feudalities, but means to be a manly and simple gentleman in any event. An American is not able to pronounce as to the verity of the type; I only know that it seems probable and that it is charming. It makes one wish that it were in Mr. James's way to paint in some story the present phase of change in England. A titled personage is still mainly an inconceivable being to us; he is like a goblin or a fairy in a story-book. How does he comport himself in the face of all the changes and modifications that have taken place and that still impend? We can hardly imagine a lord taking his nobility seriously; it is some hint of the conditional frame of Lord Warburton's mind that makes him imaginable and delightful to us.

It is not my purpose here to review any of Mr. James's books; I like better to speak of his people than of the conduct of his novels, and I wish to recognize the fineness with which he has touched-in the pretty primness of Osmond's daughter and the mild devotedness of Mr. Rosier. A masterly hand is as often manifest in the treatment of such subordinate figures as in that of the principal persons, and Mr. James does them unerringly. This is felt in the more important character of Valentin Belgarde, a fascinating character in spite of its defects,—perhaps on account of them—and a sort of French Lord Warburton, but wittier, and not so good. "These are my ideas," says his sister-in-law, at the end of a number of inanities. "Ah, you call them ideas!" he returns, which is delicious and makes you love him. He, too, has his moments of misgiving, apparently in regard to his nobility, and his acceptance of Newman on the basis of something like "manhood suffrage" is very charming. It is of course difficult for a remote plebeian to verify the pictures of legitimist society in "The American," but there is the probable suggestion in them of conditions and principles, and want of principles, of which we get glimpses in our travels abroad; at any rate, they reveal another and not impossible world, and it is fine to have Newman discover that the opinions and criticisms of our world are so absolutely valueless in that sphere that his knowledge of the infamous crime of the mother and brother of his betrothed will have no effect whatever upon them in their own circle if he explodes it there. This seems like aristocracy indeed! and one admires, almost respects, its survival in our day. But I always regretted that Newman's discovery seemed the precursor of his magnanimous resolution not to avenge himself; it weakened the effect of this, with which it had really nothing to do. Upon the whole, however, Newman is an adequate and satisfying representative of Americanism, with his generous matrimonial ambition, his vast good-nature, and his thorough good sense and right feeling. We must be very hard to please if we are not pleased with him. He is not the "cultivated American" who redeems us from time to time in the eyes of Europe; but he is unquestionably more national, and it is observable that his unaffected fellow-countrymen and women fare very well at Mr. James's hands always; it is the Europeanizing sort like the critical little Bostonian in the "Bundle of Letters," the ladies shocked at Daisy Miller, the mother in the "Pension Beaurepas" who goes about trying to be of the "native" world everywhere, Madame Merle and Gilbert Osmond, Miss Light and her mother, who have reason to complain, if any one has. Doubtless Mr. James does not mean to satirize such Americans, but it is interesting to note how they strike such a keen observer. We are certainly not allowed to like them, and the other sort find somehow a place in our affections along with his good Europeans. It is a little odd, by the way, that in all the printed talk about Mr. James—and there has been no end of it—his power of engaging your preference for certain of his people has been so little commented on. Perhaps it is because he makes no obvious appeal for them; but one likes such men as Lord Warburton, Newman, Valentin, the artistic brother in "The Europeans," and Ralph Touchett, and such women as Isabel, Claire Belgarde, Mrs. Tristram, and certain others, with a thoroughness that is one of the best testimonies to their vitality. This comes about through their own qualities, and is not affected by insinuation or by downright *petting*, such as we find in Dickens nearly always and in Thackeray too often.

The art of fiction has, in fact, become a finer art in our day than it was with Dickens and Thackeray. We could not suffer the confidential attitude of the latter now, nor the mannerism of the former, any more than we could endure the prolixity of Richardson or the coarseness of Fielding. These great men are of the past—they and their methods and interests; even Trollope and Reade are not of the present. The new school derives from Hawthorne and George Eliot rather than any others; but it studies human nature much more in its wonted aspects, and finds its ethical and dramatic examples in the operation of lighter but not really less vital motives. The moving accident is certainly not its trade; and it prefers to avoid all manner of dire catastrophes. It is largely influenced by French fiction in form; but it is the realism of Daudet rather than the realism of Zola that prevails with it, and it has a soul of its own which is above the business of recording the rather brutish pursuit of a woman by a man, which seems to be the chief end of the French novelist. This school, which is so largely of the future as well as the present, finds its chief exemplar in Mr. James; it is he who is shaping and directing American fiction, at least. It is the ambition of the younger contributors to write like him; he has his following more distinctly recognizable than that of any other English-writing novelist. Whether he will so far control this following as to decide the nature of the novel with us remains to be seen. Will the reader be content to accept a novel which is an analytic study rather than a story, which is apt to leave him arbiter of the destiny of the author's creations? Will he find his account in the unflagging interest of their development? Mr. James's growing popularity seems to suggest that this may be the case; but the work of Mr. James's imitators will have much to do with the final result.

In the meantime it is not surprising that he has his imitators. Whatever exceptions we take to his methods or his results, we cannot deny him a very great literary genius. To me there is a perpetual delight in his way of saying things, and I cannot wonder that younger men try to catch the trick of it. The disappointing thing for them is that it is not a trick, but an inherent virtue. His style is, upon the whole, better than that of any other novelist I know; it is always easy, without being trivial, and it is often stately, without being stiff; it gives a charm to everything he writes; and he has written so much and in such various directions, that we should be judging him very incompletely if we considered him only as a novelist. His book of European sketches must rank him with the most enlightened and agreeable travelers; and it might be fitly supplemented from his uncollected papers with a volume of American sketches. In his essays on modern French writers he indicates his critical range and grasp; but he scarcely does more, as his criticisms in the "The Atlantic" and "The Nation" and elsewhere could abundantly testify.

There are indeed those who insist that criticism is his true vocation, and are impatient of his devotion to fiction; but I suspect that these admirers are mistaken. A novelist he is not, after the old fashion, or after any fashion but his own; yet since he has finally made his public in his own way of storytelling—or call it character-painting if you prefer,—it must be conceded that he has chosen best for himself and his readers in choosing the form of fiction for what he has to say. It is, after all, what a writer has to say rather than what he has to tell that we care for nowadays. In one manner or other the stories were all told long ago; and now we want merely to know what the novelist thinks about persons and situations. Mr. James gratifies this philosophic desire. If he sometimes forbears to tell us what he thinks of the last state of his people, it is perhaps because that does not interest him, and a large-minded criticism might well insist that it was childish to demand that it must interest him.

I am not sure that my criticism is sufficiently large-minded for this. I own that I like a finished story; but then also I like those which Mr. James seems not to finish. This is probably the position of most of his readers, who cannot very logically account for either preference. We can only make sure that we have here an annalist, or analyst, as we choose, who fascinates us from his first page to his last, whose narrative or whose comment may enter into any minuteness of detail without fatiguing us, and can only truly grieve us when it ceases.

*W. D. Howells.*

# London Society

a) E. S. Nadal, 'Personal Recollections of Henry James', *Scribner's Magazine* (1920)

b) Justin McCarthy, *Reminiscences*, 2 vols (London: Chatto & Windus 1899), vol. ii

The two pieces included in this section, Nadal's recollections and a much briefer comment by Justin McCarthy, both focus on James's decision to settle in Europe and on his social success in London society. Whereas Nadal, a patriotic American, betrays some hostility towards James's anglophilia, McCarthy implicitly approves his decision to settle in England and writes warmly about James in a section of his book devoted to 'Americans in London'.

Ehrman Syme Nadal (1843–1922), a diplomat from Virginia, worked as a journalist in New York where he wrote articles on the London social scene, before becoming the Second Secretary of the American Legation in London. James reviewed his *Impressions of London Social Life* (1875), describing it as a 'gentlemanly book' (Edel, ii, p. 322). He and Henry James became acquainted in the late 1870s when James was living at number 3 Bolton Street, just off Piccadilly. This period saw the publication of *Daisy Miller* (1878), a great popular success. James was perceived as a highly desirable dinner guest by London hostesses, and his social aspirations emerge very clearly in the recollections of the (ostensibly) less ambitious Nadal. Nadal's colleague, the First Secretary of the American Legation, William James Hoppin, found James's popularity dispiriting. In 1879 he wrote rather sulkily in his diary:

> The great success of James leads me to inquire how it is that some people succeed so well here while others constantly fail ... I am satisfied that youth and personal appearance have a good deal to do with such matters. An old fellow like myself with an unprepossessing exterior has but a small chance. I don't write this by way of complaint. I merely state the facts. I amuse myself sufficiently without these attentions. (Edel, ii, pp. 325–6)

Nadal, like many of his fellow Americans, felt some ambivalence towards James's residence in England and eventual naturalisation. In this piece it is clear that Nadal's patriotism is irritated by James's praise of English good looks and by his distaste of American tourists. This irritation emerges most truculently towards the end of the essay when he criticises his 'incomprehensible and, it seems to me, altogether unfortunate method of speech' (p. 23).

This lack of complete harmony between the two men is also conveyed in Nadal's account of their conversation about poetry. The diplomat emerges here as a rather pedantic and literal-minded reader, anxious to select only 'the best' and perhaps not fully alert to the nuances of James's teasing 'What classical taste you've got' (p. 19). This hint that James may have found Nadal rather ridiculous is confirmed in a letter he wrote to his sister Alice in 1879: 'The little second secretary of the Legation [had] a most amiable nature but the feeblest and vaguest mind, and socially speaking, a perfect failure here – though he is not aware of it and it doesn't seem at all to have embittered him. He is a wonderful specimen of American innocence' (*Letters*, ii, p. 214).

*Pace* James, there is some acuteness in Nadal's analysis, and his observation that women are drawn to James because he 'seemed to look at women rather as women look at them' (p. 20) is telling. George Moore makes a similar observation about James's relationships with women: 'He did not carry my thoughts towards a man who had known women at first hand and intimately, but one who had watched them with literary rather than personal interest' (George Moore, *Avowals* (London: Cumann Sean-eolais na h-Eireann, 1919), p. 181). And the supposed magnetic appeal of James for women is the subject of a fantastic anecdote related by the writer and actress Elizabeth Robins:

> There was a general impression that Mr. James was much beset by the attentions of ladies. One story dates from the days when domestic electric lighting was not yet fully under control. The first of the great London establishments to install the new luxury was if I remember, Grosvenor House. At the subsequent evening party when the scene was at its most brilliant, suddenly the lights went out. As suddenly they came on, to discover – so the story went – thirteen ladies clinging to Mr. James. (Robins, pp. 171–2)

There may be some connection between Nadal's conception of James's attitude towards women, his emphasis on James's bachelor status, and his irritated account of James's somewhat caressing and proprietorial attitude towards himself: 'He seemed to have me more on his mind than I thought there was any occasion for' (p. 22) remarks Nadal, rather peevishly. Buried in this profile of the novelist we may, just possibly, detect an early allusion to James's perceived homosexuality.

Justin McCarthy (1830–1912), like Nadal, identifies Henry James as a highly popular figure on the London social scene. McCarthy was born in Cork but moved to England as a young man where he worked as a political journalist and was the editor of the radical *Morning Star* between 1864 and 1868. McCarthy continued to write for numerous periodicals including the *Fortnightly Review* and *Nineteenth Century*, and also gained success as a prolific novelist. In 1880 James reported meeting McCarthy at a dinner party given by E. D. J. Wilson of *The Times* in a letter to Thomas Sergeant Parry. Wilson described James as 'better than his novels, and a great journalist' (*Letters*, ii, p. 275).

## PERSONAL RECOLLECTIONS OF HENRY JAMES

### By E. S. Nadal

I DID not know James as a very young man. I did not make his acquaintance until some time in the seventies. The first time I saw him was at one of those afternoon parties given at the London Legation on the Fourth of July. A notice of the party would be published in the papers and any one was welcome who had a black coat, or, for that matter, a gray one. No cards were required in those days, which are now considered a necessity to keep out crooks. Mrs. Pierrepont, a graceful, pretty, and elegant-looking woman, stood at the door receiving. A rather dark and decidedly handsome young man of medium height, with a full beard, stood in the doorway and bowed rather stiffly, as if he were not to be confused with the rank and file of his compatriots. I was at once struck by his appearance, and I could see that the lady was also impressed and was wondering who he was. Later I saw him talking with Eugene Schuyler. I asked Schuyler who he was, and he told me it was James and introduced me to him. James talked about London with enthusiasm, and was charmed by the "accidental" in London, as he called it, by which no doubt he meant that something which had happened a long time ago and had ceased to be useful, was not abolished but was suffered to remain, corrected, or supplemented by something else—which was also an accident, such a fact, for instance, I suppose, as that the county-seat of Middlesex was not London but Brentford, an ancient act of Parliament permitting courts to be held in London for "the convenience of barristers." James told me he had taken rooms in Bolton Street and hoped I would come and see him there. I answered that the first rooms that I had had in London were in Bolton Street— No. 6. He said: "Mine are No. 3, the half of your old number; you can remember it by that." I happened at that time to have permission to take people over Holland House, and I went there a day or two afterward with James and the late John L. Cadwalader, who had recently been at the State Department, where he was assistant secretary under Mr. Fish. A few days afterward I took breakfast with James in his Bolton Street lodgings and he had also Cadwalader. After that I would often go there to see him. There was a slender, tall, dark, rather pretty girl who usually came to the door when I called. She was not a servant, but a relation of the landlady. James, with his quick sympathy and the keen interest he had lately acquired in English habits, said: "She's an English character. She is what they call in England a 'person.' She isn't a lady and she isn't a woman; she's a person." He told me this about her: that her risibilities were very easily affected. When he made a remark in the least jocose she would at once be overcome with laughter and would beg him to desist, saying: "Oh, please don't, Mr. James, it's quite too funny." During that summer we dined together a great deal at the Café Royal in the Quadrant, Regent Street, which had been only recently opened. This was in the summer of 1877. Later we often dined at a club in Piccadilly to which I belonged. The season was over and there was nothing to do in the evening, and after dinner we would walk in the park or about the London streets. As we walked along, James talked incessantly and with the originality and somewhat of the authority of those who read aloud to you their thoughts out of their own minds. His talk was very alert and eager. I recall at the moment one or two incidents of those walks. A little street-walker begged of us. As he gave her something, he said with feeling: "They imitate so well the tones of wretchedness." Again I remember his using the expression "This town, which I adore."

When I knew him best and saw most of him we had both just come to live in England. I expected to make diplomacy a profession. I was therefore chiefly anxious to please my masters in Washington, but I also wished incidentally to get on with the English. James had quite decided to live in London and so naturally wanted to know English society. He frankly said so. Thus, when I happened to speak with some disapprobation of the pursuit by Americans of social success in London in spite of the rudeness encountered from some of the London social leaders, he said: "I don't agree with you. I think a position in society is a legitimate object of ambition." In the things he wrote about that time I could see indications that his personal relations with English society were very much in his mind. In "An International Episode" an American woman says that an English woman had said to her, "In one's own class," meaning the middle class and meaning also that the American woman belonged to that class. The American woman says that she didn't see what right the English woman had to talk to her in that manner. This was a transcript of an incident he related to me one night when we were walking about the London streets. Some lady of the English middle class, whom he had lately visited in the country, had said to him, "That is true of the aristocracy, but in one's own class it is different," meaning, said James, "her class and mine." He did not wish to be confounded with the mass of English people and to be adjudged a place in English society in accordance with English standards. In order that this should not happen he preferred, although he expected to make England his home, to remain a foreigner. In his charming sketch "Lady Barbarina," he has a rich young doctor, an American, who proposes to and marries a young woman of the English upper class. In his proposal the doctor addresses the lady in a very spirited speech, in which there is, for James, quite a surprising degree of the sentiment of a lover. He tells her: "I love you from head to foot." To this declaration she returns a non-committal answer. She looks at him narrowly and says: "You're a foreigner." In this he was making the young lady say what he himself thought and wished to be true. I don't think he wanted to be in smart English society, because he really preferred the company of smart people. It was rather that he did not like to feel that he was shut out from that or any other kind of company. He would tell me that he wanted "to be taken seriously" by the English; that was a phrase he often made use of. He told me once that he particularly detested "that excluded feeling." I dare say also that he wanted to be enough in smart company to know what it was like. He wished to be an international novelist, and desired to know that as well as other parts of English life. Then he knew that it is perhaps truer of England than of any other country that "a box ticket takes you through the house." Other people, whose company I dare say he really preferred, artists, and people of letters, etc., would think all the more of him if he were about in the world of fashion.

The accounts of English life which, in his character of an international novelist, he wrote at that time were as a rule fairly correct, though he would now and then make a slip. In the story mentioned above, "An International Episode," he has a flirtation between an Englishman, Lord Lambeth, and a New York girl. He told me, at the time this story appeared, that certain London ladies, who were friends of his and were interested in his literary fortunes, thought he had got this young man too rough and slangy. He said, however, that he was not of that opinion. I thought the ladies were right, in one instance certainly. Lord Lambeth, in talking with the girl, speaks of bad food as "filth." I have known many smart young Englishmen, and I have never heard one of them describe food in that way, and I am sure that a young English gentleman would not so describe it in conversation with a young lady.

At that time he was rather keen upon the subject of English clubs. He liked them and wanted to become a member of one or two of them. He had his name put up for the Reform. He had no difficulty in obtaining an election, but of course one can never be quite sure of getting into a club. I remember his saying to me: "If I should fail in this, I shall then go to work and write some things and try to get an election to the Athenæum." He meant an election under the rule of that club which permits the choice annually of a certain number of men who have become distinguished in politics, literature, science, or the fine arts. He said that he had already certain friends in that club who were taking care of him. Some months after this he came in one day to see me and told me he had been elected to the Athenæum. What he said was characteristic. He had just returned from a visit to this country. He said he was in Cambridge, Mass., and started to walk in the direction of Boston, hoping to meet the postman on the way. There was a terrible blizzard and snowstorm in progress, which made England in the distance look all the more alluring. He met the postman, who put into his hands a letter from the Athenæum informing him of his election to the club. During this visit he wrote over to a friend in London that he should never be happy again till he found himself in a hansom, that vehicle not yet having been naturalized in this country.

He was a keen and eager observer. I introduced him once at a club to an English acquaintance. James said of him: "What strange hands he has." I knew the man very well and had noticed his hands, but had not given them much thought. James said: "You mean to say you never observed his hands. He has very handsome hands, but such a strange way of using them." Once we dined at a club and were sitting by the fire in the smoking-room after dinner. There were two Englishmen, whom neither of us knew, standing by the fire. One of them was a stupid-looking man who talked a great deal, and James, who had been watching the man closely, turning to me, said eagerly: "He's a fool."

He was at that time very keen and eager in observing differences between us and the English. The English scold us for this propensity, but what is more natural than that a man going from his own country to another should be interested in differences in character and manners between the peoples of the two countries? I recall this. He had been staying at a hotel in the country and had been in the habit of dining there in company with an Englishman. There was a man waiting at the table whose manners James thought unpleasantly servile. The Englishman, however, called attention to the man's excellent manners. "He thought the man had good manners," said James, "and I thought him a cringing old rascal." He thought Americans had big ears; he thought, however, that big, ugly features were more likely to be found in English than in American faces. But he thought the English very handsome. That is no doubt true; they are a handsome people. He thought that our people are not good-looking. I doubt, however, if his way of making a comparison was quite fair. In England the different kinds of people are sorted and separated; here they are mixed up together. It is not fair to compare the selected people of England with our mass. The half-starved inhabitants of Whitechapel are not handsome, nor are the operatives in English manufacturing towns. On the other hand, there is plenty of good looks among those of our people who have had the advantages of good food and lodgings and of our modern outdoor life. Of course James knew this, for he often introduced such people into his novels. A great deal of James's writing, when he first went to England, was upon these differences. But this is a subject which is soon exhausted, if the observer continues to live in the foreign country. A friend of mine, who was long our Secretary of Legation in Madrid, and who was by way of being literary, told me that when he was asked to write about Spain he found that he had nothing to say. The reason was that he saw nothing. He had got as used to the streets of Madrid as people in New York are to Broadway. This is especially true of external characteristics, of differences in looks. In my own case, when I am in a new country and have to write something about it, I am in haste to set down what I see for fear the new scene may soon lose its strangeness. Thus the man from Europe, who came to this country to write a book about it and who landed in the morning, walked up and down Broadway, and took passage home by a steamer in the afternoon, was not so wide of the mark as it might seem.

It was about the time I first knew him that he definitely made up his mind to choose Europe, and especially England, as a place to live in instead of America. It is true perhaps that his preference had always been for Europe. He told me once that he remembered a particular moment when he decided that his preference was for Europe as his part of the world. He was a boy of about fourteen at the time, and the scene was somewhere on the Continent, and he was sitting out-of-doors, looking upon such a prospect as he liked, the landscape perhaps adorned with a castle or a cathedral. It was a kind of choice of Hercules for the young globetrotter. At that moment, however, he merely decided what his preference was. I think he did not definitely decide to live in Europe until he was a man past thirty. Just before the time of my first acquaintance with him he had, in the sixties and early seventies, spent a long time here. He told me that he had then given the country a "good trial." If he was to live in Europe, I can understand why he should fix upon England. He might have made his home in Italy or in France, the language of which latter country he knew almost perfectly, although he spoke it with an accent, and I think in the end it would have been better if he had done that. But I dare say he felt that there was something thin and superficial in an American's life on the Continent. He wanted a place where his roots would be deeper than they could be in France or Italy, in which countries his acquaintances would be chiefly American. English manners and habits attracted him strongly. He liked the repose of the English character, so entirely self-contented. Then there is a certain hospitality toward foreigners in English society and also a certain resistance, and the combination attracted James. In France I believe there is very little hospitality toward the foreigner. The French are inhospitable perhaps because they are so keenly social, because they value social enjoyment so highly. A foreigner is a wet blanket, a "killjoy." But the English are not social and do not have a very keen enjoyment of society. A foreigner is not a killjoy, because there is not much social joy to kill. English society is easy to get into in a way, and yet it also offers some resistance to foreigners, for it does not like foreigners. James, I have no doubt, found a good deal of fun in the effort to overcome this resistance.

During the time James lived in this country, and for some years afterward, he wrote a good deal for *The Nation*. I did a little work at one time on that paper, and got to know the men connected with it. It was during the Grant and Greeley campaign of 1872, when I wrote some political editorials for it. James, I think, did a great deal of work for it. The tone of the paper was critical, superior, and somewhat toploftical. The other young men were of much the same disposition. Among them was Dennett, the literary critic, a tall, big fellow, strikingly handsome, with long brown hair parted in the middle, after the conventional manner of poets. He had been the class poet of 1862 at Harvard, when my old friend Charlie Grinnell was class orator, and was, I have been told, a poet of distinction, which I can well believe. He had a full brown beard and looked at you through glasses with clear, beautiful eyes, hazel in color. He was superior in a shy way. There was the managing editor, the grave, earnest, and judicious Garrison, the son of the Abolitionist, with a conscience such as you might expect a man of his paternity to have, his severity and asceticism, however, reserved almost exclusively for himself and not employed upon other people. Arthur Sedgwick, whom we have not long ago lost, was another, a handsome, *distingué* young fellow—*distingué*, indeed, he always remained. There was a fineness of perception and of instinct in him you would not expect to see associated with his somewhat heavy traits; of course he had great fineness of feeling. He was a man for whom all who knew him well had a warm affection, and whom now those of us who have survived him keenly regret and feel the absence of. Sedgwick was also superior, as were the two Adamses, who had some sort of connection with the paper. Why should they not feel so?

They were clever and young, thirty or thereabouts, and had the best intentions toward humanity. They were an honest lot, with every right to think well of themselves. I dare say they did feel their oats. The time is short in men's lives when they may feel in that lofty and confident manner. Who would grudge them their day of youthful hope and courage? They were nearly all Harvard men and were more or less connected with Cambridge. The war had been fought and the North had come out on top and Boston on top of that, and Cambridge, perhaps, in some respects on top of Boston. Doctor Holmes had lately promulgated his theory of a Brahmin caste, which flattery, of course, had been duly swallowed. These young men were of that type, although I think Dennett was a Canadian. The paper had remarkable success. Its opportunity lay in the need of an opposition to the tyranny of the party which had won the war. Everybody had been talking and thinking, or talking rather than thinking, one way. There was room for a paper which should express the sentiment of

"the honest few
Who give the fiend himself his due."

It treated literary matters in the same independent way in which it treated politics. I don't think it would now be possible for any paper to put up such a bluff and get away with it as that little paper did. We have grown less impressible, and more critical and suspicious, and we should want to see the cards. Sedgwick, who went to Washington in the winter of 1876 to watch the Hayes-Tilden affair, told me that he sat at dinner next to a young lady of whom I shall only say that she was the original of *Virginia Dare* in "Democracy," a kind-hearted girl with a clever wit. She, not knowing that Sedgwick was from Cambridge or that he was connected with *The Nation*, told him that she had just been on a visit to Cambridge, and remarked: "It's a queer place; they don't have any opinions there till Thursday morning, when a paper comes out called *The Nation*, which tells them what they are to think and say for the next week." James had a natural sympathy with the tone of the paper.

The critical things he wrote were a little superfine and would contain a good many such words as "note," "appeal," "convincing"; very convenient terms, no doubt, but which a writer who prefers freshness, modesty, and simplicity might think to savor somewhat too much of the shop and would, if possible, rather avoid. They were always elegant and pleasant, as may be said of all his things written at that time, but it seemed to me that they were somewhat deficient in point. Why they should have been so, I am sure I don't know, for he was full of intelligence and, in criticising fiction, he had a technical knowledge and experience, which must have had a special value. About 1877 I remember his telling me that he had been writing fiction a long time and had acquired some skill in it. Literary criticism, however, was scarcely his *forte*. I don't think he was what you would call a reading kind of man. His books were people. Once, when he was at my rooms in Down Street, he found Shakespeare, Milton, and some other good poetry on my table, and said with a laugh: "What classical taste you've got!" I explained that my eyes at that time were not strong, and that I chose to read poetry as the most condensed form of literature, and of course read the best.

Although I did not know him at the time he was living in America, I would hear a good deal about him, chiefly from ladies. What they invariably said of him was that he was distinguished and possessed of an inscrutability which piqued their interest and curiosity, that he was very good-looking and attractive, etc. Distinguished he was in a marked degree, both as a young man and an old one. It was one of his most striking qualities.

James, I think, found his best friends among women. They liked him for various reasons. He had fame, and they liked him for that. Then there are women who particularly value the friendship of a clever and distinguished man because it is pleasing to their vanity. Some friendships of his with women I knew, I think, had this foundation. Women liked him also for his good looks and charming manners and his innate refinement. They liked him especially for his sympathetic and delicate discernment of their own nice qualities. He seemed to look at women rather as women look at them. Women look at women as persons; men look at them as women. The quality of sex in women, which is their first and chief attraction to most men, was not their chief attraction to James. Often I did not care for his judgment of women. That is no doubt as it should be; it is a common saying in my line of business, which is horses, that it is a fortunate circumstance that all men do not prefer the same horse or the same woman. I remember his walking with me twice the length of Piccadilly, from Piccadilly Circus to Hyde Park corner and back, one afternoon descanting upon the perfections of a certain American woman he had just met, the wife of an old school friend of his. A day or two afterward I met this lady somewhere at luncheon. On being introduced to her, I thought: "Yes, you're very pretty, but you can't dance." I was put next her at the table and presently took an opportunity of asking if she liked dancing, and she said she cared nothing at all about it. I think he liked a pronounced and perhaps somewhat conscious refinement in women. There was an English woman, a spinster, who was and who always remained one of his most intimate and devoted friends, and whom I knew. She was rather pretty, and you needed only glance at her to see that she was especially what you call "nice." This lady had the somewhat extreme refinement I am speaking of. I recall as characteristic one remark of hers: she once asked me if I did not think it was vulgar to take offense.

Of all the men I ever knew he was the man whom I could least imagine with a wife. When he would be recommending matrimony to me and I would say, "Why don't you?" he would reply with quiet conviction: "I'm not a marrying man."

He may have been sorry for this later. Most men who grow old without children regret they have forfeited that kind of immortality which comes of mixing your blood with that of posterity. An American lady, the mother of children, met him in London in company with several persons who like himself were childless; she told me that he said to her: "You are the only one of us who has accomplished what is, after all, the most important and the most desirable thing in life."

In 1891 I went to London after an absence of some years, and left a card on him. A day or two afterward I found his card at my lodgings, with a letter beginning "Welcome back to old England," and asking me to lunch with him. I found him in a handsome apartment in Kensington. He had a butler of a most respectable appearance, and he had a dachshund bitch with a beautiful countenance. He sat with the dachshund in his lap much of the time. We were speaking on the subject of sex in women and were comparing European with American women in this regard. I had a notion that American women had less of this quality than European women, that in many American women it was negative, and in European women positive, and that many American girls looked like effeminate boys. There is a certain amount of truth in this, but perhaps not a great deal. James said, stroking the head of the dachshund: "She's got sex, if you like, and she's quite intelligent enough to be shocked by this conversation." He told me that his books had no sale. He said that he had written an article for the *Atlantic* on Lowell, remarking that it was too early to write anything critical about him. He said that Lowell had stayed with him during a recent visit to London and that he seemed very unhappy. I told him that I had just arranged with an English magazine for an article on Lowell, and he said, with his customary good sense: "Don't write for English magazines; write for American ones." He pointed to two large volumes on a table by his brother, the philosopher, with a fraternal pride which was pleasant to see. Of English society he seemed to be rather tired, saying that he had done it and was content for the future to let it alone. He remarked that he should never again enter an English country house accompanied by a portmanteau. He complained bitterly of the dreadful cold of the previous winter in London, but did not seem to be more attracted to his own country on that account. He expressed his abhorrence of the American women tourists, with Baedekers in their hands, he had seen during a recent visit to Dublin, saying: "Of course in any other country such people don't travel." I was not of his opinion, because I know how much nicer such people often are, and for that matter look, on closer acquaintance. He told me that he was in the habit of dining alone in his apartment. I asked: "Don't you find that dull?" He said: "No, I don't mind it." I couldn't help thinking that a mistake, for even when you dine alone at a club there is a certain amount of companionship in seeing men you know about the room. He didn't seem as happy as he used to be, and I could have wished him back in his old lodgings at No. 3 Bolton Street, "the half of my old number," without the very respectable butler, and looked after by the tall, slender, dark, rather pretty "person" with the sensitive risibilities.

James at this time had just brought out a play, which had been damned. Grant Duff had told me that he had understood that the play was liked by the people in the top galleries. I repeated this to James, who said he believed it was true. He spoke of play-writing as an infinitely difficult art, in which, however, he still had hopes of success. To anybody as fond of London as James was, it ought to have been delightful to be "damned." I don't know what the theatre was. Let us hope it was one of the good old London houses, the Haymarket, for instance, so that he should have missed nothing of the full flavor of the classic experience, and have been like Charles Lamb, who, when his play was hooted off the stage, joined the hooters, or Fielding seated behind the scenes on a first night, waiting for the verdict of the audience, a quid of chewing-tobacco stuck in his mouth, and saying to a friend who had come in from the front and told him the play was bad and ought to be withdrawn, "Let 'em find it out, damn 'em," which they presently did. These great men couldn't do it, but the artificial and conceited Bulwer could. I didn't believe James could do it. He was not dramatic, certainly not theatrical. His talent was critical and narrative. In this attempt he was moving in a direction away from rather than toward his true gift, that introvertive monologue in which he delighted, such as I used to hear from him in our nocturnal walks about the London streets.

But then monologue would not have given him a nice apartment and a combination valet and butler. The nice flat and the butler in a swallow-tail coat were perhaps the result of living in England. It used to be said that keeping a gig constituted respectability in England. But I should think now that, for an unmarried man at any rate, it is having a valet. In a country-house party every one has a valet who can afford it. Not to have one gives away the fact that you can't afford it. It is no very great expense. One could be got for $500.00 a year, and he would keep himself. Formerly it was the custom, and I dare say still is, for men who did not ordinarily keep a man to hire one to take with them to country houses. He was called a "fellow." People here don't care how a bachelor lives. There is indeed not much interest in the financial situation of any but the very rich. There is a good deal of interest in their money and a good deal of respect for it. James, in his recent visits to this country, was much struck by the increased respect for great wealth as compared with the feeling about it when he was a young man. But whether a man pays $5.00 a week for a bedroom or has a house at a rental of $5,000.00 a year, nobody cares and I doubt if very many people know. That is the case in New York, at any rate. So if James had lived here he would not have felt it necessary to be so respectable. Still he was fond of having things nice about him. During his last visit here he said to me: "You don't care how you live; I do care how I live."

During one of our dinners at the Café Royal, I once said to him: "You never make a fool of yourself, do you?" He said: "Never by any chance." He piqued himself especially upon his tact and discretion and upon never losing his head. He had indeed all of these qualities. He thought a great deal of a correct and respectable deportment. On one occasion after we had dined at the club, I took him to see some people in Kensington. I got out of the hansom first and, going up the steps, got hold in the dark of the servant's bell. At the door of a London house there are usually two bells, a visitor's and a servant's bell. James was shocked. "What," he said; "you haven't rung the servant's bell?" It made no difference, as I knew the people intimately. Indeed you can't make evening visits to people in London whom you don't know intimately. His tone toward me was often that of a Dutch uncle. He seemed to have me more on his mind than I thought there was any occasion for. He would say: "You ought to have a new silk hat," or "You ought to get a new dress coat once a year." If, on the contrary, he approved of me, he would express himself to that effect. For instance, once when I had on yellow gloves, he said: "You ought always to wear yellow gloves."

James was much interested in nice dress. At one time we had the same tailor, whose shop in Clifford Street you could see looking northward from the Burlington Arcade, the windows bulging out with flowers and inviting you of a summer afternoon to inspect the counters within, covered with pretty fabrics. The tailor was an agreeable and intelligent man, with whom James used to like to drop in and have a chat, as I did. A good many Americans went to him, among them Henry Adams and a man who knew a good deal more about the subject than any of us, Burdett Coutts. I took a number there myself.

One night I was dining alone with the Lowells, when a servant came in and said that James was at the door. He came in and sat down at the table. Presently we left and went away together. I happened to be wearing a crush-hat. It was out of the season; I suppose I was going to the theatre. He said: "What have you got an opera-hat for?" I said, perhaps with some temper: "Can't I wear a crush-hat if I want to?" He said indulgently and maternally: "Why, yes, of course." Lowell had been talking at dinner about the clever conversation at the Saturday Club in Boston. He said he found nothing like it in London. I believe he thought it better than the talk at Johnson's Club or Will's Coffee-House or even at the Mermaid Tavern. James said: "I call that provincial." "Provincial" and "parochial" he thought were words very descriptive of this country.

At one time he wanted very much to go into the diplomatic service. When Lowell was appointed Minister to Spain, I think he suggested it to Lowell, who no doubt would have been glad to have James with him. But the State Department took the view that, as Lowell himself had not had any diplomatic experience or any official or business experience of any kind, he had better have the assistance of some man of proved official capacity, and Dwight Reed, a clerk in the State Department, was appointed, who turned out an extremely good diplomatic officer and of whom Lowell had a high opinion.

I think James had the notion of a diplomatic career in his head for a long time. Meeting him one day in the street we talked about diplomatic appointments. He spoke of my connection with the Service, of which by that time I was pretty tired. I said: "You wouldn't think anything of it." He replied: "My dear fellow, that's all you know about it; I'm dying of envy." I don't doubt he would have been a very good man for such employment, though you never can be quite sure till you see a man tried. He had tact and good judgment and a great deal of common sense. I think nevertheless it would have been a mistake for James to go into diplomacy. I doubt if it is a good career for any writing man. A writing man's business is to express himself. A diplomat's business is to hold his tongue. Diplomats get very timid. They seem to get into a condition of chronic funk. I don't wonder that they do, when you consider what is expected of them. Bismarck said that it was an indiscretion for a diplomat to keep a diary. Think of that, and be thankful you were born in a free country. Certainly the effect of a diplomatic career is to make speech difficult. That would not have been good for James, who I think had by nature some difficulty in expressing himself. At least in his young days he used to say that when he was at the top of a page he never was quite sure that he should ever be able to get to the bottom of it.

I was speaking with James about

Howells, of whom he was a warm friend. He said that Howells did not like Europe and was not at home there, in which I think he must have been mistaken, and he added: "It's too much for him." Isn't living out of one's own country too much for anybody? Who but an American thinks that living in a country other than his own and getting on with the people of it is part of the whole duty of man? Certainly it is too much for any writer of books to live in a country that is not his own. An author is in pursuit of a very great prize. He wishes his country, and to some extent the rest of the world, to know his mind—an impudent ambition, at the best, it always struck me, on the part of a creature five or six feet high and with a limit of life of seventy or eighty years. There are scarcely more than a half a dozen men in a country at any one time who can accomplish this. The others may almost be said to draw blanks. It would be quite impossible to do it without the support of people's sympathy, and that sympathy a writer can scarcely have in any country but his own. It is quite true that James did reach a position among the first writers of his day in a country which was not his own, but he did it at the expense of acquiring an incomprehensible and, it seems to me, altogether unfortunate method of speech, which was, I believe, in good part the result of an incomplete sympathy.

The same remark, "It's too much for him," was once made to me about James by Mr. Howells. Some years ago Mr. Howells showed me an advertisement, which he had cut out of a newspaper, of a New York apartment-house called the "Henry James," and which he was about sending James. I was charmed, by the way, to find lately in Greensboro, N. C., which was O. Henry's home town and birthplace, a new hotel going up, which was to be the fine hotel of the place, to be called the "O. Henry." Howells said that James was not happy over there, adding: "It's too much for him." He suggested that James's friends here should be doing something to cheer him up. That no doubt was very well for Mr. Howells, with his tact and kindness and his old friendship with James, but I doubted if it would be well for other people to attempt it. I should certainly have been shy of it. James was a man so used to being on the top wave of success and so fond of being there that anything in the nature of commiseration would have been especially unpleasant to him. He was very sharp, and would have been quick to see what was meant by such expressions.

He liked to have a look of success, and I think liked particularly to have that look when he came here. James was always particularly well treated during his brief visits home. I have heard him say in London, after one of his visits to this country, that of course he never could be so great a man anywhere else as he was in his own country. Perhaps a consideration that reconciled him, if he needed to be reconciled, to living abroad was that he would be a greater man during his brief visits home than he could be if he remained here. Of course, if he had come here and stayed and have consented to be one of us hundred million molecules, we should in time have got used to him and have ceased to make much of him. He would probably have lived in New York, which was his birthplace, a fact of which he was proud. He didn't like to be taken for a Boston or Cambridge man. When this was suggested to him, he would say: "I was born in this good city of New York." So he would probably have attached himself to this town. He liked living in the country and would probably have had a little place on the Hudson and have been a commuter, and we should have met him on summer afternoons about the Grand Central Station on his way to the train, with a basket of fruit and a copy of a New York evening paper. That is a situation which would not long have been consistent with any swagger.

But James did not see fit to live in this country. I think it probable that toward the close of his life he regretted that he had made that decision. At any rate, on his last visit here he came intending to remain in this country. But I suppose he found he had deferred his return too long, and that the relations which he had formed with English people and with English life were too strong to be set aside. At the last he became a citizen of Great Britain.

Henry James is an American who may be said to have thoroughly domesticated himself in London Society, and whose books seem to belong to our literature just as much as those of Robert Louis Stevenson or Thomas Hardy. No man is more popular in London dining-rooms and drawing-rooms than Henry James, and a first night at a theatrical performance would seem incomplete if his familiar figure were not to be seen in the stalls or in one of the boxes. Henry James, too, has an interest in political life, and dines with leading public men in the London clubs which represent the one side of politics and the other. He is a delightful talker, and in his talk can develop views and ideas about every passing subject which can clothe even the trivial topics of the day with intellectual grace and meaning. Every now and then some vivid saying or some sparkling epigram comes in, and, indeed, there is only, so far as I know, one thing which Henry James never could do in any conversation—he never could be commonplace.

# Edmund Gosse, *Aspects and Impressions* (London: Cassell & Co. Ltd, 1922)

As a close friend for many years, and a warm though not uncritical admirer of James, the recollections of Edmund Gosse (1849–1928) are a valuable contribution to the biographical record, free of the exaggeration and hyperbole to be found in many posthumous accounts of Henry James. Gosse is now best known for *Father and Son* (1907), his engaging and memorable account of his relationship with his father, Philip Gosse, a naturalist who tried to reconcile science with Biblical literalism. Edmund Gosse was prolific as a poet, critic and translator. In 1875 he married Nellie Epps, then a pupil of Ford Madox Brown. He helped introduce the works of Ibsen to British audiences and worked as a translator at the Board of Trade between 1875 and 1904. Gosse was fond of gossip, prone to flattery and possessed, according to Henry James, 'a genius for inaccuracy' (*Letters*, iii, p. 338).

His strong friendship with Henry James developed in the 1880s and continued until James's death. When James was living in London he was a frequent visitor at the Gosses' house in Delamere Terrace and the two men continued to meet and correspond regularly after James settled in Rye. In a letter written to R. L. Stevenson's widow Fanny in 1896 James describes Gosse as 'the person with whom I can most freely & thoroughly communicate' (Kaplan, p. 398). In a long letter written on 10 November 1907 James expresses his deep appreciation of Gosse's recently published *Father and Son*.

> I have been reading you meanwhile with deep entrancement – spellbound from cover to cover. *F. & S.* is extraordinarily vivid & interesting, beautifully done, remarkably *much* done, & deserving to my sense to be called – which I hope you won't think a disparagement of your literary & historic, your critical achievement – the very best thing you have ever written ... Your wonderful detachment will, I daresay, in its filial light, incur some animadversion – but this is to my mind the very value & condition of the book; though indeed there are perhaps a couple of cases – places – in which I feel it go too far: not too far, I

mean, for truth, but too far for filiality, or at least for tenderness. (Horne, p. 453)

Gosse's devotion to James is conveyed in his emotional response to his friend's application for naturalisation:

> You give us the most intimate thing you possess ... it is most moving, and most cheering, a grand geste indeed ... How I rejoice to think of you as about to be *of* us in this anxious time, as you have been *with* us without fail ever since the troubles began! (Kaplan, p. 558)

This essay is significant as a profile of James's private and public life written by a friend who knew him for many years – a friend who was also an influential and perceptive literary critic. He writes particularly suggestively about James's own personal elusiveness – even in the supposedly self-revelatory prefaces, Gosse observes, 'it is as though the author felt a burning desire to confide in the reader, whom he positively button-holes in the endeavour, but that the experience itself evades him, fails to find expression, and falls stillborn, while other matters, less personal and less important, press in and take their place against the author's wish' (p. 28). Towards the end of the piece he describes his friend as 'like a fountain sealed' in his great discretion, although 'every now and then he disclosed to a friend, or rather admitted such a friend to a flash or glimpse of deeper things' (p. 52). It is interesting that Gosse describes in such detail his impression of 'deeper things' concealed by his friend. There is some evidence to suggest that Gosse, like James, may have been attracted to men. A sympathetic letter he wrote to the (unequivocally) homosexual John Addington Symonds in 1890 hints that he shares his desires, although the passage is certainly open to different interpretations (Kaplan, p. 402). In *Aspects and Impressions* his account of James's 'mysterious and poignant' (p. 53) experience of seeing a lighted lamp in a window but being unable to distinguish the face behind it has been thought by some to conceal or figure repressed homosexual desires. James apparently related the same anecdote to his friend Hugh Walpole (see section 15 in this volume), suggesting that it was indeed a moment charged with great significance for him – Walpole, interestingly, reads a more decided (though still undefined) sexual meaning into the scene. But perhaps this is a tale which, like James's own *Turn of the Screw* (1898), invites its readers not to uncover but to create a meaning, one which reflects their own assumptions and preoccupations.

# HENRY JAMES

## I

VOLUMINOUS as had been the writings of Henry James since 1875, it was not until he approached the end of his career that he began to throw any light on the practical events and social adventures of his own career. He had occasionally shown that he could turn from the psychology of imaginary characters to the record of real lives without losing any part of his delicate penetration or his charm of portraiture. He had, in particular, written the *Life of Hawthorne* in 1879, between *Daisy Miller* and *An International Episode;* and again in 1903, at the height of his latest period, he had produced a specimen of that period in his elusive and parenthetical but very beautiful so-called *Life of W. W. Story*. But these biographies threw no more light upon his own adventures than did his successive volumes of critical and topographical essays, in which the reader may seek long before he detects the sparkle of a crumb of personal fact. Henry James, at the age of seventy, had not begun to reveal himself behind the mask which spoke in the tones of a world of imaginary characters.

So saying, I do not forget that in the general edition of his collected, or rather selected, novels and tales, published from 1908 onwards, Henry James prefixed to each volume an introduction which assumed to be wholly biographical. He yielded, he said, "to the pleasure of placing on record the circumstances" in which each successive tale was written. I well recollect the terms in which he spoke of these prefaces before he began to write them. They were to be full and confidential, they were to throw to the winds all restraints of conventional reticence, they were to take us, with eyes unbandaged, into the inmost sanctum of his soul. They appeared at last, in small print, and they were extremely extensive, but truth obliges me to say that I found them highly disappointing. Constitutionally fitted to take pleasure in the accent of almost everything that Henry James ever wrote, I have to confess that these prefaces constantly baffle my eagerness. Not for a moment would I deny that they throw interesting light on the technical craft of a self-respecting novelist, but they are dry, remote, and impersonal to a strange degree. It is as though the author felt a burning desire to confide in the reader, whom he positively button-holes in the endeavour, but that the experience itself evades him, fails to find expression, and falls stillborn, while other matters, less personal and less important, press in and take their place against the author's wish. Henry James proposed, in each instance, to disclose "the contributive value of the accessory facts in a given artistic case." This is, indeed, what we require in the history or the autobiography of an artist, whether painter or musician or man of letters. But this includes the production of anecdotes, of salient facts, of direct historical statements, which Henry James seemed in 1908 to be completely incapacitated from giving, so that really, in the introductions to some of these novels in the Collected Edition, it is difficult to know what the beloved novelist is endeavouring to divulge. He becomes almost chimæra bombinating in a vacuum.

Had we lost him soon after the appearance of the latest of these prefaces—that prefixed to *The Golden Bowl*, in which the effort to reveal something which is not revealed amounts almost to an agony—it would have been impossible to reconstruct the life of Henry James by the closest examination of his published writings. Ingenious commentators would have pieced together conjectures from such tales as *The Altar of the Dead* and *The Lesson of the Master*, and have insisted, more or less plausibly, on their accordance with what the author *must* have thought or done, endured or attempted. But, after all, these would have been "conjectures," not more definitely based than what bold spirits use when they construct lives of Shakespeare, or, for that matter, of Homer. Fortunately, in 1913, the desire to place some particulars of the career of his marvellous brother William in the setting of his "immediate native and domestic air," led Henry James to contemplate, with minuteness, the fading memories of his own childhood. Starting with a biographical study of William James, he found it impossible to treat the family development at all adequately without extending the survey to his own growth as well, and thus, at the age of seventy, Henry became for the first time, and almost unconsciously, an autobiographer.

He had completed two large volumes of *Memories*, and was deep in a third, when death took him from us. *A Small Boy and Others* deals with such extreme discursiveness as is suitable in a collection of the fleeting impressions of infancy, from his birth in 1843 to his all but fatal attack of typhus fever at Boulogne-sur-Mer in (perhaps) 1857. I say "perhaps" because the wanton evasion of any sort of help in the way of dates is characteristic of the narrative, as it would be of childish memories. The next instalment was *Notes of a Son and Brother*, which opens in 1860, a doubtful period of three years being leaped over lightly, and closes—as I guess from an allusion to George Eliot's *Spanish Gypsy*—in 1868. The third instalment, dictated in the autumn of 1914 and laid aside unfinished, is the posthumous *The Middle Years*, faultlessly edited by the piety of Mr. Percy Lubbock in 1917. Here the tale is taken up in 1869, and is occupied, without much attempt at chronological order, with memories of two years in London. As Henry James did not revise, or perhaps even re-read, these pages, we are free to form our conclusion as to whether he would or would not have vouchsafed to put their disjected parts into some more anatomical order.

Probably he would not have done so. The tendency of his genius had never been, and at the end was less than ever, in the direction of concinnity. He repudiated arrangement, he wilfully neglected the precise adjustment of parts. The three autobiographical volumes will always be documents precious in the eyes of his admirers. They are full of beauty and nobility, they exhibit with delicacy, and sometimes even with splendour, the qualities of his character. But it would be absurd to speak of them as easy to read, or as fulfilling what is demanded from an ordinary biographer. They have the tone of Veronese, but nothing of his definition. A broad canvas is spread before us, containing many figures in social conjuncture. But the plot, the single "story" which is being told, is drowned in misty radiance. Out of this *chiaroscuro* there leap suddenly to our vision a sumptuous head and throat, a handful of roses, the glitter of a satin sleeve, but it is only when we shut our eyes and think over what we have looked at that any coherent plan is revealed to us, or that we detect any species of composition. It is a case which calls for editorial help, and I hope that when the three fragments of autobiography are reprinted as a single composition, no prudery of hesitation to touch the sacred ark will prevent the editor from prefixing a skeleton chronicle of actual dates and facts. It will take nothing from the dignity of the luminous reveries in their original shape.

Such a skeleton will tell us that Henry James was born at 2 Washington Place, New York, on April 15th, 1843, and that he was the second child of his parents, the elder by one year being William, who grew up to be the most eminent philosopher whom America has produced. Their father, Henry James the elder, was himself a philosopher, whose ideas, which the younger Henry frankly admitted to be beyond his grasp, were expounded by William James in 1884, in a preface to their father's posthumous papers. Henry was only one year old when the family paid a long visit to Paris, but his earliest recollections were of Albany, whence the Jameses migrated to New York until 1855. They then transferred their home to Europe for three years, during which time the child Henry imbibed what he afterwards called "the European virus." In 1855 he was sent to Geneva for purposes of education, which were soon abandoned, and the whole family began an aimless wandering through London, Paris, Boulogne-sur-Mer, Newport, Geneva, and America again, nothing but the Civil War sufficing to root this fugitive household in one abiding home.

Henry James's health forced him to be a spectator of the war, in which his younger brothers fought. He went to Harvard in 1862 to study law, but was now beginning to feel a more and more irresistible call to take up letters as a profession, and the Harvard Law School left little or no direct impression upon him. He formed a close and valuable friendship with William Dean Howells, seven years his senior, and the pages of the *Atlantic Monthly*, of which Howells was then assistant editor, were open to him from 1865. He lived for the next four years in very poor health, and with no great encouragement from himself or others, always excepting Howells, at Cambridge, Massachusetts. Early in 1869 he ventured to return to Europe, where he spent fifteen months in elegant but fruitful vagabondage. There was much literary work done, most of which he carefully suppressed in later life. The reader will, however, discover, tucked away in the thirteenth volume of the Collected Edition, a single waif from this rejected epoch, the tale called *A Passionate Pilgrim*, written on his return to America in 1870. This visit to Europe absolutely determined his situation; his arrival in New York stimulated and tortured his nostalgia for the old world, and in May, 1872, he flew back here once more to the European enchantment.

Here, practically, the biographical information respecting Henry James which has hitherto been given to the world ceases, for the fragment of *The Middle Years*, so far as can be gathered, contains few recollections which can be dated later than his thirtieth year. It was said of Marivaux that he cultivated no faculty but that *de ne vivre que pour voir et pour entendre*. In a similar spirit Henry James took up his dwelling in fashionable London lodgings in March, 1869. He had come from America with the settled design of making a profound study of English manners, and there were two aspects of the subject which stood out for him above all others. One of these was the rural beauty of ancient country places, the other was the magnitude—"the inconceivable immensity," as he put it —of London. He told his sister, "The place sits on you, broods on you, stamps on you with the feet of its myriad bipeds and quadrupeds." From his lodgings in Half Moon Street, quiet enough in themselves, he had the turmoil of the West End at his elbow, Piccadilly, Park Lane, St. James's Street, all within the range of a five minutes' stroll. He plunged into the vortex with incredible gusto, "knocking about in a quiet way and deeply enjoying my little adventures." This was his first mature experience of London, of which he remained until the end of his life perhaps the most infatuated student, the most "passionate pilgrim," that America has ever sent us.

But his health was still poor, and for his constitution's sake he went in the summer of 1869 to Great Malvern. He went alone, and it is to be remarked of him that, social as he was, and inclined to a deep indulgence in the company of his friends, his habit of life was always in the main a solitary one. He had no constant associates, and he did not shrink from long periods of isolation, which he spent in reading and writing, but also in a concentrated contemplation of the passing scene, whatever it might be. It was alone that he now made a tour of the principal English cathedral and university towns, expatiating to himself on the perfection of the weather—"the dozen exquisite days of the English year, days stamped with a purity unknown in climates where fine weather is cheap." It was alone that he made acquaintance with Oxford, of which city he became at once the impassioned lover which he continued to be to the end, raving from Boston in 1870 of the supreme gratifications of Oxford as "the most dignified and most educated" of the cradles of our race. It was alone that during these enchanting weeks he made himself acquainted with the unimagined loveliness of English hamlets buried in immemorial leafage and whispered to by meandering rivulets in the warm recesses of antiquity. These, too, found in Henry James a worshipper more ardent, it may almost be averred, than any other who had crossed the Atlantic to their shrine.

Having formed his basis for the main construction of his English studies, Henry James passed over to the Continent, and conducted a similar pilgrimage of entranced obsession through Switzerland and Italy. His wanderings, "rapturous and solitary," were, as in England, hampered by no social engagement; "I see no people to speak of," he wrote, "or for that matter to speak to." He returned to America in April, 1870, at the close of a year which proved critical in his career, and which laid its stamp on the whole of his future work. He had been kindly received in artistic and literary circles in London; he had conversed with Ruskin, with William Morris, with Aubrey de Vere, but it is plain that while he observed the peculiarities of these eminent men with the closest avidity, he made no impression whatever upon them. The time for Henry James to "make an impression" on others was not come yet; he was simply the well-bred, rather shy, young American invalid, with excellent introductions, who crossed the path of English activities, almost without casting a shadow. He had published no book; he had no distinct calling; he was a deprecating and punctilious young stranger from somewhere in Massachusetts, immature-looking for all his seven-and-twenty years.

Some further uneventful seasons, mainly spent in America but diversified by tours in Germany and Italy, bring us to 1875, when Henry James came over from Cambridge with the definite project, at last, of staying in Europe "for good." He took rooms in Paris, at 29 Rue de Luxembourg, and he penetrated easily into the very exclusive literary society which at that time revolved around Flaubert and Edmond de Goncourt. This year in Paris was another highly critical period in Henry James's intellectual history. He was still, at the mature age of thirty-two, almost an amateur in literature, having been content, up to that time, to produce scarcely anything which his mature taste did not afterwards repudiate. *The Passionate Pilgrim* (1870), of which I have spoken above, is the only waif and stray of the pre-1873 years which he has permitted to survive. The first edition of this short story is now not easy of reference, and I have not seen it; the reprint of 1908 is obviously, and is doubtless vigorously, re-handled. Enough, however, remains of what must be original to show that, in a rather crude, and indeed almost hysterical form, the qualities of Henry James's genius were, in 1869, what they continued to be in 1909. He has conquered, however, in *A Passionate Pilgrim*, no command yet over his enthusiasm, his delicate sense of beauty, his apprehension of the exquisite colour of antiquity.

From the French associates of this time he derived practical help in his profession, though without their being aware of what they gave him. He was warmly attracted to Gustave Flaubert, who had just published *La Tentation de St. Antoine*, a dazzled admiration of which was the excuse which threw the young American at the feet of the Rouen giant. This particular admiration dwindled with the passage of time, but Henry James continued faithful to the author of *Madame Bovary*. It was Turgenev who introduced him to Flaubert, from whom he passed to Guy de Maupassant, then an athlete of four-and-twenty, and still scintillating in that blaze of juvenile virility which always fascinated Henry James. In the train of Edmond de Goncourt came Zola, vociferous over his late tribulation of having *L'Assommoir* stopped in its serial issue; Alphonse Daudet, whose recent *Jack* was exercising over tens of thousands of readers the tyranny of tears; and François Coppée, the almost exact coeval of Henry James, and now author of a *Luthier de Crémone*, which had placed him high among French poets. That the young American, with no apparent claim to attention except the laborious perfection of his French speech, was welcomed and ultimately received on terms of intimacy in this the most exclusive of European intellectual circles is curious. Henry James was accustomed to deprecate the notion that these Frenchmen took the least interest in him: "they have never read a line of me, they have never even persuaded themselves that there was a line of me which anyone could read," he once said to me. How should they, poor charming creatures, in their self-sufficing Latin intensity, know what or whether some barbarian had remotely "written"? But this does not end the marvel, because, read or not read, there was Henry James among them, affectionately welcomed, talked to familiarly about "technique," and even about "sales," like a fellow-craftsman. There must evidently have developed by this time something modestly "impressive" about him, and I cannot doubt that these Parisian masters of language more or less dimly divined that he too was, in some medium not by them to be penetrated, a master.

After this fruitful year in Paris, the first result of which was the publication in London of his earliest surviving novel, *Roderick Hudson*, and the completion of *The American*, Henry James left his "glittering, charming, civilized Paris" and settled in London. He submitted himself, as he wrote to his brother William in 1878, "without reserve to that Londonizing process of which the effect is to convince you that, having lived here, you may, if need be, abjure civilization and bury yourself in the country, but may not, in pursuit of civilization, live in any smaller town." He plunged deeply into the study of London, externally and socially, and into the production of literature, in which he was now as steadily active as he was elegantly proficient. These novels of his earliest period have neither the profundity nor the originality of those of his middle and final periods, but they have an exquisite freshness of their own, and a workmanship the lucidity and logic of which he owed in no small measure to his conversations with Daudet and Maupassant, and to his, at that time almost exclusive, reading of the finest French fiction. He published *The American* in 1877, *The Europeans* and *Daisy Miller* in 1878, and *An International Episode* in 1879. He might advance in stature and breadth; he might come to disdain the exiguous beauty of these comparatively juvenile books, but now at all events were clearly revealed all the qualities which were to develop later, and to make Henry James unique among writers of Anglo-Saxon race.

His welcome into English society was remarkable if we reflect that he seemed to have little to give in return for what it offered except his social adaptability, his pleasant and still formal amenity, and his admirable capacity for listening. It cannot be repeated too clearly that the Henry James of those early days had very little of the impressiveness of his later manner. He went everywhere, sedately, watchfully, graciously, but never prominently. In the winter of 1878-79 it is recorded that he dined out in London 107 times, but it is highly questionable whether this amazing assiduity at the best dinner-tables will be found to have impressed itself on any Greville or Crabb Robinson who was taking notes at the time. He was strenuously living up to his standard, "my charming little standard of wit, of grace, of good manners, of vivacity, of urbanity, of intelligence, of what makes an easy and natural style of intercourse." He was watching the rather gross and unironic, but honest and vigorous, English upper-middle-class of that day with mingled feelings, in which curiosity and a sort of remote sympathy took a main part. At 107 London dinners he observed the ever-shifting pieces of the general kaleidoscope with tremendous acuteness, and although he thought their reds and yellows would have been improved by a slight infusion of the Florentine harmony, on the whole he was never weary of watching their evolutions. In this way the years slipped by, while he made a thousand acquaintances and a dozen durable friendships. It is a matter of pride and happiness to me that I am able to touch on one of the latter.

It is often curiously difficult for intimate friends, who have the impression in later years that they must always have known one another, to recall the occasion and the place where they first met. That was the case with Henry James and me. Several times we languidly tried to recover those particulars, but without success. I think, however, that it was at some dinner-party that we first met, and as the incident is dubiously connected with the publication of the *Hawthorne* in 1879, and with Mr. (now Lord) Morley, whom we both frequently saw at that epoch, I am pretty sure that the event took place early in 1880. The acquaintance, however, did not "ripen," as people say, until the summer of 1882, when in connexion with an article on the drawings of George Du Maurier, which I was anxious Henry James should write—having heard him express himself with high enthusiasm regarding these works of art—he invited me to go to see him and to talk over the project. I found him, one sunshiny afternoon, in his lodgings on the first floor of No. 3 Bolton Street, at the Piccadilly end of the street, where the houses look askew into Green Park. Here he had been living ever since he came over from France in 1876, and the situation was eminently characteristic of the impassioned student of London life and haunter of London society which he had now become.

Stretched on the sofa and apologizing for not rising to greet me, his appearance gave me a little shock, for I had not thought of him as an invalid. He hurriedly and rather evasively declared that he was not that, but that a muscular weakness of his spine obliged him, as he said, "to assume the horizontal posture" during some hours of every day in order to bear the almost unbroken routine of evening engagements. I think that this weakness gradually passed away, but certainly for many years it handicapped his activity. I recall his appearance, seen then for the first time by daylight; there was something shadowy about it, the face framed in dark brown hair cut short in the Paris fashion, and in equally dark beard, rather loose and "fluffy." He was in deep mourning, his mother having died five or six months earlier, and he himself having but recently returned from a melancholy visit to America, where he had unwillingly left his father, who seemed far from well. His manner was grave, extremely courteous, but a little formal and frightened, which seemed strange in a man living in constant communication with the world. Our business regarding Du Maurier was soon concluded, and James talked with increasing ease, but always with a punctilious hesitancy, about Paris, where he seemed, to my dazzlement, to know even a larger number of persons of distinction than he did in London.

He promised, before I left, to return my visit, but news of the alarming illness of his father called him suddenly to America. He wrote to me from Boston in April, 1883, but he did not return to London until the autumn of that year. Our intercourse was then resumed, and, immediately, on the familiar footing which it preserved, without an hour's abatement, until the sad moment of his fatal illness. When he returned to Bolton Street—this was in August, 1883—he had broken all the ties which held him to residence in America, a country which, as it turned out, he was not destined to revisit for more than twenty years. By this means Henry James became a homeless man in a peculiar sense, for he continued to be looked upon as a foreigner in London, while he seemed to have lost citizenship in the United States. It was a little later than this that that somewhat acidulated patriot, Colonel Higginson, in reply to someone who said that Henry James was a cosmopolitan, remarked, "Hardly! for a cosmopolitan is at home even in his own country!" This condition made James, although superficially gregarious, essentially isolated, and though his books were numerous and were greatly admired, they were tacitly ignored alike in summaries of English and of American current literature. There was no escape from this dilemma. Henry James was equally determined not to lay down his American birthright and not to reside in America. Every year of his exile, therefore, emphasized the fact of his separation from all other Anglo-Saxons, and he endured, in the world of letters, the singular fate of being a man without a country.

The collection of his private letters, therefore, which has just been published under the sympathetic editorship of Mr. Percy Lubbock, reveals the adventures of an author who, long excluded from two literatures, is now eagerly claimed by both of them, and it displays those movements of a character of great energy and singular originality which circumstances have hitherto concealed from curiosity. There was very little on the surface of his existence to bear evidence to the passionate intensity of the stream beneath. This those who have had the privilege of seeing his letters know is marvellously revealed in his private correspondence. A certain change in his life was brought about by the arrival in 1885 of his sister Alice, who, in now confirmed ill-health, was persuaded to make Bournemouth and afterwards Leamington her home. He could not share her life, but at all events he could assiduously diversify it by his visits, and Bournemouth had a second attraction for him in the presence of Robert Louis Stevenson, with whom he had by this time formed one of the closest of his friendships. Stevenson's side of the correspondence has long been known, and it is one of the main attractions which Mr. Lubbock held out to his readers that Henry James's letters to Stevenson are now published. No episode of the literary history of the time is more fascinating than the interchange of feeling between these two great artists. The death of Stevenson, nine years later than their first meeting, though long anticipated, fell upon Henry James with a shock which he found at first scarcely endurable. For a long time afterwards he could not bring himself to mention the name of R. L. S. without a distressing agitation.

In 1886 the publication of *The Bostonians*, a novel which showed an advance in direct or, as it was then styled, "realistic" painting of modern society, increased the cleft which now divided him from his native country, for *The Bostonians* was angrily regarded as satirizing not merely certain types, but certain recognizable figures in Massachusetts, and that with a suggestive daring which was unusual. Henry James, intent upon making a vivid picture, and already perhaps a little out of touch with American sentiment, was indignant at the reception of this book, which he ultimately, to my great disappointment, omitted from his Collected Edition, for reasons which he gave in a long letter to myself. Hence, as his works now appear, *The Princess Casamassima*, of 1886, an essentially

London adventure story, takes its place as the earliest of the novels of his second period, although preceded by admirable short tales in that manner, the most characteristic of which is doubtless *The Author of Beltraffio* (1885). This exemplifies the custom he had now adopted of seizing an incident reported to him, often a very slight and bald affair, and weaving round it a thick and glittering web of silken fancy, just as the worm winds round the unsightly chrysalis its graceful robe of gold. I speak of *The Author of Beltraffio,* and after thirty-five years I may confess that this extraordinarily vivid story was woven around a dark incident in the private life of an eminent author known to us both, which I, having told Henry James in a moment of levity, was presently horrified and even sensibly alarmed to see thus pinnacled in the broad light of day.

After exhausting at last the not very shining amenities of his lodgings in Bolton Street, where all was old and dingy, he went westward in 1886 into Kensington, and settled in a flat which was both new and bright, at 34 De Vere Gardens, Kensington, where he began a novel called *The Tragic Muse,* on which he expended an immense amount of pains. He was greatly wearied by the effort, and not entirely satisfied with the result. He determined, as he said, "to do nothing but short lengths" for the future, and he devoted himself to the execution of *contes.* But even the art of the short story presently yielded to a new and, it must be confessed, a deleterious fascination, that of the stage. He was disappointed—he made no secret to his friends of his disillusion—in the commercial success of his novels, which was inadequate to his needs. I believe that he greatly over-estimated these needs, and that at no time he was really pressed by the want of money. But he thought that he was, and in his anxiety he turned to the theatre as a market in which to earn a fortune. Little has hitherto been revealed with regard to this "sawdust and orange-peel phase" (as he called it) in Henry James's career, but it cannot be ignored any longer. The memories of his intimate friends are stored with its incidents, his letters will be found to be full of it.

Henry James wrote, between 1889 and 1894, seven or eight plays, on each of which he expended an infinitude of pains and mental distress. At the end of this period, unwillingly persuaded at last that all his agony was in vain, and that he could never secure fame and fortune, or even a patient hearing from the theatre-going public by his dramatic work, he abandoned the hopeless struggle. He was by temperament little fitted to endure the disappointments and delays which must always attend the course of a dramatist who has not conquered a position which enables him to browbeat the tyrants behind the stage. Henry James was punctilious, ceremonious, and precise; it is not to be denied that he was apt to be hasty in taking offence, and not very ready to overlook an impertinence. The whole existence of the actor is lax and casual; the manager is the capricious leader of an irresponsible band of egotists. Henry James lost no occasion of dwelling, in private conversation, on this aspect of an amiable and entertaining profession. He was not prepared to accept young actresses at their own valuation, and the happy-go-lucky democracy of the "mimes," as he bracketed both sexes, irritated him to the verge of frenzy.

It was, however, with a determination to curb his impatience, and with a conviction that he could submit his idiosyncrasies to what he called the "passionate economy" of play-writing, that he began, in 1889, to dedicate himself to the drama, excluding for the time being all other considerations. He went over to Paris in the winter of that year, largely to talk over the stage with Alphonse Daudet and Edmond de Goncourt, and he returned to put the finishing touches on *The American*, a dramatic version of one of his earliest novels. He finished this play at the Palazzo Barbaro, the beautiful home of his friends, the Daniel Curtises, in Venice, in June, 1890, thereupon taking a long holiday, one of the latest of his extended Italian tours, through Venetia and Tuscany. Edward Compton had by this time accepted *The American*, being attracted by his own chances in the part of Christopher Newman. When Henry James reappeared in London, and particularly when the rehearsals began, we all noticed how deeply the theatrical virus had penetrated his nature. His excitement swelled until the evening of January 3rd, 1891, when *The American* was acted at Southport by Compton's company in anticipation of its appearance in London. Henry James was kind enough to wish me to go down on this occasion with him to Southport, but it was not possible. On the afternoon of the ordeal he wrote to me from the local hotel: "After eleven o'clock to-night I *may* be the world's—you know—and I may be the undertaker's. I count upon you and your wife both to spend this evening in fasting, silence, and supplication. I will send you a word in the morning, a wire if I can." He was "so nervous that I miswrite and misspell."

The result, in the provinces, of this first experiment was not decisive. It is true that he told Robert Louis Stevenson that he was enjoying a success which made him blush. But the final result in London, where *The American* was not played until September, 1891, was only partly encouraging. Henry James was now cast down as unreasonably as he had been uplifted. He told me that "the strain, the anxiety, the peculiar form and colour of the ordeal (not to be divined in the least in advance)" had "sickened him to *death*." He used language of the most picturesque extravagance about the "purgatory" of the performances, which ran at the Opera Comique for two months. There was nothing in the mediocre fortunes of this play to decide the questions whether Henry James was or was not justified in abandoning all other forms of art for the drama. We endeavoured to persuade him that, on the whole, he was not justified, but he swept our arguments aside, and he devoted himself wholly to the infatuation of his sterile task.

*The American* had been dramatized from a published novel. Henry James now thought that he should do better with original plots, and he wrote two comedies, the one named *Tenants* and the other *Disengaged,* of each of which he formed high expectations. But, although they were submitted to several managers, who gave them their customary loitering and fluctuating attention, they were in every case ultimately refused. Each refusal plunged the dramatist into the lowest pit of furious depression, from which he presently emerged with freshly-kindled hopes. Like the moralist, he never was but always to be blest. *The Album* and *The Reprobate*—there is a melancholy satisfaction in giving life to the mere names of these stillborn children of his brain—started with wild hopes and suffered from the same complete failure to satisfy the caprice of the managers. At the close of 1893, after one of these "sordid developments," he made up his mind to abandon the struggle. But George Alexander promised that, if he would but persevere, he really and truly would produce him infallibly at no distant date, and poor Henry James could not but persevere. "I mean to wage this war ferociously for one year more," and he composed, with infinite agony and deliberation, the comedy of *Guy Domvile*.

The night of January 5th, 1895, was the most tragical in Henry James's career. His hopes and fears had been strung up to the most excruciating point, and I think that I have never witnessed such agonies of parturition. *Guy Domvile*—which has never been printed—was a delicate and picturesque play, of which the only disadvantage that I could discover was that instead of having a last scene which tied up all the threads in a neat conclusion, it left all those threads loose as they would be in life. George Alexander was sanguine of success, and to do Henry James honour such a galaxy of artistic, literary, and scientific celebrity gathered in the stalls of the St. James's Theatre as perhaps were never seen in a London playhouse before or since. Henry James was positively storm-ridden with emotion before the fatal night, and full of fantastic plans. I recall that one was that he should hide in the bar of a little public-house down an alley close to the theatre, whither I should slip forth at the end of the second act and report "how it was going." This was not carried out, and fortunately Henry James resisted the temptation of being present in the theatre during the performance. All seemed to be going fairly well until the close, when Henry James appeared and was called before the curtain—only to be subjected—to our unspeakable horror and shame—to a storm of hoots and jeers and catcalls from the gallery, answered by loud and sustained applause from the stalls, the whole producing an effect of hell broke loose, in the midst of which the author, as white as chalk, bowed and spread forth deprecating hands and finally vanished. It was said at the time, and confirmed later, that this horrible performance was not intended to humiliate Henry James, but was the result of a cabal against George Alexander.

Early next morning I called at 34 De Vere Gardens, hardly daring to press the bell for fear of the worst of news, so shattered with excitement had the playwright been on the previous evening. I was astonished to find him perfectly calm; he had slept well and was breakfasting with appetite. The theatrical bubble in which he had lived a tormented existence for five years was wholly and finally broken, and he returned, even in that earliest conversation, to the discussion of the work which he had so long and so sadly neglected, the art of direct prose narrative. And now a remarkable thing happened. The discipline of toiling for the caprices of the theatre had amounted, for so redundant an imaginative writer, to the putting on of a mental strait-jacket. He saw now that he need stoop no longer to what he called "a meek and lowly review of the right ways to keep on the right side of a body of people who have paid money to be amused at a particular hour and place." Henry James was not released from this system of vigorous renunciation without a very singular result. To write for the theatre the qualities of brevity and directness, of an elaborate plainness, had been perceived by him to be absolutely necessary, and he had tried to cultivate them with dogged patience for five years. But when he broke with the theatre, the rebound was excessive. I recall his saying to me, after the fiasco of *Guy Domvile*, "At all events, I have escaped for ever from the foul fiend Excision!" He vibrated with the sense of release, and he began to enjoy, physically and intellectually, a freedom which had hitherto been foreign to his nature.

## II

THE abrupt change in Henry James's outlook on life, which was the result of his violent disillusion with regard to theatrical hopes and ambitions, took the form of a distaste for London and a determination, vague enough at first, to breathe for the future in a home of his own by the sea. He thought of Bournemouth, more definitely of Torquay, but finally his fate was sealed by his being offered, for the early summer months of 1896, a small house on the cliff at Point Hill, Playden, whence he could look down, as from an "eagle's nest," on the exquisite little red-roofed town of Rye and over the wide floor of the marsh of Sussex. When the time came for his being turned out of this retreat, he positively could not face the problem of returning to the breathless heat of London in August, and he secured the Vicarage in the heart of Rye itself for two months more. Here, as earlier at Point Hill, I was his guest, and it was wonderful to observe how his whole moral and intellectual nature seemed to burgeon and expand in the new and delicious liberty of country life. We were incessantly in the open air, on the terrace (for the Vicarage, though musty and dim, possessed, like the fresher Point Hill, a sea-looking terrace), sauntering round the little town, or roving for miles and miles over the illimitable flats, to Winchelsea, to Lydd, to the recesses of Walland Marsh—even, on one peerless occasion, so far afield as to Midley Chapel and the Romneys.

Never had I known Henry James so radiant, so cheerful or so self-assured. During the earlier London years there had hung over him a sort of canopy, a mixture of reserve and deprecation, faintly darkening the fullness of communion with his character; there always had seemed to be something indefinably non-conductive between him and those in whom he had most confidence. While the playwriting fit was on him this had deepened almost into fretfulness; the complete freedom of intercourse which is the charm of friendship had been made more and more difficult by an excess of sensibility. Henry James had become almost what the French call a *buisson d'épines*. It was therefore surprising and highly delightful to find that this cloud had ceased to brood over him, and had floated away, leaving behind it a laughing azure in which quite a new and charming Henry James stood revealed. The summer of 1896, when by a succession of happy chances I was much alone with him at Rye, rests in my recollection as made exquisite by his serene and even playful uniformity of temper, by the removal of everything which had made intercourse occasionally difficult, and by the addition of forms of amenity that had scarcely been foreshadowed. On reflection, however, I find that I am mixing up memories of June at Point Hill and of September at the Vicarage with the final Rye adventure, which must now be chronicled. When he was obliged to turn out of his second refuge, he returned to London, but with an ever-deepening nostalgia for the little Sussex town where he had been happy. In the following summer the voice of Venice called him so loudly that he stayed in London longer than usual, meaning to spend the autumn and winter in Italy. He thought meanwhile of Bournemouth and of Saxmundham. He went on his bicycle round the desolate ghost of Dunwich, but his heart was whispering "Rye" to him all the while. Nothing then seemed available, however, when suddenly the unexpected vacancy of the most eligible residence conceivable settled, in the course of a couple of days, the whole future earthly pilgrimage of Henry James. The huge fact was immediately announced in a letter of September 25th, 1897:

I am just drawing a long breath from having signed—a few moments since—a most portentous parchment: the lease of a smallish, charming, cheap old house in the country—down at Rye—for 21 years. (It was built about 1705.) It is exactly what I want and secretly and hopelessly coveted (since knowing it) without dreaming it would ever fall. But it *has* fallen—and has a beautiful room for you (the King's Room—George II's —who slept there); together with every promise of yielding me an indispensable retreat from May to October (every year). I hope you are not more sorry to take up the load of life that awaits, these days, the hunch of one's shoulders than I am. You'll ask me what I mean by "life." Come down to Lamb House and I'll tell you.

There were the most delightful possibilities in the property, which included a small garden and lawn, the whole hemmed in by a peaceful old red wall, plentifully tapestried with espaliers. The noble tower of Rye church looked down into it, and Henry James felt that the chimes sounded sweetly to him as he faced his garden in monastic quiet, the little market-town packed tightly about him, yet wholly out of sight.

Meanwhile the intellectual release had been none the less marked than the physical. The earliest result of his final escape from the lures of the Vivian of the stage had been the composition of a novel, *The Spoils of Poynton*, in a manner entirely different from that of his earlier long romances. This was published in 1897, and in the meantime he had set to work on a longer and more ambitious romance, *What Maisie Knew*. In these he began the exercise of what has been called his "later manner," which it would be out of proportion to attempt to define in a study which purports to be biographical rather than critical. It is enough to remind the reader familiar with Henry James's writings that in abandoning the more popular and conventional method of composition he aimed at nothing less than a revolution in the art of the novelist. While thus actively engaged in a new scheme of life, he found it more and more difficult to break "the spell of immobility" which enveloped him. He who had been so ready to start on any call of impulse in any direction found it impossible to bring himself to respond, at Christmas, 1897, to the appeal of Madame Alphonse Daudet to come over to Paris to grace the obsequies of her illustrious husband. The friends—

and the author of *Jack* was the most intimate of James's Parisian acquaintances—had not met after 1895, when Daudet had spent a month in London mainly under the charge of Henry James, since which time the French novelist's life had been sapped and drained from him by a disease the symptoms of which were beginning to be painfully manifest when he was with us in London. The old French friends were now disappearing. Their places in Henry James's affection were partly filled by Paul Bourget and by Maurice Barrès, whose remarkable and rather "gruesome" book, *Les Déracinés*, now supplied James with an endless subject of talk and reflection.

The first novel actually completed at Lamb House was *The Awkward Age*, which was ready for the printers early in 1898. The ecstasy with which he settled down to appreciate his new surroundings is reflected in that novel, where the abode of Mr. Longdon is neither more nor less than a picture of Lamb House. It was a wonderful summer and autumn, and, as Henry James said: "The air of the place thrilled all the while with the bliss of birds, the hum of little lives unseen, and the flicker of white butterflies." The MS. of *The Awkward Age* was no sooner finished than he took up the germ of an incident dimly related to him years before at Addington, by Archbishop Benson, and wove it into *The Turn of the Screw*, a sort of moral (or immoral) ghost story which not a few readers consider to be the most powerful of all his writings, and which others again peculiarly detest. I admit myself to be a hanger-on of the former group, and I have very vivid recollections of the period when *The Turn of the Screw* was being composed. The author discussed it with a freedom not usual with him. I remember that when he had finished it he said to me one day: "I had to correct the proofs of my ghost story last night, and when I had finished them I was so frightened that I was afraid to go upstairs to bed!"

By the close of 1898 he had got rid of the flat in De Vere Gardens, which had become a mere burden to him, and had taken what he called an "invaluable south-looking,

Carlton-Gardens-sweeping bedroom " at the Reform Club in Pall Mall, which served his brief and sudden pilgrimages to town for many seasons. Lamb House, in the course of this year, became his almost exclusive residence, and it is to be noted that at the same time a remarkable change came over the nature of his correspondence. He had been a meticulous but not very inspired letter-writer in early youth; his capacity for epistolary composition and his appetite for it had developed remarkably in the middle years (1882-1890). During the hectic period of his theatrical ambition it had dwindled again. But when he settled finally at Rye, spreading himself in luxurious contentment within the protection of his old brick garden-wall, the pink and purple surface of which stood in his fancy as a sort of bodyguard of security passed down for that particular purpose through mild ages of restfulness, as soon as he sat, with his household gods about him, in the almost cotton-woolly hush of Lamb House, he began to blossom out into a correspondent of a new and splendid class. The finest and most characteristic letters of Henry James start with his fifty-fifth year, and they continue to expand in volume, in richness and in self-revelation almost to the close of his life. On this subject Mr. Percy Lubbock, than whom no one has known better the idiosyncrasies of Henry James, has described his method of correspondence in a passage which could not be bettered:

> The rich apologies for silence and backwardness that preface so many of his letters must be interpreted in the light, partly indeed of his natural luxuriance of phraseology, but much more of his generous conception of the humblest correspondent's claim on him for response. He could not answer a brief note of friendliness but with pages of abounding eloquence. He never dealt in the mere small change of intercourse; the postcard and the half-sheet did not exist for him; a few lines of enquiry would bring from him a bulging packet of manuscript, overwhelming in its disproportion. No wonder that with this standard of the meaning of a letter he often groaned under his postal burden. He discharged himself of it, in general, very late at night; the morning's work left

him too much exhausted for more composition until then. At midnight he would sit down to his letter-writing and cover sheet after sheet, sometimes for hours, with his dashing and not very readable script. Occasionally he would give up a day to the working off of arrears by dictation, seldom omitting to excuse himself to each correspondent in turn for the infliction of the "fierce legibility" of type.

This amplitude of correspondence was the outcome of an affectionate solicitude for his friends, which led him in another direction, namely, in that of exercising a hospitality towards them for which he had never found an opportunity before. He did not, however, choose to collect anything which might remotely be called "a party"; what he really preferred was the presence of a single friend at a time, of a companion who would look after himself in the morning, and be prepared for a stroll with his host in the afternoon, and for a banquet of untrammelled conversation under the lamp or on the expanse of the lawn after the comfortable descent of nightfall.

His practice in regard to such a visitor was always to descend to the railway station below the town to welcome the guest, who would instantly recognize his remarkable figure hurrying along the platform. Under the large soft hat would be visible the large pale face, anxiously scanning the carriage-windows and breaking into smiles of sunshine when the new-comer was discovered. Welcome was signified by both hands waved aloft, lifting the skirts of the customary cloak, like wings. Then, luggage attended to, and the arm of the guest securely seized, as though even now there might be an attempt at escape, a slow ascent on foot would begin up the steep streets, the last and steepest of all leading to a discreet door which admitted directly to the broad hall of Lamb House. Within were, to right and left, the pleasant old rooms, with low windows opening straight into the garden, which was so sheltered and economized as to seem actually spacious. Further to the left was a lofty detached room, full of books and lights, where in summer Henry James usually wrote, secluded from all possible disturbance. The ascent of arrival from the railway grew to be more and more interesting as time went on, and as the novelist became more and more a familiar and respected citizen, it was much interrupted at last by bows from ladies and salaams from shopkeepers; many little boys and girls, the latter having often curtsied, had to be greeted and sometimes patted on the head. These social movements used to inspire in me the inquiry: "Well, how soon are you to be the Mayor-Elect of Rye?" a pleasantry which was always well received. So obviously did Henry James, in the process of years, become the leading inhabitant that it grew to seem no impossibility. Stranger things had happened! No civic authority would have been more conscientious and few less efficient.

His outward appearance developed in accordance with his moral and intellectual expansion. I have said that in early life Henry James was not "impressive"; as time went on his appearance became, on the contrary, excessively noticeable and arresting. He removed the beard which had long disguised his face, and so revealed the strong lines of mouth and chin, which responded to the majesty of the skull. In the breadth and smoothness of the head—Henry James became almost wholly bald early in life—there was at length something sacerdotal. As time went on, he grew less and less Anglo-Saxon in appearance and more Latin. I remember once seeing a Canon preaching in the Cathedral of Toulouse who was the picture of Henry James in his unction, his gravity, and his vehemence. Sometimes there could be noted—what Henry would have hated to think existing—a theatrical look which struck the eye, as though he might be some retired *jeune premier* of the Français, *jeune* no longer; and often the prelatical expression faded into a fleeting likeness to one or other celebrated Frenchman of letters (never to any Englishman or American), somewhat of Lacordaire in the intolerable scrutiny of the eyes, somewhat of Sainte-Beuve, too, in all except the mouth, which, though mobile and elastic, gave the impression in rest of being small. All these comparisons and suggestions, however, must be taken as the barest hints, intended to mark the tendency of Henry James's radically powerful and unique outer appearance. The beautiful modelling of the brows, waxing and waning under the stress of excitement, is a point which singularly dwells in the memory.

It is very difficult to give an impression of his manner, which was complex in the extreme, now restrained with a deep reserve, now suddenly expanding, so as to leave the auditor breathless, into a flood of exuberance. He had the habit of keeping his friends apart from one another; his intimacies were contained in many watertight compartments. He disliked to think that he was the subject of an interchange of impressions, and though he who discussed everybody and everything with the most penetrating and analysing curiosity must have known perfectly well that he also, in his turn, was the theme of endless discussion, he liked to ignore it and to feign to be a bodiless spectator. Accordingly, he was not apt to pay for the revelations, confidences, guesses and what not which he so eagerly demanded and enjoyed by any coin of a similar species. He begged the human race to plunge into experiences, but he proposed to take no plunge himself, or at least to have no audience when he plunged.

So discreet was he, and so like a fountain sealed, that many of those who were well acquainted with him have supposed that he was mainly a creature of observation and fancy, and that life stirred his intellect while leaving his senses untouched. But every now and then he disclosed to a friend, or rather admitted such a friend to a flash or glimpse of deeper things. The glimpse was never prolonged or illuminated, it was like peering down for a moment through some chasm in the rocks dimmed by the vapour of a clash of waves. One such flash will always leave my memory dazzled. I was staying alone with Henry James at Rye one summer, and as twilight deepened we walked together in the garden. I forget by what meanders we approached the subject, but I suddenly found that in profuse and enigmatic language he was recounting to me an experience, something that had happened, not something repeated or imagined. He spoke of standing on the pavement of a city, in the dusk, and of gazing upwards across the misty street, watching, watching for the lighting of a lamp in a window on the third storey. And the lamp blazed out, and through bursting tears he strained to see what was behind it, the unapproachable face. And for hours he stood there, wet with the rain, brushed by the phantom hurrying figures of the scene, and never from behind the lamp was for one moment visible the face. The mysterious and poignant revelation closed, and one could make no comment, ask no question, being throttled oneself by an overpowering emotion. And for a long time Henry James shuffled beside me in the darkness, shaking the dew off the laurels, and still there was no sound at all in the garden but what our heels made crunching the gravel, nor was the silence broken when suddenly we entered the house and he disappeared for an hour.

But the gossamer thread of narrative must be picked up once more, slight as it is. Into so cloistered a life the news of the sudden loss of Edward Burne-Jones in June, 1898, fell with a sensation; he had "seen the dear man, to my great joy, only a few hours before his death." In the early spring of the next year Henry James actually summoned resolution to go abroad again, visiting at Hyères Paul Bourget and the Vicomte Melchior de Vogüé (of whose *Le Roman Russe* and other essays he was a sturdy admirer), and proceeding to Rome, whence he was "whirled by irresistible Marion Crawford off to Sorrento, Capri, Naples," some of these now seen for the first time. He came back to England and to Lamb House at the end of June, to find that his novel of *The Awkward Age,* which was just published, was being received with a little more intelligence and sympathetic comprehension than had been the habit of greeting his productions, what he haughtily, but quite justly, called "the lurid asininity" of the Press in his regard now beginning to be sensibly affected by the loyalty of the little clan of those who saw what he was "driving at" in the new romances, and who valued it as a pearl of price. Nevertheless, there was still enough thick-witted denunciation of his novels to fill his own "clan" with anger, while some even of those who loved him best admitted themselves bewildered by *The Awkward Age*. Nothing is more steadily cleared away by time than the impression of obscurity that hangs over a really fine work of imagination when it is new. Twenty years have now passed, and no candid reader any longer pretends to find this admirable story "bewildering."

The passing of old friends was partly healed by the coming of new friends, and it was about this time that Mr. H. G. Wells, Mr. Rudyard Kipling, and Mr. W. E. Norris began to be visited and corresponded with. In 1900 and 1901 Henry James was slowly engaged, with luxurious throes of prolonged composition, in dictating *The Ambassadors*, which he "tackled and, for various reasons, laid aside," only to attack it again "with intensity and on the basis of a simplification that made it easier" until he brought it successfully through its voluminous career. In the summer of 1902 Mrs. Wharton, who had dedicated to him, as a stranger, her novel of *The Valley of Decision*, became a personal acquaintance, and soon, and till the end, one of the most valued and intimate of his friends. This event synchronized with the publication of his own great book, *The Wings of a Dove*. It was followed by *The Golden Bowl*. He now turned from such huge schemes as this—which in his fatigue he described as "too inordinately drawn out and too inordinately rubbed in"—to the composition of short stories, in which he found both rest and refreshment.

On this subject, the capabilities of the *conte* as a form of peculiarly polished and finished literature, he regaled me—and doubtless other friends—at this time with priceless observations. I recall a radiant August afternoon when we sallied from his high abode and descended to the mud of the winding waters of the Brede, where, on the shaky bridge across the river, leaning perilously above the flood,

Henry James held forth on the extraordinary skill of Guy de Maupassant, whose posthumous collection, *Le Colporteur,* had just reached him, and on the importance of securing, as that inimitable artist so constantly secured, one straight, intelligible action which must be the source of all vitality in what, without it, became a mere wandering anecdote, more or less vaguely ornamented. Henry James was at this time, I think, himself engaged upon the series of short stories which ultimately appeared under the title of *The Better Sort,* each one, as he said, being the exhibition of a case of experience or conduct. He collected and published in these years several such volumes of short compositions, in which he endeavoured, and admirably effected his endeavour, to combine neatness of handling with that beauty of conception which became more and more the object of his passionate desire. The reader naturally recalls such perfect specimens of his craft as *The Real Right Thing* and *The Beast in the Jungle.*

For many years he had let his fancy toy with the idea of returning, on a visit only, to America. In 1904 this project really took shape, and the long-debated journey actually took place. He terminated another extended romance, *The Golden Bowl,* and in August set sail for New York, ostensibly for the purpose of writing a book of American impressions. The volume called *The American Scene,* published in 1906, gives his account of the adventure, or rather of certain parts of it. He lived through the first autumn with his family in the mountains of New Hampshire, and, after a sojourn in Cambridge, spent Christmas in New York. He then went south in search of warmth, which he found at last in Florida. By way of Chicago, St. Louis, and Indianapolis he reached California in April, 1905. He delivered in various American Colleges two lectures, specially written for the purpose, which came out as a little volume in the United States, but have not yet appeared in England. His impressions of America, in the volume which he published after his return, stop with Florida, and give therefore no record of the extreme pleasure which he experienced in California, of which his private letters were full. He declared, writing on April 5th, 1905, from Coronado Beach, that "California has completely bowled me over. . . . The flowers, the wild flowers, just now in particular, which fairly *rage* with radiance over the land, are worthy of some purer planet than this. . . . It breaks my heart to have so stinted myself here"; but return eastward was imperative, and in August, 1905, he was back again safe in the silence of Lamb House.

Throughout the following autumn and winter he was, as he said, "squeezing out" his American impressions, which did not flow so easily as he had hoped they would. Many other enterprises hung temptingly before him, and distracted his thoughts from that particular occupation. Moreover, just before his plan for visiting the United States had taken shape, he had promised to write for a leading firm of English publishers "a romantical-psychological-pictorial-social" book about London, and in November, 1905, he returned to this project with vivacity. There is a peculiar interest about works that great writers mean to compose and never succeed in producing, and this scheme of a great picturesque book about London is like a ghost among the realities of Henry James's invention. He spoke about it more often and more freely than he did about his solid creations; I feel as though I had handled and almost as though I had read it. Westminster was to have been the core of the matter, which was to circle out concentrically to the City and the suburbs. Henry James put me under gratified contribution by coming frequently to the House of Lords in quest of "local colour," and I took him through the corridors and up into garrets of the Palace where never foreign foot had stepped before. There was not, to make a clean breast of it, much "local colour" to be wrung out, but Henry James was indefatigable in curiosity. What really did thrill him was to stand looking down from one of the windows of the Library on the Terrace, crowded with its motley afternoon crew of Members of both Houses and their guests of both sexes. He liked that better than to mingle with the throng itself, and he should have written a superb page on the scene, with its background of shining river and misty towers. Alas! it will not be read until we know what songs the Sirens sang.

All through the quiet autumn and winter of 1906 he was busy preparing the collective and definite, but far from complete, edition of his novels and tales which began to appear some twelve months later. This involved a labour which some of his friends ventured to disapprove of, since it included a re-writing into his latest style of the early stories which possessed a charm in their unaffected immaturity. Henry James was conscious, I think, of the arguments which might be brought against this reckless revision, but he rejected them with violence. I was spending a day or two with him at Lamb House when *Roderick Hudson* was undergoing, or rather had just undergone, the terrible trial; so the revised copy, darkened and swelled with MS. alterations, was put into my hands. I thought—I dare say I was quite mistaken —that the whole perspective of Henry James's work, the evidence of his development and evolution, his historical growth, were confused and belied by this wholesale tampering with the original text. Accordingly I exclaimed against such dribbling of new wine into the old bottles. This was after dinner, as we sat alone in the garden-room. All that Henry James—though I confess, with a darkened countenance—said at the time was, "The only alternative would have been to put the vile thing"— that is to say the graceful tale of *Roderick Hudson*— "behind the fire and have done with it!" Then we passed to other subjects, and at length we parted for the night in unruffled cheerfulness. But what was my dismay, on reaching the breakfast-table next morning, to see my host sombre and taciturn, with gloom thrown across his frowning features like a veil. I inquired rather anxiously whether he had slept well. "Slept!" he answered with dreary emphasis. "Was I likely to sleep when my brain was tortured with all the cruel and—to put it plainly to you—monstrous insinuations which you had brought forward against my proper, my necessary, my absolutely inevitable corrections of the disgraceful and disreputable style of *Roderick Hudson?*" I withered, like a guilty thing ashamed, before the eyes that glared at me over the coffee-pot, and I inly resolved that not one word of question should ever escape my lips on this subject again.

Early in 1907 he was tempted once more, after so long absence, to revisit France. While in America he had acquired the habit of motoring, which he learned to enjoy so much that it became the greatest physical pleasure of his life, and one which seemed definitely to benefit his health. He motored through a great part of France, and then proceeded to his beloved Italy, where he spent some radiant summer days under the pines near Vallombrosa, and later some more with his lifelong friend Mrs. Curtis in her wonderful Palazzo Barbaro in Venice. Ten weeks in Paris must be added to the foreign record of this year, almost the last of those which Henry James was able to dedicate to the Latin world that he loved so well and comprehended so acutely. The "nightmare," as he called it, of his Collected Edition kept him closely engaged for months after his return—it ultimately ran into a range of twenty-four volumes—but he was also sketching a novel, *The Ivory Tower,* which was to embody some of his American recollections; this was never finished. He met new friends of the younger generation, such as Hugh Walpole and Rupert Brooke, and they gave him great happiness.

He seemed to be approaching old age in placidity and satisfaction when, towards the end of 1909, he was seized by a mysterious group of illnesses which "deprived him of all power to work and caused him immeasurable suffering of mind." Unfortunately his beloved brother William was also failing in health, and had come to Europe in the vain search for recovery; their conditions painfully interacted. The whole year 1910 was one of almost unmitigated distress. Henry accompanied Mr. and Mrs. William back to their home in New Hampshire, where in the autumn not only the eminent philosopher, but a third brother, Robertson James, died, leaving Henry solitary indeed, and weighed upon by a cloud of melancholy which forbade him to write or almost to speak. Out of this he passed in the spring of 1911, and returned to Lamb House, where he had another sharp attack of illness in the autumn of 1912. It was now felt that the long pale winters over the marsh at Rye were impossible for him, and the bedroom at the Reform Club insufficient. He therefore rented a small flat high up over the Thames in Cheyne Walk, where he was henceforth to spend half of each year and die. He sat, on the occasion of his seventieth birthday, to Mr. Sargent for the picture which is now one of the treasures of the National Portrait Gallery; this was surprisingly mutilated, while being exhibited at the Royal Academy, by a "militant suffragette"; Henry James was extraordinarily exhilarated by having been thus "impaired by the tomahawk of the savage," and displayed himself as "breasting a wondrous high-tide of postal condolence in this doubly-damaged state." This was his latest excitement before the war with Germany drowned every other consideration.

The record of the last months of Henry James's life is told in the wonderful letters that he wrote between the beginning of August, 1914, and the close of November, 1915. He was at Rye when the war broke out, but he found it absolutely impossible to stay there without daily communication with friends in person, and, contrary to his lifelong habit, he came posting up to London in the midst of the burning August weather. He was transfigured by the events of those early weeks, overpowered, and yet, in his vast and generous excitement, himself overpowering. He threw off all the languor and melancholy of the recent years, and he appeared actually grown in size as he stalked the streets, amazingly moved by the unexpected nightmare, "the huge horror of blackness" which he saw before him. "The plunge of civilization into the abyss of blood and darkness by the wanton feat of these two infamous autocrats" made him suddenly realize that the quiet years of prosperity which had preceded 1914 had been really, as he put it, "treacherous," and that their perfidy had left us unprotected against the tragic terrors which now faced our world. It was astonishing how great Henry James suddenly seemed to become; he positively loomed above us in his splendid and disinterested faith. His first instinct had been horror at the prospect; his second anger and indignation against the criminals; but to these succeeded a passion of love and sympathy for England and France, and an unyielding but anxious and straining confidence in their ultimate success. Nothing could express this better than the language of a friend who saw him constantly and studied his moods with penetrating sympathy. Mr. Percy Lubbock says:

To all who listened to him in those days it must have seemed that he gave us what we lacked—a voice; there was a trumpet note in it that was heard nowhere else and that alone rose to the height of the truth.

The impression Henry James gave in these first months of the war could not be reproduced in better terms. To be in his company was to be encouraged, stimulated and yet filled with a sense of the almost intolerable gravity of the situation; it was to be moved with that "trumpet note" in his voice, as the men fighting in the dark defiles of Roncevaux were moved by the sound of the oliphant of Roland. He drew a long breath of relief in the thought that England had not failed in her manifest duty to France, nor "shirked any one of the implications of the Entente." When, as at the end of the first month, things were far from exhilarating for the Allies, Henry James did not give way to despair, but he went back to Rye, possessing his soul in waiting patience, "bracing himself unutterably," as he put it, "and holding on somehow (though to God knows what!) in presence of the perpetrations so gratuitously and infamously hideous as the destruction of Louvain and its accompaniments."

At Lamb House he sat through that gorgeous tawny

September, listening to the German guns thundering just across the Channel, while the advance of the enemy through those beautiful lands which he knew and loved so well filled him with anguish. He used to sally forth and stand on the bastions of his little town, gazing over the dim marsh that became sand-dunes, and then sea, and then a mirage of the white cliffs of French Flanders that were actually visible when the atmosphere grew transparent. The anguish of his execration became almost the howl of some animal, of a lion of the forest with the arrow in his flank, when the Germans wrecked Reims Cathedral. He gazed and gazed over the sea south-east, and fancied that he saw the flicker of the flames. He ate and drank, he talked and walked and thought, he slept and waked and lived and breathed only the War. His friends grew anxious, the tension was beyond what his natural powers, transfigured as they were, could be expected to endure, and he was persuaded to come back to Chelsea, although a semblance of summer still made Rye attractive.

During this time his attitude towards America was marked by a peculiar delicacy. His letters expressed no upbraiding, but a yearning, restrained impatience that took the form of a constant celebration of the attitude of England, which he found in those early months consistently admirable. In his abundant and eloquent letters to America he dealt incessantly on the shining light which events were throwing on "England's moral position and attitude, her predominantly incurable good-nature, the sublimity or the egregious folly, one scarcely knows which to call it, of her innocence in face of the most prodigiously massed and worked-out intentions of aggression." He admitted, with every gesture of courtesy, that America's absence from the feast of allied friendship on an occasion so unexampled, so infinitely momentous, was a bitter grief to him, but he was ready to believe it a necessity. For his own part, almost immediately on his return to London in October, 1914, Henry James began to relieve the mental high pressure by some kinds of practical work for which nothing in his previous life had fitted him, but into which he now threw himself with even exhausting ardour. He had always shrunk from physical contact with miscellaneous strangers, but now nothing seemed unwelcome save aloofness which would have divided him from the sufferings of others. The sad fate of Belgium particularly moved him, and he found close to his flat in Cheyne Walk a centre for the relief of Belgian refugees, and he was active in service there. A little later on he ardently espoused the work of the American Volunteer Motor Ambulance Corps. His practical experiences and his anxiety to take part in the great English movement for relief of the Belgians and the French are reflected in the essays which were collected in 1919 under the title of *Within the Rim*.

We were, however, made anxious by the effect of all this upon his nerves. The magnificent exaltation of spirit which made him a trumpeter in the sacred progress of the Allies was of a nature to alarm us as much as it inspirited and rejoiced us. When we thought of what he had been in 1911, how sadly he had aged in 1912, it was not credible that in 1915 he could endure to be filled to overflowing by this tide of febrile enthusiasm. Some of us, in the hope of diverting his thoughts a little from the obsession of the war, urged him to return to his proper work; and he responded in part to our observations, while not abandoning his charitable service. He was at work on *The Ivory Tower* when the war began, but he could not recover the note of placidity which it demanded, and he abandoned it in favour of a novel begun in 1900 and then laid aside, *The Sense of the Past*. He continued, at the same time, his reminiscences, and was writing the fragment published since his death as *The Middle Years*. But all this work was forced from him with an effort, very slowly; the old sprightly running of composition was at an end, the fact being that his thoughts were now incessantly distracted by considerations of a far more serious order.

The hesitations of Mr. Wilson, and Henry James's conviction that in the spring of 1915 the United States government was "sitting down in meekness and silence under the German repudiation of every engagement she solemnly took with " America, led to his taking a step which he felt to be in many respects painful, but absolutely inevitable. His heart was so passionately united with England in her colossal effort, and he was so dismally discouraged by the unending hesitation of America, that he determined to do what he had always strenuously refused to do before, namely, apply for British naturalization. Mr. Asquith (then Prime Minister), Sir George Prothero (the Editor of the *Quarterly Review*), and I had the honour and the gratification of being chosen his sponsors. In the case of so illustrious a claimant the usual formalities were passed over, and on July 26th, 1915, Henry James became a British subject. Unhappily he did not live to see America join the Allies, and so missed the joy for which he longed above all others.

But his radiant enthusiasm was burning him out. In August he had a slight breakdown, and his autumn was made miserable by an affection of the heart. He felt, he said, twenty years older, but "still, I cultivate, I at least attempt, a brazen front." He still got about, and I saw him at Westminster on the evening of November 29th. This was, I believe, the last time he went out, and two days later, on the night between the 1st and the 2nd of December, he had a stroke. He partly rallied and was able to receive comfort from the presence of his sister-in-law, Mrs. William James, who hurried across the Atlantic to nurse him. At the New Year he was awarded the highest honour which the King can confer on a British man of letters, the Order of Merit, the insignia of which were brought to his bedside by Lord Bryce. On February 28th, 1916, he died, within two months of his 73rd birthday. His body was cremated, and the funeral service held at that "altar of the dead " which he had loved so much, Chelsea Old Church, a few yards from his own door.

1920.

# Jacques-Emile Blanche, *Portrait of a Lifetime* (London: Dent, 1937)

This piece, based on a slight acquaintance and published long after James's death, perhaps contributes more to the 'Legend of the Master' than to the record of James's life. The account of James's conversation, for example, can be seen as a rhetorical exercise, inviting comparison with other equally extravagantly creative accounts (such as Muriel Draper's in section 16), as much as an attempt at accurate representation.

Jacques-Emile Blanche (1861–1942) was a successful and fashionable French artist whose paintings included portraits of Marcel Proust and Aubrey Beardsley. Although connected with Manet and Degas, Blanche's own paintings were comparatively traditional in style. He was introduced to James in 1908 by Edith Wharton who commissioned James's portrait. She thought it the most successful portrait of James ever painted although James himself seems to have been less convinced, confiding in a letter to Ellen 'Bay' Emmet (an artist who had painted James in 1900) that Blanche's portrait made him look 'very big and fat and uncanny and "brainy" and awful' (*Letters*, iv, p. 500). Wharton recalls the sittings in her memoir, *A Backward Glance*:

> It was in that year, I think that James, through my intervention, sat to Blanche for the admirable portrait which distressed the sitter because of the 'Daniel Lambert' curve of the rather florid waistcoat; and during those sittings, and on other occasions at the Blanches', he made many new acquaintances, and renewed some old friendships. (Wharton, p. 306)

In *Portrait of a Lifetime* Blanche, like Nadal and Howells *inter alia*, is preoccupied by the question of James's nationality, comparing him with his fellow American exile, the painter John Singer Sargent. Blanche's criticisms of the latter's own later portrait of James are entertainingly direct: 'His portrait of Henry James lacks psychological insight. Of his model, so complex and so finely shaded in his sensibility, he has made a business man from the provinces' (p. 68).

Blanche came from an educated, intellectual background (his father was an eminent pathologist) and he was thus well acquainted with French literary culture and writes perceptively about the influence of French writers on the works of James. The comparison he draws between James and Proust is a particularly suggestive one. There are many affinities between these two pioneers of the modern novel and it is a pity that we cannot establish whether James read *Du Côté de Chez Swann* (1913) – he certainly possessed a copy presented to him by Edith Wharton – and, if so, what he thought of it (Edel, v, p. 500).

If Henry James chatted with Sargent during his sittings as he did when I painted him, he did so presumably as one born American to another. In a letter to Miss Norton he confessed that he felt the lack of that sympathy which his intelligent countrymen showed, for in England every play of feeling is corked up. He had become a confirmed Cockney. Moore's fiasco when he wanted to turn Irishman again was but a literary episode. Henry James, who after the Great War had become a naturalized Englishman, discovered that certain minds, made uneasy by their conscience, build up defences and sometimes succumb. Yet Sargent, even had he returned to his own country and worked there, would nevertheless have been corked up. From Europe he might have written in such a strain as did Henry James to his brother William, the philosopher, in 1888: '. . . I have not the least hesitation in saying that I aspire to write in such a way that it would be impossible to an outsider to say whether I am at a given moment an American writing about England or an Englishman writing about America (dealing as I do with both countries), and, so far from being ashamed of such an ambiguity, I should be exceedingly proud of it, for it would be highly civilized. You are right in surmising that it must often be a grief to me not to get more time for reading—though not in supposing that I am "hollowed out inside" by the limitations my existence has too obstinately attached to that exercise, combined with the fact that I produce a great deal. At times I read almost as much as my wretched little *stomach* for it literally will allow, and on the whole I get much more time for it as the months and years go by. I touched the bottom, in the way of missing time, during the first half of my long residence in London—and traversed then a sandy desert in that respect—where, however, I took on board such an amount of human and social information that if the same necessary alternatives were presented to me again I should make the same choice. . . . The great thing is to be *saturated* with something—that is, in one way or another, with life; and I chose the form of my saturation. Moreover, you exaggerate the degree to which my writing takes it out of my mind, for I try to spend only the interest of my capital. . . .

'I have seen a great many (that is, more than usual) Frenchmen in London this year: they bring me notes of introduction —and the other day, the night before coming away, I entertained at dinner (at a club) the French Ambassador at Madrid (Paul Cambon), Xavier Charmes of the French Foreign Office, G. du Maurier, and the wonderful little Jusserand, the chargé d'affaires in London, who is a great friend of mine, and to oblige and relieve whom it was I invited the two other diplomatists, his friends, whom he had rather helplessly on his hands. There is the *real* difference—a gulf from the English (or the American) to the Frenchman, and *vice versa* (still more); and not from the Englishman to the American'.

In my opinion these lines are of capital importance. Would Sargent have subscribed to them? I have my doubts, but his painting speaks for itself. His portrait of Henry James lacks psychological insight. Of his model, so complex and so finely shaded in his sensibility, he has made a business man from the provinces. His writings stand in antithesis to his compatriot Sargent's painting, which I should term Esperanto.

Mr. Henry James senior was of Irish extraction; he had been an assiduous reader of Swedenborg. Speculative, religious and moralizing by temperament, like his son William, he failed to understand the attraction which sinful and futile humanity in the carnival of Society exerted on his novelist son. But it was he who brought all his family to Europe for educative purposes. One day, about 1906, as Henry James and I were leaving the Ritz in Paris after lunching with Bernhard Berenson, he told us about his early childhood. He saw himself at the age of just over one year at the Place Vendôme; he was to be educated in Paris. In 1856 he went to the Ecole Fezandié and during the years 1859-60 to the Institut Rochette in Geneva. In the Louvre and the Luxembourg museum the plastic arts were revealed to him. He frequented the Quartier Latin as Carl Van Vechten did later—with the Americans, it was a tradition. James, who was older than the author of *Peter Whaffle*, vowed to himself that he would write books in the style which the Latin races considered their own. In his magisterial preface to *The Reverberator* (the edition revised and corrected by him) he reminds us why ' "international" light lay thick, from period to period, on the general scene of my observation', and how all things set themselves out so that they take on an international character—and he believes very genuinely that this is a 'happy circumstance'. His countrymen, from whom he has removed himself and whom he visits only as a guest, have shed their relationship as cousins, and he finds them stripped and in their 'state of innocence', and this induces him to take pains not to resemble them. Their 'negative aspects', said he, were always manifest to him, although he looked above and beyond their collective heads, yet with a passionate desire that they should be worthy of his love. But soon his scepticism got the better of him and he went away to breathe a more stimulating air in England, the country with a 'perfect civilization'. After 1918, when Sargent was back from the United States, where he had completed the decoration for the Boston library, he advised all his fellow artists to make their home in that country where civilization would be at its highest during the twentieth century.

How appalled both would be to-day—Henry James and John Sargent died in good time.

When Henry James laboured to reply to someone it took him some time to start—he was like a heavy aeroplane taking off. The patient—that is to say, the person for whom a conversation with him was a first experience and who managed to extract a few sentences from him, began to feel weak when confronted with the effort of their birth. What anguish before the noun, the adjective, or adjectives rather, saw daylight clear and definite, expelled from the cavity of his lips which moved as if he were chewing gum. Or again, one might fancy oneself standing by a well, pulling a rope that made the pulley grate. Slowly the bucket ascends, knocking against the sides. It is lifted over the edge and emptied; the water is limpid and sweet. In its complacency, length, wealth of incidents and digressions, we can only compare the Jamesian sentence with Proust's. When he spoke, all his efforts could be read on his brow; his watchful eyes sparkled intently, focused on the person to whom he was talking. But for this piercing look, one might have gone to sleep—and this did once actually happen in my presence—I have forgotten the trend of the conversation. The stupendous work of elimination, the implicit examination of what he imposed upon himself in order to formulate for the reader that which was nearest to the truth and to life, resolved itself into a delicate madrigal for certain women of fashion who were unknown to him, a nutshell tossed on a stormy sea. *The Pattern in the Carpet*, the one story which must survive even if the others be lost, a real labyrinth without an outlet, matches his marvellous conversation and his correspondence.

The children of one of these admirers longed to hear Henry James at their mother's house, and to see the author of *What Maisie Knew*. Without telling him I arranged an innocent ambush. At tea-time James appeared, and the compliments he paid Mrs. S. N. were in the most exaggerated Henry James manner, even more so than I could possibly have promised the younger members of the family, who were hidden behind a screen. They were hard put to restrain the torrent of their mirth, and though the sounds were exceedingly muffled, I recognized the voices of these rogues. Following that event, and for years after, when one of them imitated Henry James, there were snorts and puffs and heavy breathing in their attempt to find the monumental word—but that word never came. Knowing nothing, or very little, about our hostess, and imagining her quite other than she actually was, James set himself to charm her by developing an abracadabral theory about Paris stores; the dresses and fashions were described with a bravura and a flaunting of the floral ornaments and patchouli of the Second Empire. When I wanted to lead him back to literature, he shook his head to give me to understand that this was not the right place—for when he came in he had made up his mind that he was with business people who had no comprehension of the artist's troubles and anxieties.

Generally when he came up to London from Rye for a rehearsal of a play or an appointment with a publisher, he stayed at the Reform Club, and we took our lunch together. He attracted no attention, he was merely one member amongst many whose heads were hidden behind the large newspapers they were reading. Some were writing letters, others going up or coming down the steps of an imposing staircase. James jealously maintained his incognito, always in fear that one of the attendants might hand him a card of some visitor, and these he looked upon as the curse of London. His clinging fear of being confronted with a caller drove him to shelter behind the assertion that he was at home to no one, and so, on one occasion, Joseph Conrad, who had come with a manuscript, was not admitted to his presence. Nevertheless, these two became fast friends, as everyone knows.

A French publisher, Stock, had asked me to write a book of recollections about my sitters, and the suggested title was to be *Mes Modèles*. Those represented were Maurice Barrès, Thomas Hardy, Marcel Proust, Henry James, André Gide, and George Moore. In Henry James's works I cast about to find passages which, when translated, would give my readers the clearest impression of his style. Walter Berry, the most discerning of James's friends, as he also was of Proust, parried my question, 'Can one term Henry James a man of outstanding mind?'

'To start with, what according to you is an outstanding mind? Is it one that treats abstruse problems?'

'It is', I replied, 'one which leads us to enter upon paths of whose existence we were unaware. Proust goes always further, he uses a probe at every turn of phrase, he astonishes and dominates us by the all-embracing extent of his search. Few are the things and the human characteristics that he has not enlightened, whilst James has made a single category his field of exploration.' Walter Berry laughed. 'Allow me to remind you of certain endings of his books, which you should translate. Besides, do not the wise tell us that all atoms are alike in constitution and that each atom has its own existence, like that of a universe, and that it obeys the same laws?'

'Yes, Berry, James has gone very far, much further than those that came before him, but his characters, whether they be exceptional or artificial, are portrayed in a style that partakes of Vermeer and Cubism. His art is static, he lacks the dynamic power of those moralists who have created generous types. He is fantastic in an Anglo-Saxon mode, his strange humour would escape the French reader—just as do certain aspects of Proust's.'

Whereupon Berry retorted: 'Doubtless you are right; Shakespeare will never appeal to you Frenchmen'.

I protested that this proposition no longer held true. Shakespeare's plays in our day drew the largest audiences. Henry James, though he might be no Shakespeare, nor yet a Racine, a Montaigne, an Honoré de Balzac, nor even a Stendhal, must be classed amongst the forerunners of Freud, with those who delved into the subconscious, into suppressions. On the other hand, as a dramatic author he was a failure. If his pieces had no success, the reason must be ascribed to the writer who considered that the same type of precious and pruned dialogue could with as much advantage be used on the stage as in his books. The majority of his heroes express themselves by innuendo, for they are hampered by the conventions of their surroundings, whose over-ornamental façade is all that a novelist less incisive would see. Yet a student of the soul uncovers behind this shell passions as burning, embryonic intrigues the more difficult to exteriorize, as unbecomingness constrains these beings, constantly acting, to slip like rabbits into burrows when a hunter tracks them.

Henry James often spoke to me of Racine's princes and princesses, saying that these are singularly difficult to consider as human beings, to accept as individuals in their classical majesty, but that they are nevertheless more interesting to examine than the creatures drawn by realists such as Zola—and I agree with him.

He expressed his contempt for, and horror of, Zola's vulgarity. Yet, to-day, Zola, in spite of his defects, is rising in general esteem. James at first admired him, as he had also appreciated Alphonse Daudet—however, here is one of his sayings: 'The Frenchmen I see all seem to me wonderful the first time—but not so much at all the second'.

I could not let this remark pass and one day I asked him whether he had ever taken the trouble or had had the opportunity of becoming intimate with a genuine Frenchman of merit—but this is not an occasion for reproaching my dear friend Henry James with his preference for the work of certain French writers, whose merit he exaggerated, or whose acquaintance he had but superficially made.

# Henry James and Scandal

a) Violet Hunt, 'The Last Days of Henry James', *Daily Mail* (1 March 1916)

b) Violet Hunt, *The Flurried Years* (London: Hurst & Blackett Ltd, 1926)

c) Vincent O'Sullivan, *Aspects of Wilde* (London: Constable & Co., 1936)

Like the previous piece by Jacques-Emile Blanche, the extracts included in this section illustrate how the 'legend' of Henry James was constructed and refined. The novelist and literary hostess Violet Hunt (1862–1942) was considered daring in the 1890s – the English counterpart of the earthy and racy French novelist Colette. Although as a girl she was described by Oscar Wilde as 'the sweetest Violet in England', in later life she was nicknamed 'Violent Hunt' (Hardwick, pp. 27–8). She knew James from an early age as he was acquainted with her father, the painter Alfred Hunt, and used to visit the family at their house on Campden Hill. James certainly read Violet Hunt's novels, but was not an uncritical admirer. In 1900 he wrote her a rather slippery letter after she had sent him her latest novel, *The Human Interest*:

> I am extremely struck by its cleverness & expertness – your acuteness of mind & skill of hand. Of course I don't, in my battered & wrinkled stage of life & reflection, read any fiction *naivement* & unquestioningly – the eternal critic within me insists on his rights & takes his ease, or his fun, as he goes – & he, precisely, was set in motion, – which he isn't on every occasion, by any means. He made, in short, his account of the affair. But I have no right whatever to thrust him on you – that was by no means what your graceful offering invited. (Horne, p. 336)

Hunt's friendship with James was disrupted when she became involved with a married man, the writer and editor Ford Madox Ford, then known as Ford Madox Hueffer (see headnote to section 12). Ford printed some of her stories in the *English Review*, and employed her as a manuscript reader before eventually becoming her lover. Hunt and Ford later lived together as man and wife although Ford was never divorced – in fact his wife Elsie Hueffer was awarded £300 damages in a libel suit after Ford and Hunt claimed to be legally married (Hardwick, p. 116).

The first piece reprinted here, which appeared in the *Daily Mail* shortly after James's death, was later expanded and revised in Hunt's volume of reminiscences, *The Flurried Years*. Here she is clearly anxious to emphasise the closeness of her relationship with James as well as his high opinion of her work. Nadal would probably have placed her in the category of 'women who particularly value the friendship of a clever and distinguished man because it is pleasing to their vanity' (p. 19). Hunt appears to want to hint at a kind of romantic frisson in their relationship – even when describing a conversation about the War there is something about her breathless style and novelettish lexis which suggests, most improbably, that a scene of passion may ensue. Hunt's characteristically mannered style becomes even more brittle in the revised piece – her insistence on referring to her lover as 'the editor' throughout is particularly arch. Only here does she make reference to any tension between James and herself, though she is careful to emphasise her own innocence, James's exaggerated prudery, and the strength of their later reconciliation. She may be suspected of exaggeration herself, on all three counts, and the alterations she makes to her account of James's words is another indication of unreliability (see the Introduction, p. xiii).

Despite his misgivings about her conduct James did later resume his friendship with Violet Hunt and his diary for 1912 records that he met her and Ford and 'went home with them for half an hour' (*Notebooks*, p. 357). In fact his break with the couple had as much to do with 'form' as morality – it was the scandal and publicity attached to Hunt's affair which seems to have been the real problem, for James was not troubled in this way by Edith Wharton's more discreetly conducted liaison with Morton Fullerton.

Another testimonial to James's avoidance even of indirect involvement in any sexual intrigue is offered by Vincent O' Sullivan in *Aspects of Wilde*. Here the anecdote apparently reported by Wilde reflects the gulf which separated Maupassant and James, despite their shared mastery of the short story. Whereas Maupassant was considered scandalously earthy and direct, Henry James is famed for his elusive reticence.

O'Sullivan (c. 1868–1940) was born in New York but moved to England as a young man. Here he became acquainted with many prominent figures of the *fin-de-siècle* including Oscar Wilde and Aubrey Beardsley. He tried his hand at most literary forms, producing a novel, short stories, poems, plays and prose sketches as well as his study of the 1890s literary scene, *Aspects of Wilde*. It is for this work, and some of his tales of the macabre, that he is chiefly remembered.

# THE LAST DAYS OF HENRY JAMES.

## ONE OF US.

### By VIOLET HUNT.

"He is dying, madam," the porter at No. 21, Carlyle-mansions said. "A set-back!" said the lady, who came down the stairs and joined me. She had been right into the flat and "seen Peggy." The doctor had given them fresh hope since the morning. And yet I have lost my "trusty, rusty Henry James."

Germany has killed him. It is the Kaiser whom we must arraign for the murder of a British subject. For in thus grieving and horrifying Henry James to death he has deprived us of our great acquisition, the best brain in America, which our own sorrows had gained for us. It has not profited us long. But there was more joy in heaven when James came over than if Mr. Bryan had repented.

"Why precisely did you do it?" I asked when I thanked him.

"My dear Purple Patch," he answered, "because I wanted to be able to say 'We' when I talked about an advance."

And during those last months he said "We" so hard, he took the affairs of "Us" so much to heart, that it killed him. Throwing himself into the struggle with all the enthusiasms of a general, a politician, and a literary man, his over-tasked sensorium could not stand the strain. "Anything I can do, anything I can write——" No appeal went unregarded. He was thinking in the spring of giving lectures to aid recruiting . . . He allowed himself to be interviewed in the great cause. It must not be forgotten that "We" included the magnificent French, for whom he had a love that passeth the love of man for woman.

*Mr. Henry James.*

His art was French rather than English; he impressed that on me often. To the English mind he conceded its *jardin secret* where the world of ideas, even the science of *le mot juste*, flourished though withdrawn. It was there, it was mysteriously inspiring our arms. He read aloud to me his article for the "Book of France," . . . His voice, strong, deep, a wonderful organ for a man of his age, trembled . . . his accents were of a poignancy. . . . I was stirred beyond measure, and I exclaimed, impertinent, on a wave of enthusiasm which earned my pardon: "I didn't believe that you could have been so passionate!"

He had risen and was walking shyly away from me towards a bookcase. He turned an eye, *narquois*, reflective, devilish, calmly-wise—the Henry James eye, in fact—full upon me, and with a little laugh, designed to ward off any attempt to attack his supreme bachelordom, declared:

"Madam, don't forget that I am not addressing a woman, but a nation!"

* * * *

I used to go there on the understanding that I talked of nothing but the war. I should perhaps find him fairly well and going out in a taxicab; or rather poorly, with his feet on a cushion and his "old pain" in possession. Still, we would talk of the war. He would almost rudely, assuming the privilege of an invalid, suppress any inappropriate resumption of the gossip in which he had used to delight. What he wanted then from one was the hint, the grain, from which he fostered his mightier, wider imaginings. I used to suffer, like other people, from the truncated anecdote. He always arrested the progress of a story as soon as he had got all he wanted out of it, and left you with the point of it on your hands. One consoled oneself with the reflection that he had probably got another "Turn of the Screw" out of your tale of some childish aberration, or some more "Spoils of Poynton" from your reminiscences of your old north-country aunt.

What he wanted to hear nowadays was what you had gathered about Zeppelin defences while you were staying at an anti-aircraft station on the east coast, or whether you thought recruiting good at Cardiff, whence you had come recently, or were the streets reassuringly full of khaki? And what did soldiers back from the front tell you, and could you bring the tired officer to see him who riding along from the battle of the Marne had come upon the mysterious château of Pierrefonds beyond Noyon and had made a detour to see it?

I remember his passionate cherishing of young Rupert Brooke, not very well even then. I remember seeing his hand on the beautiful young man's knee, and how proudly he drove him home after lunch. He could not even speak of Rupert Brooke after he had died. And it was perhaps after that that he cared so much to help, that he was even willing to be comprehended of the people. Shyly he said to me, "I want to read you something. I should be obliged if you would listen carefully and tell if I am comprehensible. They tell me"—he turned his head away—" that I am obscure. . . ." Then, with a touch of his old, sly humour, he said, " You will think that I am experimenting on a vile body. . . . One of my oldest friends."

Miss Violet Hunt.

That was true. I remember Henry James when he was really Henry James junior, come to London and fêted everywhere on the strength of a little story in the *Cornhill*. He was tall, rather thick-set, with an olive skin. "Mamma," I said, "he looks as if he ought to be wearing earrings!" This was the impression made on a child by this Elizabethan, with his dark, silky beard and deep, wonderful eyes. He had been to a tea-party, "chaperoning himself," so the lady who made the society pars of that day described his demureness, his reticence, his air always of perfect acquaintance with the facts of every case, a sage not to be taken unawares or at a disadvantage.

He had a house in De Vere-gardens, and he came to see us. He had a house in Rye, and I went to see him in my purple coat and cap that earned me my nickname. We used to walk along the links at Rye with the dachshund Max—on the end of a long chain—who sometimes succeeded in wrapping us round lamp-posts all the way back to High-street.

Then we would go back to the Lamb House, and Mr. James would leave me to my own devices and enter "La Maison de Péché," as we called the kiosk where he dictated. And—and —well, I knew him too well to write about him! I cannot single out the detachable touches of personality from the mass of coherent intimacy of years. It is all welded together, as it were, in one long Jamesian sentence.

I have the sense of a stream of tendency making for literary righteousness, with *le mot juste* threaded upon it. I am conscious only of the charming, polished, clear-throated utterance; the exciting fits of intolerance, the artillery of this great intellect playing on all undeserved and shoddy reputations. He was both cruel and kind; a block of beneficent ice, with a pulse of fierce life informing it. I shall never look upon his like again.

Conrad and James were, more or less, our mentors—interchangeable. They both sermonised us both. I had known Henry James longer than the editor had, but he had the advantage of me as regards Conrad, and I think he loved Conrad more than I loved James. Henry James was kinder, less selfish; Conrad was ruder, and more lovable. The editor adored Conrad. I never heard him speak of Conrad without the most reverent affection, though he did allow himself to chip at him sometimes to me. In matters of literature his attitude was servile, positively. To James he posed merely as *le jeune homme modeste*, but his native arrogance appeared to be completely obliterated when Conrad was in the room. He imitated him, even to the point of cultivating in himself some one or other of Conrad's phobias. All great men have phobias. He used to say he suffered from agoraphobia—or was it claustrophobia? They seem to me very interchangeable. A breakdown in the street or a breakdown in a drawing-room, the market-place or the field? The Lake District is less lonely than a long street in Bloomsbury where I have seen the editor weaken and totter. These two confessed to sharing " queer sensations of being no longer in this world " as they sat writing. " Heart thumps, head swims ! "—" It's funny, but startling." The thought of a journey made either of them tremble. " I shirk going out into the road. . . . I get over-excited and worried with new faces. . . . Something peculiar with me ! "

Not so very peculiar for such cattle as these ! How one recognises the symptoms of nervous breakdown that assail all men who subsist on their own nervous energy, and, peradventure, keep a family with it ! To feel, as soon as a journey is threatened, that one is not coming back again, is an elementary sensation of the kind. I always feel it myself. And suicide ! Every author thinks of suicide when he cannot get *le mot juste*, or is spinning a web of fiction like the spider in a gale ; to adopt Conrad's expressive phrase, " making an effort for copy or die ! " It seems simpler almost to die. " The latter the easier feat—and so beautifully final ! "

The interchange of these *Morituri te Salutant* is just the waving of the arms resorted to after an effort of conversation, the awful yawn of satiety, the sense of virtue gone out of one.

The doyen of the Review, Henry James, lived mostly in London now, " chaperoning himself." *Modeste Mignon* I called him, after Balzac. He never, so far as I know, honoured the office—which was also a drawing-room—with his presence. I don't believe he ever set foot in it. The purlieus of literature were not for him ; he preferred to live among his raw material in marble halls in the wealthy North ; on Aubusson carpets in Paris. But he used to come to see me in my house, nicely *montée* for entertaining, and to any one of my three clubs. He delighted in my Saturdays at the Socialist New Reform Club, where the members consumed eggs beaten up in glasses, where the walls were of a duck-coloured green, and the three windows after dark enjoyed a view of the glittering pharos advertising Sir Thomas Dewar's excellent whiskey outlined on a screen of Whistler blue. Mr. Bernard Shaw appropriately tenants that room now.

It was quite unnecessary to be careful to whom you introduced H. J., for if you were too particular, took too much care of him, you might lose him a chance of meeting a Mona Maltravers or a Princess Casamassima.

Nobody bored him; he took care of that. That immunity was included in the careful chaperoning of himself for which he was noted. I used to suffer, as other people did who told him anything that might amuse him, from the summarily truncated anecdote. He would hold up a story as soon as he had got all he needed out of it; extend a finger—" Thank you, I've got as much —all I want "—and leave you with the point of your anecdote on your hands. You consoled yourself with the reflection that he might have perhaps got another *Turn of the Screw* out of your relation of some childish aberration, or some more *Spoils of Poynton* from your reminiscence of your old North Country aunt.

My rattling, roaring, social existence seemed to hold all sorts of queer lures and baits for him. I was his " purple patch "—the Medusa head by which he envisaged the less refined happenings of life and made his little cautious descents into reality, the violet ray in his so pure spectrum. I don't believe that in all his days he ever came nearer to passion, to the stark human nature of things, as at that time when I tried to force him down into the arena to fight for me. I ought to have known better. I had had a hint. Once I mentioned a dead friend whom I had loved very much—and I actually used the word of awe in this connection. It was at breakfast in Lamb House. H. J. left his poached egg on cereals and, rising with a little nervous cough, courteously drew my attention to the picture of his mother which hung over the sideboard!

★   ★   ★   ★   ★

"Lamb House,
"Rye,
"Sussex.
"*October* 31*st*, 1909.

"MY DEAR VIOLET,—Yes, indeed, I am at Rye—where else should I be? For I am here pretty well always and ever, and less and less anywhere else. There are advantages preponderant in that; but there are also drawbacks; one of which is that I am liable to go so long without seeing you. But to this, on the other hand, there are possible remedies—as, for instance, that of your conceivably (I hope) coming down here for a couple of nights before very long. Is this thinkable to you? Not unaware as you are of my homely and solitary state, my limited resources, my austere conditions, and frugal though earnest hospitality. I am more and more aged, infirm, and unattractive, but I make such a stand as I can, and shall be very glad to see you if you can brave the adventure or face such a tiresome displacement on such meagre terms. We can have a long jaw (with lots of arrears to make up), and, weather permitting, eke a short walk. The *week-end* would suit me (though I am not restricted to that) of almost any of the next weeks, and you could perhaps then take the Saturday a.m. train and get here for luncheon—in which case we could take even two walks. Let me know what I may hope, and that health and peace attend you, and believe me to be,

" Yours ever,
" HENRY JAMES."

I accepted with the usual heartily expressed elation —that was merely respect—but I think I really rather loved Henry James; I had known him so long, and as a plastic schoolgirl. But it was not to be. My pitch was queered damnably. . . . There had been signs . . . rumblings. . . . One evening I got a short note from H. G. much distracted by something " the veracious Pinker " had told him. He did hope I wasn't going to get into another mess—any mess—a particular mess he had heard of? Dear H. G.!

Pinker always knew everything, and was always looking out to do something kind and apposite with his knowledge. And a week after I had accepted I received letters from Henry James which decidedly knocked the first nail into my coffin. For observe the change of title— a change subtle and cruel!

" DEAR VIOLET HUNT,—I should be writing to you to-night to say that it would give me great pleasure to see you on Saturday next had I not received by the same post which brought me your letter one from ———, which your mention of the fact that you have known the writing of it enables me thus to allude to as depriving, by its contents, our projected occasion of indispensable elements of frankness and pleasantness. I deeply lament and deplore the lamentable position in which I gather you have put yourself. . . . It affects me as painfully unedifying, and that compels me to regard all agreeable or unembarrassed communications between us as impossible. I can neither suffer you to come down to hear me utter those homely truths, nor pretend at such a time to free or natural discourse of other things on a basis of avoidance of what must now be most to the front in your own consciousness, or what in a very unwelcome fashion disconcerts mine. Otherwise, "*es wäre so schön gewesen!*" But I think you will understand, on a moment's further reflection, that I can't write to you otherwise than I do, or that I am very sorry indeed to have to do it.

"Believe me, then, in very imperfect sympathy,
"Yours,
"HENRY JAMES."

I wrote, and he replied:

". . . I am obliged to you for your letter of Wednesday last, but, with all due consideration for it, I do not see, I am bound to tell you, that it at all invalidates my previous basis of expression to you. It appeared from that . . . that the person best qualified to measure the danger feared for your reputation, and I really don't see how an old friend of yours *could* feel or pronounce your being in a position to permit of this anything but lamentable, lamentable, oh, lamentable! What sort of a friend is it that would say less? I wasn't for a moment pretending to characterize the nature of the relations . . . that may conduce to that possibility . . . but your position! If I had to speak of it again I am afraid I could only speak of it as lamentable. . . . I, however, deprecate the discussion of private affairs of which I wish to hear nothing whatever. And, neither knowing or willing to know anything of the matter, it was exactly because I didn't wish to that I found conversing with you at all to be in prospect impossible. That was the light in which I didn't—your term is harsh !—*forbid* you my house ; but deprecated the idea of what would otherwise have been so interesting and welcome a *tête-à-tête* with you. I am very sorry to have had to lose it, and I am yours in regret,

" HENRY JAMES.

"*November 5th*, 1909."

It was represented to him that he had more or less put himself in the position of a judge, and vehemently he disclaimed it. He didn't " for a moment pretend to judge, qualify, or deal with any act of conduct of V. H.'s in the connection, as a part, matter of . . . that whole quantity being none of my business and destined to remain so. . . . I deplored or lamented the situation in which you had landed or were going to land her. . . . I don't see how an old friend of hers can be indifferent to that misfortune. . . ."

" But these things surely are your own affair. . . . I wish you very heartily that your complications may work out for you with some eventual ' Peace with honour.' "

Then I wrote to my dear Henry James passionately, speaking for myself, declaring that, for my part, I wasn't in a " lamentable position " at all. That I had nothing to do but speak the truth and defend myself if what he feared should come to pass. I said that I thought it very hard that he should turn against me, and that, though I was sorry I might not come to Lamb House, I quite understood that it might be inconvenient and unpleasant to him to have me under his roof. I wanted him to believe that I should listen humbly enough to home truths from him if only a certain amount of the sympathy on which I had learned to count was behind it.

I assured him in plain language, using the stock, stereotyped expression consecrated by long use, that I was " innocent," and could not be dragged into anything, and that, as for the other details, could he not, if he was ever in the least interested in me, come and see me in town and let me tell him how I stood. I impressed upon him that he ought to count it to me that I had put him in possession of certain facts, and could very easily have paid my visit to Lamb House even at the risk of involving him in a scandal and selfishly grabbed my pleasure at the expense of his ease.

For one knew that the one thing Henry really dreaded was being mixed up with life in any way, or entangled in anything that went on outside the drawing-room door. He was in no sense a man of the world. And, being what he was, would it not have savoured of social meanness if, through mere contact, I were to procure the soilure of the white hem of Henry's robe of innocence? And there it should rest. If he, on his side, had not compassed the man's virtue of being *sans peur*, I had acted according to my own conscience and should retain the woman's of being *sans reproche*, so far as he was concerned. So that was that!

★ ★ ★ ★ ★

During this dreary acreage of time, big with menace, fraught with ominous trifles, there were " moments," satisfactions—sops to one's vanity, if nothing else. I went to stay at Smeeth, and my host gave me a message from Mr. Conrad—ill in bed—to the effect that he was grateful to me for " being so good to his friend." The editor, still smarting, for me, from Mr. James's *laches*, was not particularly pleased to hear it and wrote quite sarcastically of a letter he had himself just received from his hero, blessing him in his incomings and outgoings, but " in a circumscribed sort of way ; the outcome, as you may imagine, of a Polish Jew, plus lower-middle-class British Puritanism." Comic, the association of Conrad and the British middle class ! And was he a Jew ? Oh, nonsense ! The editor was dyspeptic or riding one of his high horses that day. " It pleases me to bring these people to their knees. 'Enery will be the next, you will see."

And he was.

For that little *rixe* of last year was really all 'Enery's old-maidishness of spirit. He was like the ladies of Cranford, providing themselves with umbrellas and goloshes for fear of a possible downpour ; clogs, lest they stepped into little pools of passion, dreading such effects of emotion as might subsist outside the four walls of a drawing-room and are not properly announced by the butler. He always, from that time, called me the " Purple Patch," and in 1913 he told me to " go on being one " and giving him teas at my club.

Later, ashamed of what I will call his *inburst*, he confessed to Mrs. P. that he " had simply kept out of it because I am too old to be mixed up in messes." He kept out of mischief by not getting into it, as old Mrs. Frank Hill used to say. The one bright spot, Mrs. P. said, seemed to have been that I had written and warned him that there might be a slight atmosphere of mess about me. There were several counts on which my presence in court might have been required. Supposing I had " called " him ! 'Enery would have died. America would have squirmed. No, I would not bring whatever it was into the house, as one says of scarlet fever or measles.

And he had dilated to Mrs. P. on Mary Martindale, her charm, her beauty, which gave me something nice to tell Mary, for she was always too humble. She knew 'Enery very well. He had always admired her.

He had been ill again, and I had written to enquire. He replied. I was " Dear Violet " again !

" Lamb House,
" *February* 14*th*, 1910.

" . . . Don't measure my extreme appreciation of your most kind letter by this delay, or by these informal, invalidical signs. I have had to wait to be able to form the latter at all presentably—after a dreary little relapse, from which I am again picking up; and my letters have to be rare and feeble scrawls of which this is a pattern. It was a charming charity in you to write, and everything you tell me a breath of your roaring London world (gracefully and considerately bedimmed a little), wafted into a sick-room that at the end of six or seven weeks has become dismally tedious. I have turned the corner (round which convalescence has kept tantalisingly hiding and staying; I'm after it—or close on its heels probably now.) I am mostly sitting up *without* the prospect of tumbling back into the sheets of platitude. And I rejoice in your brave account of your own heroisms. They come to me like vague, confused strains and boom-booms of a Wagner opera—that there are women of confirmed genius who take ravenous nieces to London balls ; I mean for the incredible Valkyrie air of *Götterdämmerung* of it. Mrs. Clifford tells me you have written—just published—something very strange and fine and fierce somewhere ; would it overtax the shaken nerves of your enfeebled yet unconquered and all-faithful old

" HENRY JAMES."

I gave a series of " afternoons." They always amused my mother and were within her competence. As I was fastening the last hook of the Beauty's frock upstairs I heard the voice of the editor, who was like a child before a party, looking out of the window on the stairs into the porch. It expressed the deepest satisfaction, as if all was well in the best of all possible worlds:

" Here's James! "

Soon, settled in for the afternoon, surrounded by adoring ladies, the recluse of Rye sat complacent, holding my last new Persian kitten between his open palms, talking animatedly to the Beauty, who could not talk but *looked*. He quite forgot the poor beast, which was too polite and too squeezed between the upper and the nether millstone of the great man's hands, to remind him of its existence, and I dared not rescue it until the sentence on which Mr. James was engaged was brought to a close—inside of half an hour.

Everybody came to me. I suppose it was the Beauty's spell. Her photograph adorned Henry James's mantelpiece at Rye for long after.

★ ★ ★ ★ ★

And 'Enery! The way these authors came up to time! Henry James, gouty, dyspeptic, short-sighted, could do nothing—but he did that magnificently! He had moved into a flat in Chelsea, started a brougham, and entertained the British Army in the widest sense of the word. Drawing-rooms interested him no longer. Peggy, a niece, was living somewhere round about, the daughter of his brother William, author of one of the most widely interesting, most psychological of books, the material of half a dozen novels buried in accounts of the varieties of religious " dopes "—for so he seems to me to envisage them, but most reverently. His brother, Henry, had never talked religion; he now talked Army, thought Army, and died Army—quite suddenly!

No one expected it. Like little Miles, I think the great man's heart broke because of another apparent turpitude —because America was so slow coming in.

" He is dying, madam! " the porter at 21 Carlyle Mansions said to me one evening when I went there, not expecting to see him, but to enquire after a slight cold that had been announced. " A little set-back," said the lady of next door, who came down the stairs from his flat and asked me to go in to tea with her. There was no need for me to ring, for she had been right into the flat and had " seen Peggy." He *was* ill, indeed, but that very morning the doctor had given them all fresh hopes. . . .

And yet, before the morning, I had lost my " trusty, rusty Henry James."

Which of them killed the Premier British Subject—Germany or America? Germany murdered Americans in the *Lusitania*, but America only came in after murdering her own Henry James with her delays. He did not live to see the two reconcilements, but in England there was surely more joy when Henry James came over than if even President Wilson himself had repented. By the time Henry died we had got used to thinking that was impossible, and doubtless Henry was no more optimistic than the nation to which he now belonged. I had asked him, using the pauses to which he had, as it were, trained me :

" Why, Mr. James, precisely, did you do it ? "

He answered, " My dear Purple Patch, chiefly because I wanted to be able to say *We*—with a capital—when I talked about an Advance."

I suppose that, during those last few months, he said *We* so hard, took the affairs of *Us* so much to heart, that it gave him the stroke from which he died. Paralysed he was, all up that side that leaves the brain comparatively free.

Henry James could not legally belong to two nations at once, like Joseph Leopold, but I was never allowed to forget that *We* included the French. I shall never forget his rage when I told him of how Mrs. Fisher (Adrienne Dayrolles), who had played for him in *Guy Domville*, had been lunching with some ladies of the English upper classes who were doing all sorts of war work, and doing it very nicely, too. They were bragging of " our men " at Ypres, justly enough, but one of them, less British than the others, had sufficient detachment to observe the angry dismay of a Frenchwoman whose countrymen were being quite unconsciously left out of this pæan. With the high courtesy of her race, and it is to be feared some of its stupidity, she put in a word for Mrs. Fisher's benefit, saying, with a note of flippant patronage, " And the *French* did very well, *too* ! "

He boiled. I boiled. We boiled together. That kind of thing happened too often, and Henry James's sympathies, if anything, were rather more with the country that had produced Flaubert, the original seeker of *le mot juste*, that now old-fashioned slogan. The war has killed *le mot juste*. But the uses of his sympathy naturally fell to the country of his adoption—" Anything I can do, anything I can write ! " No war appeal went unregarded ; he even allowed himself to be interviewed. The chaste Henry ! He ceased to " chaperon " himself. Words were put into his mouth—ineptitudes ! Greater love hath no man than he lay down his *style* for his friend. He was so willing to help that he was eager to be comprehended of the people.

Mary Robinson asked him to write an article for the *Book of France* and she would translate it. It would appear here in English, too. He said to me, shyly :

" I want you to let me read you something I have written. Perhaps you would be kind enough to tell me if I am comprehensible ? They tell me "—he turned his head away—" that I am obscure. . . ."

A pause. He was preparing apologies . . . for the immense compliment he was going to pay me . . . sweetly clumsy : " You must not think that I am preparing to experiment on a vile body . . . yours . . . I just remembered that you were one of my oldest friends."

He read . . . standing . . . walking up and down in the front part of the room a long way from where I sat. But I heard. His voice, strong, resonant—the wonderful voice that old invalid men can muster when put to it—trembled, not from feebleness, but from emotion. Emotion, in Henry James! It was all perfectly clear, and of a poignancy! That was because he was in love with his subject. France, *la belle France* . . . intensely feminine, a bit of a cat, as I always see her. She stood there personified. No real woman could have resisted a real lover pleading in such a voice as that for *le don de l'amoureuse Merci*. Listening, I was stimulated to boldness—actual impertinence, it seemed to me ten minutes afterwards. But he was not angry; he knew that his reading had provoked the boldness that had borne me on the wave of enthusiasm which must earn me my forgiveness. It was an old man's slinky triumph. One for me, too, for twice this day I had succeeded in making Henry shy.

I said, " Mr. James! . . . I did not know you could be so—*passionate*!" I had sought and found *le mot juste*.

He turned and glared a little . . . a frown that was really a smile . . . he was gratified at the tremendous effect he had produced on this woman he always persisted in calling a frivolous *mondaine*. He walked towards a bookcase at the other end of the room to give himself a countenance . . . and time. . . . He also had to find *le mot juste*!

He found it. He turned on me an eye, *narquois*, reflective, stork-like, a little devilish, calmly wise—the Henry James eye, in fact—and, with a little pompous laugh . . . the male warding off any attack that the persevering female might possibly be contemplating against his supreme bachelordom :

"Ah, madam, you must not forget that in this article I am addressing—not a Woman, but a Nation!"

Of course, he had gout now, like any good old English gentleman. Sometimes when I went to see him he would have his foot—both feet—swathed in linen bandages, laid out helplessly on a chair in front of him—" My old pain in possession "—very much annoyed if I dropped my glove or something that, however near his chair, he could not pick up for me. He stooped for things in excess—embarrassingly—and I have known such a contretemps cloud a whole afternoon. He would be a little untidy, perhaps, dressing-gown unequally disposed over night-gear, looking what he was—a thoroughly ugly man, with eyes dull, dyspeptic and inward, flat and deep set, like landlocked bays, gloomy, relieved at times by the harbour-lights of humour—a stony twinkle of innocent malice. He was all good—*herzen's gut*, as poor little Elizabeth Schultz used to say of the editor.

But, well or ill, it was understood that we talked in these days of war and nothing but war. There was to be no resumption of the Society gossip in which he used to delight. It was what one had gathered about Zeppelin defences while staying at an anti-aircraft station at Shingle Street, on the east coast, or whether one thought the recruiting good at Cardiff or at Redcar, where one would have lived for a month or two. Were the streets nicely full of khaki? Had I really seen a ten-shilling piece in that remote corner of Wales? Several? And what did the many men I must have met tell me about their respective experiences, and could I bring Mr. Stacke, the wounded officer of my acquaintance to see him who, after the battle of the Marne, riding into Paris, had made a détour to see the Château de Pierrefonds? And he would wear him next his heart, for he loved to think of an officer as a Bayard who had not altogether lost his love of the arts. Rupert Brooke, a little wounded but able to come to lunch, he cherished like a son. I remember seeing his hand laid on the knee of the young soldier-poet like a benediction. We would drive him home after lunch in the carriage. He must be petted . . . must not walk, even if he could. . . .

He would never speak of Rupert Brooke after he had died.

He sometimes, but not often, spoke to me of Conrad who had sent *his* son and had so far got him safe, but never knew whether he was to be allowed to keep him— until the end.

Wilde told me that when Maupassant visited London he was the guest of Henry James. James took him to the Exhibition at Earl's Court and they dined in the restaurant. Maupassant said: 'There's a woman sitting over there that I'd like to have. Go over and get her for me.'

James was horribly shocked.

'But, my dear friend, I can't do that. She may be perfectly respectable. In England you have to be careful.'

After a few minutes, Maupassant spotted another woman.

'Surely, you know her at least? I could do quite well with her if you'll get her for me. Ah, if I only knew English!'

When James had refused for about the fifth time, Maupassant observed sulkily: 'Really you don't seem to know anybody in London.'

That James had refused to do what he asked from motives of prudery and respectability never occurred to him.

# A. C. Benson, *Memories and Friends* (London: John Murray, 1923)

Arthur Christopher Benson (1862–1925) was acquainted with James for many years, and although not such a close friend as Edmund Gosse, his account of James (derived partly from his own diary entries) offers a sober and sensitive evaluation of his works as well as a warm testimony to his personal qualities. Benson was the second son of Edward White Benson, Archbishop of Canterbury. The Archbishop was himself an admirer of James's works – as Benson remarks in *Memories and Friends* he once quoted from *Roderick Hudson* in a sermon – and James was acquainted with both the Archbishop's sons, Edward Frederic Benson and Arthur Christopher Benson. E. F. Benson (the author of the popular Mapp and Lucia novels) also wrote reminiscences of Henry James, although these are perhaps more entertaining than they are reliable (see Nowell-Smith, p. xxiii–xxviii, for a detailed discussion of E. F. Benson). A. C. Benson was a highly sensitive man, prone to bouts of depression and anxiety. However he was also a prolific essayist, literary critic and poet, whose compositions included the words to 'Land of Hope and Glory'. At the time of his first meeting with James, Benson had just been appointed a master at Eton. He later became a Fellow of Magdalene College, Cambridge, and was elected Master of the College in 1915. James and A. C. Benson remained friends and Benson was invited to stay with James in Rye in 1900. He recorded his impressions of James as an attentive if slightly unnerving host in his diary:

> H.J. works hard; he establishes me in a little high-walled white parlour, very comfortable, but is full of fear that I am unhappy. He comes in, pokes the fire, presses a cigarette on me, puts his hand on my shoulder, looks inquiringly at me, and hurries away. His eyes are *piercing*. (*The Diary of Arthur Christopher Benson*, ed. by Percy Lubbock (London: Hutchinson & Co., 1926), p. 47)

A. C. Benson's account in *Memories and Friends* of the effect of his father's ghostly anecdote on James is fully corroborated in James's own notes on the incident. Although *The Turn of the Screw* was not published until 1898 the core features of this highly successful tale had already taken root in James's mind:

> Note here the ghost-story told me at Addington (evening of Thursday 10th), by the Archbishop of Canterbury: the mere vague, undetailed, faint sketch of it – being all he had been told (very badly and imperfectly), by a lady who had no art of relation, and no clearness: the story of the young children (indefinite number and age) left to the care of servants in an old country-house, through the death, presumably, of parents. The servants, wicked and depraved, corrupt and deprave the children; the children are bad, full of evil, to a sinister degree. (*Notebooks*, p. 109)

Among Benson's works was a study of Walter Pater, which James read with particular interest and pleasure:

> I am much moved to write to you; so, hang it, I let myself go! This beautiful crisis has risen from my perusal of your infinitely interesting & accomplished volume on Pater, under the charm of which, as I lay it down, I so feel myself – the charm of a wrought nearer proximity to you as well as to W.H.P. – that I can no more *not* write than I could turn my back on you in silence after a personal hour. (Horne, p. 433)

This letter was written in 1906 and at this period Benson might have found it difficult to reciprocate such fulsome praise. He found James's 'late' style impenetrable and in 1905 wrote in his diary:

> I am baffled. I suppose I am not subtle in mind. I hate H.J.'s obscurity and finesse of thought – I hate his involved style. I feel I am near beautiful things and cannot see them. I am in a mist, and I don't think that a mist which conceals beautiful things is better than a mist which conceals ugly things. It is the mist which I see. (Miranda Seymour, *Henry James and His Literary Circle 1895-1915* (Boston: Houghton Mifflin Company, 1989), p. 117)

In *Memories and Friends* he is more reticent, acknowledging the difficulties of James's late style but in the most respectful terms: 'I must frankly confess that while I regard the later books with a reverent admiration for their superb fineness and the concentrated wealth of expression – they are hard work – they require unflagging patience and continuous freshness of apprehension' (p. 108). Despite this reservation, Benson's reminiscences are full of admiration for James – although he writes appreciatively about James's fiction Benson perhaps reserves his greatest enthusiasm for his exuberantly eloquent appreciation of James's conversation – 'like the steam hammer, it could smite and bang an incandescent mass, but it could also crack a walnut or pat an egg' – and his letters – 'the epigram melts out, to be replaced by the far finer and deeper gift of metaphor – never simile, but a hidden image tinging the sentence with colour' (p. 108).

And, with its loving attention to detailed reminiscences of memorable meetings and visits, the piece is also testimony to James's capacity to inspire great affection even in those (like Benson) who were not his very closest friends.

## XI

## HENRY JAMES

It was a hot Sunday in the July of 1884, soon after I had taken my degree. I was to go as a Master to Eton in the January following, and I had obtained leave to reside at Cambridge in the interval and to improve my mind. There were but a few undergraduates in residence, and I was enjoying the idyllic liberty of the Long Vacation, when it was possible to read, undistracted by lectures, and to choose one's own amusements. I went to luncheon with Fred Myers, in his fine, secluded house, with its long, ingeniously screened garden. There was always in that house the presence of some influence larger and more graceful than the academic culture, which gave a sense of pleasing mystery and rich associations. That day there were two guests—one a girl of singular beauty and charm, who bewildered me by the contrast between her extreme and delicate youthfulness and the aplomb and finish of her talk. This was Miss Laura Tennant, who was soon to marry Alfred Lyttelton. The other, a small, pale, noticeable man, with a short, pointed beard, and with large, piercingly observant eyes. He was elegantly dressed in a light grey suit, with a frock-coat of the same material, and in the open air he wore a white tall hat. His name was mentioned, and it transported me with delight—Mr. Henry James. I knew some of his books well; indeed, my father had quoted *Roderick Hudson* shortly before in a University sermon—" my ecclesiastical passport," as Henry James said smilingly to me—and he was one of my chief literary heroes. He talked little and epigrammatically. He had not yet acquired, or he did not display, that fine conversational manner of his later years, which I shall try hereafter to describe. The luncheon passed for me in ecstatic pleasure; I was permitted to escort the two to the service at King's, and to give them tea afterwards in my big panelled rooms looking out at the back over lawn and river and immemorial elms. I made two good friends that day—two friendships that never lapsed nor were obliterated. And I recollect a dim consciousness at the time that the attention of Henry James was bent indulgently and benignantly upon me, that he was definitely concerned with me, extracting from me the data, so to speak, of a little personal problem which he deigned to observe. The sense of this was deeply and subtly flattering, combined as it was with a far-reaching sort of goodwill.

He never lost touch with me from that hour. Two or three meetings stand out prominently in my mind at subsequent dates. I lunched with him at De Vere Gardens, and was called for after luncheon by my mother, who came in. When we departed, Henry James, who was wearing a black velvet smoking-jacket, with red frogs, put on his tall hat and came down to the street. He suddenly became aware of his unaccustomed garb at the side of the carriage, and hurriedly retreated to the shelter of the porch, where he stood, waving mute and intricate benedictions till we drove away. Again, he came to stay with us at Addington on the day after the collapse of one of his plays. He talked, I remember, to my mother and myself with great good-humour of the failure, and went on to speak of his other writing. He said that hitherto he seemed to himself to have been struggling in some dim water-world, bewildered and hampered by the crystal medium, and that he had suddenly got his head above the surface, with a new perspective and an unimpeded vision. This referred, no doubt, to the later style which he developed, so wholly different in its complex substance from the clearer and thinner manner of the earlier books. He and my father, on that occasion, found much to say to each other. Indeed it was not long after that date that he presented me with his *Two Magics*, saying that I should at once guess the reason of the gift. I read the book, but could not divine the connection. He then told me that it was on that visit that my father had told him a story which was the germ of that most tragical and even appalling story, *The Turn of the Screw*. My father took a certain interest in psychical matters, but we have never been able to recollect any story that he ever told which could have provided a hint for so grim a subject.

Again, I went once to stay with him at Rye in his stately and beautiful little house. He told me with deprecating courtesy that his mornings were closely engaged; and if I remember rightly, one heard him dictating in an adjoining room to the click of a typewriter; but he paid me short visits to shower down stamps or stationery or cigarettes beside me, to place his hand upon my shoulder, and ask if I was well bestowed. In the afternoons we walked together, and he even took me, in search of social distraction, to tea at some club or other, where he seemed on very easy terms with his neighbours. On another occasion he came down to dine with me at Eton, when I had a boarding-house. He was to have stayed the night, but he excused himself on the score of illness; and when he appeared, it was obvious that he was suffering: he was very pale, and had a gouty lameness which gave him much discomfort. But he talked energetically, and even came with me into the boys' passages to see two or three boys whose parents he knew. He limped distressfully, but he was full of attention and observation. He commented admiringly on pictures and furniture, he asked the boys whimsical little questions, and heard them with serious discernment. He ought certainly to have been in bed; and I never saw so complete a triumph of courtesy and genuine interest over bodily pain. Latterly, I used to engage myself to dine or lunch in his company at the Athenæum. You would see him enter, serious and grave, with compressed lips—he was clean-shaven in the later years—breasting the air with a decisive and purposeful walk; and then he would catch sight of you, and his eyes and lips would expand in a half-ironical and wholly indulgent smile—his mood was always indulgent. The meal itself was always a curious affair; he would get engaged in talk, look with absent-minded surprise at his food, and then, becoming aware that he was belated, take a few mouthfuls and send his plate away—it was impossible to persuade him to a leisurely consumption. The last time that I saw him he was lunching at the Athenæum, and I went up to him—he had a companion—and said that I only came for a passing benediction. He put his hand on my arm and said : " My dear Arthur, my mind is so constantly and continuously bent upon you in wonder and goodwill that any change in my attitude could be only the withholding of a perpetual and settled felicitation." He uttered his little determined, triumphant laugh, and I saw him no more.

Such sentences as the above seemed in later days to spring without the least premeditation from his lips. Without premeditation, I say, because they welled up out of a reservoir of fancy, emotion, and language which seemed inexhaustible. But the extreme and almost tantalising charm of his talk lay not only in his quick transitions, his exquisite touches of humour and irony, the width and force of his sympathy, the range of his intelligence, but in the fact that the whole process of his thought, the qualifications, the resumptions, the interlineations, were laid bare. The beautiful sentences, so finished, so deliberate, shaped themselves audibly upon the air. It was like being present at the actual construction of a little palace of thought, of improvised yet perfect design. The manner was not difficult to imitate : the slow accumulation of detail, the widening sweep, the interjection of grotesque and emphatic images, the studied exaggerations ; but what could not be copied was the firmness of the whole conception. He never strayed loosely, as most voluble talkers do, from subject to subject. The *motif* was precisely enunciated, reversed, elongated, improved upon, enriched, but it was always, so to speak, strictly contrapuntal. He dealt with the case and nothing but the case ; he completed it, dissected it, rounded it off. It was done with much deliberation, and even with both repetition and hesitation. But it was not only irresistibly beautiful, it was by far the richest species of intellectual performance that I have ever been privileged to hear. I must frankly confess that while I regard the later books with a reverent admiration for their superb fineness and the concentrated wealth of expression—they are hard work—they require unflagging patience and continuous freshness of apprehension. But his talk had none of this weighted quality. It was not exactly conversation: it was more an impassioned soliloquy; but his tone, his gestures, his sympathetic alertness made instantly and abundantly clear and sparkling, what on a printed page often became, at least to me, tough and coagulated. There was certainly something pontifical about it—not that it was ever solemn or mysterious; but you had the feeling that it was the natural expansiveness of a great mind and a deep emotion, even when his talk played, as it often did, half-lambently and half-incisively, over the characters and temperaments of friends and acquaintances. It was minute, but never trivial; and there was tremendous force in the background. Like the steam-hammer, it could smite and bang an incandescent mass, but it could also crack a walnut or pat an egg. It was perfectly adjusted, delicately controlled.

Then, again, there were his letters. I have myself a large bundle of them; glancing at them, I notice the same sense of growing freedom and controlled exuberance. The earlier ones are serious and a little ceremonious; the epigram melts out, to be replaced by the far finer and deeper gift of metaphor—never simile, but a hidden image tinging the sentence with colour. How liberal he was! A friendly bulletin would produce a document like a great tapestry of complex sentences rolling out, parenthesis after parenthesis, yet all dominated and directed. How royal were his compliments! How fertile his encouragement!

"Nardi parvus onyx eliciet cadum."

Yet there was often a strict justice in the background, which had its own secret word to say, touching a weak point with a genial emphasis, and never failing to give a sound warning. His letters always had that special note of intimacy, which FitzGerald defines, that they instantly recalled the tones of his voice; indeed, this was the characteristic of all his later writing, that it ever more and more aspired to a conversational utterance. All was conceived from the point of view of unhampered speech. But I do not feel sure that his letters and his talk were not an even higher achievement than his writings, because they were suffused with a sense of definite relation. His sense of relation, his personal interest and affection were so strong, that his writings in their loneliness, their isolation, miss, I think, that added charm of expression. I mean that they did not evoke quite the whole man. In his talk he was perhaps careless of his auditors, but never oblivious of them. He was bent upon satisfying himself, upon completely embodying his thought, but the listeners were there; while, in his letters, the thought of the particular correspondent was always in his mind; so that as the wave of words broke and regathered itself, it was always making for one well-defined point. "I respond," as he once wrote to me, "to the lightest touch of a friendly hand"; and as I turn through the letters, year after year, I am almost amazed at the intentness with which he observed, depicted, and glorified the smallest features of the background upon which he saw me, and how largely he interpreted the least hint or gesture of life. He used to write of himself ironically and deprecatingly. He deplores in one of his letters, in reply to a question of mine as to what he was actually doing, his inability ever to say " the egotistical thing," upon doing which " seriously and yet unaffectedly " he declared that the expression of personality depended. " I am trying, in fact," he wrote, " to answer the dear little deadly question of *how to do it* "; and this, he affirmed, constituted the preoccupation of his life.

His letters always carried with them an extraordinary stimulus—the stimulus of one's being so generously realised as a distinct personality. He had a quite clear picture of one's performance and quality, and even of one's purpose, which gave a touch of dignity and aim to the pursuit, however scrambling and impulsive it might be.

He had, moreover, a conriant curiosity as to the details of any circumstance or situation. I used to think that you could not please him more than by telling him the whole of a story in which friends or acquaintances were involved. I wrote him once a letter giving some further particulars of a case we had been discussing, and apologised for descending to such minute details. " I don't think," he replied, " that we see anything about our friends unless we see all—so far as in us lies—and there is surely no care we can take for them as to turn our mind upon them liberally. . . . The virtue of that 'ruder jostle' that you speak of so happily, is that it shakes out more aspects and involves more impressions."

He always urged upon one the duty of plunging wholly into experiences, not lingering half-heartedly on the edge of them. "If there be a wisdom," he once wrote to me, "in not feeling, to the last throb, the great things that happen to us, it is a wisdom that I shall never either know or esteem. Let your soul live—it's the only life that isn't on the whole a sell."

Complex and delicate as his whole intellectual and emotional nature was, he was yet wholly simple in one respect: in his need for affection. That stands out above any and every impression of him. It was not that he put criticism aside, or that he ever saw his friends' performances and exploits in anything but the clearest light; but he combined with this perfect distinctness of vision a deep craving for simple, sincere, outspoken affection which made him beyond anyone that I have ever known the most loyal and tender of friends. He responded eagerly and ardently to any proffer of friendship; he could not bear to disappoint; and I used to be deeply touched by the way that the smallest message of interest and goodwill would evoke a warm and cordial expression of delight and pleasure. "Yours faithfully and constantly" was a common signature of his; and if one did not see him or hear from him for a time, there was always a sense, on resuming relations, that there was a dedicated space in his mind and heart in which one was securely enshrined. He must have had, I imagine, wide groups and circles of friends who can never have come into contact with each other; but each relation once formed was always quite permanent and distinct. He was thus one of the few persons I have ever known who really solved that most difficult of all problems—how, namely, to combine the claims of an intellect which was for ever and instantaneously weighing and judging qualities, actions, temperaments, with a freedom and a delicacy almost without parallel, and with the unflinching certainty of touch which accompanies the skilled exercise of psychological diagnosis. Intellectual compromise and condescension were difficult enough to him, and in a general way his judgment of literary conception and craftsmanship was unhesitating and severe. But there was an even further difficulty. His own temperament was so instinctively high-minded, so utterly remote from all spite or jealousy or baser faults, that you would have believed it difficult to him not to be censorious, impossible almost for him to have faced the contact with uglier or coarser motives. But here, I think, his artistic greatness was most clearly revealed. He had the power, only granted to the supreme imaginative artist, of being able to shut off the moral light, to observe, to record, to create, with a relentless fidelity, and not to condemn. There is no sense of partisanship in his written work. He does not take a side, or yield to the pleasure of ruthlessly immersing his baser characters in the consequences of their faults. Take the case of Gilbert Osmond, that supreme and heartless egotist in *The Portrait of a Lady*. The book represents his complete triumph, from his own point of view, over all the finer and gentler characters whom he had pressed into his service. Gilbert Osmond never repents, is never abashed, never humiliated. He holds his own and goes on his way rejoicing, perfectly certain that his view of the world is both just and lofty. Few writers could have resisted the temptation to turn the tables on him. But Henry James does not give vitality to his villains, if that is not too crude a word to use, by projecting himself, as Robert Browning did, into their reasoning faculties. Henry James is never an impassioned advocate, advancing the baser point of view by means of an intellectual sympathy. He has the passionless insight of Shakespeare; he does not skilfully present the case of his puppets; he simply embodies them.

The result of this was that in actual life he could see cruder and even baser natures at work, with astonishment perhaps, but without disgust; and thus when it came to human relationships, he was able to form natural and simple ties with a tolerance, and indeed with an eagerness, which gave no smallest sense of either condescension or reserved judgment. He only demanded that his friends and acquaintances should show themselves as they were; and indeed he had a certain kindly relish for situations when his friends, as he called it, " struck the hour "—that is to say, behaved and acted as it was natural to expect them to behave and act. He never felt it to be disloyal to see his friends in the brightest and strongest of lights, and still less did he feel it his business to modify and improve them; but his loyalty and his faithfulness to a relation once formed were perfect; and perhaps his only diplomacy consisted in the good-natured avoidance of situations in which his friends should do themselves less than justice.

Indeed, as I remember with pride and gratitude the steady, almost fatherly, kindness he showed me, unruffled by any misunderstanding, any sense of unfulfilled claims, I can only describe him in two words which are lightly used, but which seem to me to be the ultimate words that can be applied to human character. He was noble, and he was generous —noble in the sense that he gave himself freely and unsparingly, acting instinctively from the finest and freest of motives ; and generous in the way in which he did not resent or mistrust ; he forgave, he condoned, he continued to love. I never doubted his affection, and I was often surprised at the constancy and intentness with which it was lavished upon me.

I have known no artist who was both so absorbed and buried in his work, and who at the same time failed to recognise the larger and fuller claim of life. Indeed, he seemed entirely absorbed in both art and life alike. As a rule, as the years go on, the dedicated artist retires more and more into the stronghold of art, and bestows upon life his tired and exhausted moods. But Henry James, through some fiery vitality of emotion, continued, alone of all the men I have ever known, to be continuously equal to the double claim. I have seen him ill, fatigued, melancholy, but never either dreary or listless ; it was always " a situation " with which he had to deal : " You go on talking while I deal with this cup of tea," I remember his saying—it evoked his energies, and he had his part to play. He never took refuge behind anything, or considered himself to be excused. " One has to be *equal* to things," I can hear him say ; and what could be more characteristic than the gay words he spoke to a friend in the first days of his last illness ? He was describing the attack itself ; " ' So it's come at last '—I said to myself—' the distinguished thing ! ' " With such high courage, seriousness touched with irony, did he meet the last situation.

My knowledge of Henry James does not entitle me

to speak more completely or authoritatively than I have done. My friendship with him was a long and tranquil affair, intermitted but never interrupted. I never claimed his unique regard, and yet for all that, I felt, as many are feeling, that I had a perfectly secure and definite place in his heart. His picture looks down at me as I write, open-eyed, with the small controlled mouth, as though preparing for some gentle, deliberate utterance. He sits in a carelessly flung attitude, his brow lined by observation and concentration, which all melted so swiftly into that firm, half-questioning, half-caressing look, which seemed to indicate the focussing of all the elements and memories of the friendship, and to say, " Where are you exactly now ? Let me see." It was always that, the same tender regard, the same critical appreciation, determined to investigate and add any new development to the old store ; and the best of it was, that, though you realised the intellectual solvent, the critical appraisement of what was intimate and personal, at the basis of it all lay a great simplicity which received you open-armed, and loved you for being exactly what you were, and for no more complex reason.

# Detachment and Morality

a) Desmond MacCarthy, *Portraits* (London: Putnam, 1931)
b) F. M. Colby, 'The Queerness of Henry James', *Bookman* (1902)

Desmond MacCarthy (1877–1952) was associated with the Bloomsbury Group and promoted the works of avant-garde artists including Matisse and Van Gogh. From 1920 to 1927 he was the literary editor of *The New Statesman* and published a number of works of literary criticism. At one point he was proposed as a suitable editor of James's letters (*Letters*, i, pp. xvii–xviii). MacCarthy's description of James's conversation in later life nicely conveys the privilege (and peril) experienced by his interlocutors. His analysis suggests James's humorous awareness of his own reputation, particularly when he reports James's response to his observation that Carlyle was a master of 'the art of mountaining mole-hills':

> A look of droll sagacity came over his face, and turning sideways to fix me better and to make sure I grasped the implication, he said: 'Ah! but for that, where would *any of us be*?' (p. 122)

Also striking is his report of how James once offered a glimpse of his usually concealed inner life. When MacCarthy recoils from and articulates the impression given of James's complete detachment from others, James is surprisingly and vigorously forthcoming, warning the younger man: 'Yes, it is solitude. If it runs after you and catches you, well and good. But for heaven's sake don't run after *it*. It is absolute solitude' (p. 124). According to MacCarthy, although James was detached, even aloof, his detachment enabled him to observe more finely and acutely than other writers, to be 'the master in fiction of the art of distinguishing' (p. 135) even though his characters existed in a different medium from 'real life', one 'entirely composed of personal relations, aesthetic emotions, and historic associations' (p. 135).

Frank Moore Colby (1865–1925) was an American critic, editor and essayist. His harsh judgment on the morality of James's novels contrasts with the views of James's friends, A. C. Benson and

Desmond MacCarthy. Whereas Benson is frustrated by the sense that James's late style conceals beauty from its readers, Colby is convinced that opacity is a fig leaf for immorality. And where MacCarthy saw the most refined moral consciousness in James's late novels, Colby concludes that he is dissolute and appears to judge him by the standards of his least admirable characters, confirming the analysis made by Benson (and earlier by W. D. Howells) that James places moral and intellectual demands on his readers because he does not instruct them what to think of the characters and events he portrays. Although the responses of MacCarthy and Colby are thus polarised, it may be that both are aware of something problematic about James's sexual identity. MacCarthy (echoing Nadal) notes that he was struck 'by how much woman there seemed to be in him' (p. 122). It might be thought anachronistic to suggest a connection between Colby's hostility and his use of the word 'queerness'. But although the *OED* suggests that 'queer' was not used as a synonym for homosexual until 1922, Hugh Stevens makes a convincing case for this usage being current much earlier (Hugh Stevens, *Henry James and Sexuality* (Cambridge: Cambridge University Press, 1998), p. 12).

## HENRY JAMES

IN Henry James's later letters his voice is audible; nor is this surprising, for his letters were often dictated, and his conversation, in its search for the right word, its amplifications, hesitations and interpolated afterthoughts, resembled dictation. This sounds portentous, not to say boring; indeed, it was at times embarrassing. But—and this made all the difference—he was fascinating. The spell he exercised by his style was exercised in his conversation. Phrases of abstruse exaggerated drollery or of the last intellectual elegance flowered in it profusely. At first you might feel rather conscience-stricken for having set in motion, perhaps by a casual question, such tremendous mental machinery. It seemed really too bad to have put him to such trouble, made him work and weigh his words like that; and if, through the detestable habit of talking about anything rather than be silent, you had started a topic in which you were not interested, you might be well punished. There was something at once so painstaking, serious and majestical in the procedure of his mind that you shrank from diverting it, and thus the whole of your little precious time with him might be wasted. This often happened in my case during our fifteen years' acquaintance, and I still regret those bungled opportunities.

In conversation he could not help giving his best, the stereotyped and perfunctory being abhorrent to him. Each talk was thus a fresh adventure, an opportunity of discovering for himself what he thought about books and human beings. His respect for his subject was only equalled, one noticed, by his respect for that delicate instrument for recording and comparing impressions, his own mind. He absolutely refused to hustle it, and his conversational manner was largely composed of reassuring and soothing gestures intended to allay, or anticipate, signs of impatience. The sensation of his hand on my shoulder in our pausing rambles together was, I felt, precisely an exhortation to patience. "Wait," that reassuring pressure seemed to be humorously saying, " wait. I know, my dear fellow, you are getting fidgety; but wait —and we shall enjoy together the wild pleasure of discovering what 'Henry James' thinks of this matter. For my part, I dare not hurry him!" His possession of this kind of double consciousness was one of the first characteristics one noticed; and sure enough we would often seem both to be waiting, palpitating with the same curiosity, for an ultimate verdict. At such moments the working of his mind fascinated me, as though I were watching through a window some hydraulic engine, its great smooth wheel and shining piston moving with ponderous ease through a vitreous dusk. The confounding thing was that the great machine could be set in motion by a penny in the slot!

I remember the first time I met him (the occasion was an evening party) I asked him if he thought London " beautiful "—an idiotic question; worse than that, a question to which I did not really want an answer, though there were hundreds of others (some no doubt also idiotic) which I was longing to ask. But it worked. To my dismay it worked only too well. "London? Beautiful?" he began, with that considering slant of his massive head I was to come to know so well, his lips a little ironically compressed, as though he wished to keep from smiling too obviously. "No: hardly beautiful. It is too chaotic, too ——" then followed a discourse upon London and the kind of appeal it made to the historic sense, even when it starved the aesthetic, which I failed to follow; so dismayed was I at having, by my idiot's question, set his mind working at such a pitch of concentration on a topic indifferent to me. I was distracted, too, by anxiety to prove myself on the spot intelligent; and the opportunity of interjecting a comment which might conceivably attain that object seemed to grow fainter and fainter while he hummed and havered and rolled along. How should I feel afterwards if I let slip this chance, perhaps the last, of expressing my admiration and my gratitude! At the end of a sentence, the drift of which had escaped me, but which closed, I think, with the words " find oneself craving for a whiff of London's carboniferous damp," I did however interrupt him. Enthusiasm and questions (the latter regarding *The Awkward Age*, just out) poured from my lips. A look of bewilderment, almost of shock, floated for a moment over his fine, large, watchful, shaven face, on which the lines were so lightly etched. For a second he opened his rather prominent hazel eyes a shade wider, an expansion of the eyelids that to my imagination seemed like the adjustment at me of the lens of a microscope; then the great engine was slowly reversed, and, a trifle grimly, yet ever so kindly, and with many reassuring pats upon the arm, he said: "I understand, my dear boy, what you mean—and I thank you." (Ouf! What a relief!)

He went on to speak of *The Awkward Age*. " Flat " was, it appeared, too mild an expression to describe its reception, " My books make no more sound or ripple now than if I dropped them one after the other into mud." And he had, I learnt to my astonishment, in writing that searching diagnosis of sophisticated relations, conceived himself to be following in the footsteps, " of course, with a difference," of the sprightly Gyp! Hastily and emphatically I assured him that where I came from, at Cambridge, his books were very far from making no ripple in people's minds. At this he showed some pleasure; but I noticed then, as often afterwards, that he was on his guard against being gratified by appreciation from any quarter. He liked it—everybody does, but he was exceedingly sceptical about its value. I doubt if he believed that anybody thoroughly understood what, as an artist, he was after, or how skilfully he had manipulated his themes; and speaking with some confidence for the majority of his enthusiastic readers at that time, I may say he was right.

He was fully aware of his idiosyncrasy in magnifying the minute. I remember a conversation in a four-wheeler (" the philosopher's preference," he called it) about the married life of the Carlyles. He had been re-reading Froude's *Life of Carlyle*, and after remarking that he thought Carlyle perhaps the best of English letter-writers, he went on to commiserate Mrs. Carlyle on her dull, drudging life. I protested against "dull," and suggested she had at least acquired from her husband one source of permanent consolation and entertainment, namely the art of mountaining mole-hills. A look of droll sagacity came over his face, and turning sideways to fix me better and to make sure I grasped the implication, he said: " Ah! but for that, where would *any of us* be? "

Once or twice I went a round of calls with him. I remember being struck on these occasions by how much woman there seemed to be in him; at least it was thus I explained the concentration of his sympathy upon social worries (the wrong people meeting each other, etc., etc.), or small misfortunes such as missing a train, and also the length of time he was able to expatiate upon them with interest. It struck me that women ran on in talk with him with a more unguarded volubility than they do with most men, as though they were sure of his complete understanding. I was amazed, too, by his standard of decent comfort; and his remark on our leaving what appeared to me a thoroughly well-appointed, prosperous house, " Poor S., poor S.—the stamp of unmistakable poverty upon everything!" has remained in my memory. I never ventured to ask him to my own house; not because I was ashamed of it, but because I did not wish to excite quite unnecessary commiseration. He would have imputed himself; there were so many little things in life he minded intensely which I did not mind at all. I do not think he could have sat without pain in a chair, the stuffing of which was visible in places. His dislike of squalor was so great that surroundings to be tolerable to him had positively to proclaim its utter impossibility. " I can stand," he once said to me, while we were waiting for our hostess in an exceptionally gilt and splendid drawing-room, " a great deal of gold." The effects of wealth upon character and behaviour attracted him as a novelist, but no array of terms can do justice to his lack of interest in the making of money. He was at home in describing elderly Americans who had acquired it by means of some invisible flair, and on whom its acquisition had left no mark beyond perhaps a light refined fatigue (His interest in wealth was therefore the reverse of Balzacian); or in portraying people who had inherited it. Evidence of ancient riches gave him far more pleasure than lavishness, and there we sympathized; but above all the signs of tradition and of loving discrimination exercised over many years in conditions of security soothed and delighted him. " Lamb House," his home at Rye, was a perfect shell for his sensibility. He was in the habit of speaking of its " inconspicuous little charm," but its charm could hardly escape anyone; so quiet, dignified and *gemütlich* it was, within, without.

But an incident comes back to me which struck me as revealing something much deeper in him than this characteristic. It occurred after a luncheon party of which he had been, as they say, " the life." We happened to be drinking our coffee together while the rest of the party had moved on to the verandah. " What a charming picture they make," he said, with his great head aslant, " the women there with their embroidery, the . . ." There was nothing in his words, anybody might have spoken them; but in his attitude, in his voice, in his whole being at that moment, I divined such complete detachment, that I was startled into speaking out of myself: " I can't bear to look at life like that," I blurted out, " I want to be in everything. Perhaps that is why I cannot *write*, it makes me feel absolutely alone. . . ." The effect of this confession upon him was instantaneous and surprising. He leant forward and grasped my arm excitedly: " Yes, it is solitude. If it runs after you and catches you, well and good. But for heaven's sake don't run after *it*. It is absolute solitude." And he got up hurriedly and joined the others. On the walk home it occurred to me that I had for a moment caught a glimpse of his intensely private life, and, rightly or wrongly, I thought that this glimpse explained much: his apprehensively tender clutch upon others, his immense pre-occupation with the surface of things and his exclusive devotion to his art. His confidence in himself in relation to that art, I thought I discerned one brilliant summer night, as we were sauntering along a dusty road which crosses the Romney marshes. He had been describing to me the spiral of depression which a recent nervous illness had compelled him step after step, night after night, day after day, to descend. He would, he thought, never have found his way up again, had it not been for a life-line thrown to him by his brother William; perhaps the only man in whom he admired equally both heart and intellect. What stages of arid rejection of life and meaningless yet frantic agitation he had been compelled to traverse! " But," and he suddenly stood still, " but it has been good "—and here he took off his hat, baring his great head in the moonlight—" for my genius." Then, putting on his hat again, he added, " Never cease to watch whatever happens to you."

Such was Henry James the man. For Henry James the writer I shall attempt to find a formula.

He was a conscious artist, who knew more clearly than most English novelists what he wished to do and how he must set about it. That fiction need not be formless, and that a novelist's mastery is shown in unfolding a situation to which every incident contributes, was the lesson that his books could teach a generation, persuaded to the contrary by dazzling achievements in an opposite manner. To Henry James the novel was not a hold-all into which any valuable observations and reflections could be stuffed; nor was it merely peptonized experience. He was an artist and a creator. Of course the world he created bore a vital relation to experience, as all fiction must if it is to bewitch and move us; but the characters in that world, in whose fate and emotions he interested us, existed in a medium which was not the atmosphere we ordinarily breathe. That medium was his own mind. Just as there is a world called " Dickens," another called " Balzac," so there is a world called " Henry James." When we speak of the " reality " of such worlds, we only mean that we have been successfully beguiled. We are really paying homage to the shaping imagination of a creator. How independent of the actual world are characters in fiction, and how dependent for their vitality upon the world in which they are set, becomes clear the moment we imagine a character moved from one imaginary world into another. If Pecksniff were transplanted into *The Golden Bowl*, he would become extinct; and how incredible would " the Dove " be in the pages of *Martin Chuzzlewit*! The same holds good of characters constructed piecemeal from observation, when introduced into a world created by an overflow of imagination. They become solecisms, either they kill the book or the book kills them. The unforgivable artistic fault in a novelist is failure to maintain consistency of tone. In this respect Henry James never failed. His characters always belonged to his own world, and his world was always congruous with his characters. What sort of a world was it? And what were its relations to our common experience which made it interesting? There is no need to separate the answers to these two questions, which the work of every creative artist prompts. The answer to the one will suggest the answer to the other.

It is important to emphasize at once Henry James's power of creating his own world because, in every novelist who possesses that power, it is the most important faculty. Yet in his case it has often been overlooked. Critics have found in his work so much else to interest them: his style, his methods, his subtlety. From their comments it might be supposed that his main distinction lay in being a psychologist, or an observer, or an inventor of a fascinating, but—so some thought—an indefensible style. Yet to regard him primarily as an observer or psychologist or as a maker of phrases, is not only to belittle him, but to make the mistake we made when first Ibsen came into our ken. It seems hardly credible that we should have taken Ibsen for a realist, but we did. Despite his rat-wife, wild-duck, his towers and ice-churches; despite the strange intensity of his characters, which alone might have put us on the right track; despite the deep-sea pressure of the element in which they had their being; despite the perverse commonness of the objects which surrounded them—as of things perceived in some uncomfortable dream—it was under the banner of realism that Ibsen's battle was fought for him. Because his characters threw such a vivid light on human nature and our predicaments, we mistook them for photographs. And yet we meant by " an Ibsen character " was as clear to us as what " a Dickens character " meant. The fact that we understand each other, when we speak of a " Henry-James character," is the proof that his imagination, too, was essentially creative.

Most great novelists have given to their creations an excess of some faculty predominant in themselves. Thus Meredith's characters are filled to an unnatural degree with the beauty and courage of life, while Balzac gives to his a treble dose of will and appetite. The men and women in Henry James's novels, the stupid as well as the intelligent, show far subtler powers of perception than such men and women actually have. It was only by exaggerating, consciously or unconsciously, that quality in them, that he could create a world that satisfied his imagination. With this exception his work is full of delicately observed actualities. His men and women are neither more heroic, nor single-hearted, nor more base than real people; and, if allowance be made for their superior thought-reading faculties and the concentration of their curiosity upon each other, events follow one another in his stories as they would in real life. The reader may sometimes find himself saying: " Would anyone, without corroborative evidence act on such a far-fetched guess as that? " But he will never find himself saying (granted of course the super-subtlety of these people), " That is not the way things happen." Whether his characters are children of leisure and pleasure, jaded journalists, apathetic or wily disreputables, hard-working or dilatory artists, they are all incorrigibly pre-occupied with human nature; with watching their own emotions, and the complex shifting relations and intimate dramas around them. There is a kind of collected self-consciousness and clairvoyance about them all. They watch, they feel, they compare notes. There is hardly a minor character in his later books, not a butler or a telegraph clerk, who, if he opens his lips twice, does not promptly show the makings of a gossip of genius. There are other equally important generalizations to be made about the people of Henry James's world, but this is the most comprehensive. For the critic this peculiarity has a claim to priority, not on aesthetic grounds, but because it leads to the centre of his subject: what was the determining impulse which made Henry James create the particular world he did?

In that astonishing record of imaginative adventure, *The American Scene*, he continually refers to himself as the " restless analyst," speaking of himself as a man " hag-ridden by the twin demons of observation and imagination." The master-faculty of Henry James was this power of analysing his impressions, of going into them not only far but, as they say in Norse fairy-tales, " far and farther than far." Indeed, there are only three other novelists whom a passion for finality in research and statement has so beset, for whom the sole condition of a Sabbath's rest was the assurance that everything that there was to be said had been at any rate attempted:—Proust, Balzac (with whom the later Henry James had more sympathy than with any other fellow-craftsman) and Dostoevsky. The last two were very different men from himself, labouring in other continents. Dostoevsky's subject is always the soul of man, and ultimately its relation to God; his deepest study is man as he is when he is alone with his soul. In Henry James, on the contrary, the same passion of research is directed to the social side of man's nature, his relations to his fellow-men. The universe and religion are as completely excluded from his books as if he had been an eighteenth-century writer. The sky above his people, the earth beneath them, contains no mysteries for them. He is careful never to permit them to interrogate these. Mr. Chesterton has called Henry James a mystic; the truth is that he is perhaps the least mystical of all writers who have ever concerned themselves with the inner life. Mysticism would have shattered his world; it is not the mystical which attracts him, but a very different thing, the mysterious, that is to say, whatever in life fascinates by being hidden, ambiguous, illusive and hard to understand. And this brings us again straight up to the question of his directing impulse as an artist.

It was to conceive the world in a light which (a religious interpretation of man's nature being excluded) would give most play to his master faculties of investigation. It was an impulse, or rather a necessity, to see people in such a way as made them, their emotions and their relations to each other, inexhaustible subjects for the exploring mind. A single formula for a writer is justly suspect; but entertain this one for a moment on approval. It may prove to be " the pattern in the carpet."

In the first place, it explains his choice of themes. His long career was a continual search for more and more recondite and delicate ones. He begins with cases of conscience, and in these already the shades seemed fine to his contemporaries, and the verdicts to depend upon evidence not always visible to " twelve good men and true." Then the formula explains his early fondness—long before he had found a method of constructing a world of recondite possibilities—for ending with that substitute for mystery, the note of interrogation. It explains also his excitement in discovering Europe, especially those secluded corners of European society where dark deposits of experience might be postulated without extravagance. (In *his* America everything was depressingly obvious.) It explains his passionate interest in the naive consciousness of his Americans when confronted with Europeans who possessed more complex standards and traditions. Did they or did they not understand? It explains his later interest in children, in whom it is so puzzling to fix the moment of dawning comprehension. It explains his marked preference for faithful failure as a subject over the soon exhausted interest of success. It explains in a measure his comparative lack of interest in the life of the senses (there is no mystery in the senses compared with the mind); also his efforts to keep in the background, so that they might gather an impenetrable portentousness, crude facts, such as professional careers, adulteries, swindles and even murders, which nevertheless, for the sake of the story, had sometimes to go through the empty form of occurring in his books. It explains the attraction a magnificently privileged class had for his art, his " Olympians," whose surroundings allowed latitude to the supposition of a wonderfully richer consciousness. It explains the almost total exclusion from his world of specimens of labouring humanity, to whom no such complexity can be with any plausibility attributed—a dustman in the world of Henry James is an inconceivable monster. It accounts, too, for the blemishes in his books; for his refusal to admit that such a thing as a molehill *can* exist for a man with eyes in his head, and (how it seems to fit!) for his reluctance, even when occasion demanded it, to call a spade anything so dull and unqualified as a spade. It explains the fascination of his style, which conveyed amazingly the excitement of a quest, the thrill of approaching some final precision of statement. And above all, it explains why he came to endow his men and women with more and more of his own penetration, tenderness and scrupulousness, till at last he created a world worthy of his own master faculty, in which human beings, when confronted, saw mysteries in one another's gestures, and profundities in their words, and took joy in each other's insight, like brave antagonists in each other's strength; a world in which they could exclaim about one another that they were " wonderful " and " beautiful," where they belonged to, or fought with each other, on levels of intimacy which had never been described before.

The words, which he found to describe the characters in this world that he loved, are unrivalled for revealing delicacy. His method is to present them to us through some other character dowered with his own power of appreciation. Mrs. Stringham in *The Wings of the Dove* is, for instance, the medium through which we first catch a glimpse of Milly. She is first conscious of the immense rich extravagant background of New York from which Milly springs, and of which " the rare creature was the final flowering "; next of " a high, dim, charming ambiguous oddity which was even better " in Milly herself, who seemed, on top of all that, to enjoy boundless freedom, the freedom of the wind in the desert. " It was unspeakably touching to be so equipped and yet to have been reduced by fortune to little humble-minded mistakes.... She had arts and idiosyncrasies of which no great account could have been given, but which were a daily grace if you lived with them; such as the art of being almost tragically impatient and yet making it light as air; of being inexplicably sad and yet making it clear as noon; of being unmistakably gay and yet making it as soft as dusk."

Although this world is peopled with subtler men and women than that of any other novelist, the crown does not go to the clever. It is tempting to describe him as an inveterate moralist, who, finding ordinary scales too clumsy to weigh finer human qualities, employs instead aesthetic weights and measures. The consequent reversal of the verdict was one of his favourite themes. " There are no short cuts," he seemed to say, " to being beautiful; to be beautiful you must be really good." He made us understand better the meaning of intimacy and the beauty of goodness.

If one were to attempt to suggest the morality or philosophy behind his books in a sentence, " There are no short cuts to a good end " would serve the purpose. What are Maggie Verver and " Milly " but beautiful examples of " the long road," or Kate Croy and Charlotte Stant but instances of the disastrous " short cut "? Where does the failure and vulgarity of the set in *The Awkward Age*, Mrs. Brookenham and her friends, lie? Surely, in their attempt to take by storm the charms of refinement and the refinements of intimacy. In many short stories, recent and early, we find the same drama; the contrast between the charms and superiorities (even the physical beauties) which have been won, paid for, as it were, by suffering, thought and sympathy, and those which have been appropriated by money, sheer brute brain, or self-assertion. Whether the contrast is between houses or manners or faces or minds, the same law is insisted on that *there is no short cut to beauty.* It is curious that just as no other author has noted so subtly the liberating power of wealth, those aspects of it in which it may be even symbolized by " the wings of a dove," bringing the inaccessible within reach, enabling a noble imagination to gratify itself, lending sometimes to a character, through the consciousness of its possession, an intensified charm, making some virtues just what they ought to be by making them easy; so no other author has insisted more subtly upon the beauty which wealth cannot buy, cannot add to, cannot diminish. How often in his books the failures are the successes, and the man or woman " who gets there " is, to the artist's eye, the one who fails!

Up to the age of seventeen, like most boys, I read not only without discrimination, but without any clear idea that anybody ever discriminated in such matters. I had only one classification for novels, the " good " and the " rotten." The latter were a very small class; nearly all were " good." Dickens was, of course, superbly good; but Wilkie Collins was also good, and so were Miss Corelli, Stanley Weyman, Scott, Miss Braddon, and a host of others whose names are forgotten, *Vanity Fair* was good, but so was *The Deemster* and *She.* It never entered my head that people did not say and do what in books authors made them, or that the writer ever left out anything which would have made the situation or characters more interesting. My attitude (except where Dean Farrar's school stories were concerned) was one of boundless acceptance. It never struck me that the explanation why life, as reflected in novels, was sometimes dull, could be that it was not reflected in them properly. I was very fond, however, of " good expressions," a phrase which in my private vocabulary covered indifferently any words which pleased me, wherever I found them—in Milton, Dickens, Keats, or Sir William Harcourt's public speeches. I often missed them in books which I otherwise thoroughly enjoyed. One day I had to make a slow long cross-country journey from Eton, and m'tutor lent me two small volumes called *The American*, just the right size for the side pocket. These, I found, were full of " good expressions." The book (but not for this reason) had, I see now, a profound effect on me. At the time I thought I had merely enjoyed it very much, but something else had happened—I had discovered the art and the resource of the observer. Henceforward life was to be not merely a matter of doing things and wanting things, or of things happening to oneself; there was another resource of inexhaustible interest always to hand— one could stand still and take things in.

Nevertheless my own generation, when we discovered Henry James, read him on the whole for his substance, for precisely that side of his work which appears now to be wearing thin. Our generation, at least that part of it with which I was best acquainted and most at home, was interested in those parts of experience which could be regarded as ends in themselves. Morality was either a means to attaining these goods of the soul, or it was nothing— just as the railway system existed to bring people together and to feed them, or the social order that as many " ends " as possible should be achieved. These ends naturally fined themselves down to personal relations, aesthetic emotions and the pursuit of truth. We were perpetually in search of distinctions; our most ardent discussions were attempts to fix some sort of a scale of values for experience. The tendency was for the stress to fall on feeling rightly rather than upon action. It would be an exaggeration to say we cared not a sprat either for causes or for our own careers (appetite in both directions comes with eating, and we had barely begun to nibble); but those interests were subordinate. Henry James was above all a novelist of distinctions; he was, indeed, the master in fiction of the art of distinguishing. His philosophy amounted to this: to appreciate exquisitely was to live intensely. We suspected, I remember, that he over-valued subtlety as an ingredient in character, and was perhaps too " social " in his standards, employing, for instance, " charm " too often as the last test of character. But whether or not we always agreed with his estimate of values, he was pre-eminently interested in what interested us; that is to say, in disentangling emotions, in describing their appropriate objects and in showing in what subtle ways friendships might be exquisite, base, exciting, dull or droll. That his characters were detached from the big common struggling world, that its vague murmur floated in so faintly through their windows, that they moved and had their being in an environment entirely composed of personal relations, aesthetic emotions, and historic associations, seemed to us unimportant limitations to his art. Nor were we particularly interested in the instincts or the will compared with the play of the intelligence. What was the will but a means, a servant? Or what were the instincts but the raw stuff out of which the imagination moulded a life worth contemplating?

It still seems to me, on the whole, a sound philosophy; only the fiction which reflects these things to exclusion of all else now appears to me to shut out much which is both more absorbing and more important than I once supposed—even also to falsify the flavour of those very experiences on which it exclusively dwells.

I have described Henry James's youthful audience during those years when his books in his later manner were appearing, because such a description indicates the angle from which his work must always appear important. He cared immensely for spiritual decency; nothing in life beguiled him into putting anything before that. He had a tender heart, an even more compassionate imagination, but a merciless eye.

I knew him for over fifteen years, but I only saw him at long intervals. In spite of admiration and curiosity, I left our meetings entirely to chance, for I soon discovered two daunting facts about him. Firstly, that he was easily bored (not merely in an ordinary but in an excruciating sense of the word), and secondly, that he minded intensely the dislocations and disappointments which are inevitable in all human relations. They made him groan and writhe and worry. The measure of how much he minded them could be read in the frequency, extravagance and emphasis of his signals that all was really well, across even those small rifts (to him they had the horror of gulfs) which absence and accident open up between people. Many have not understood the elaborate considerateness which is so marked in his correspondence. As I read Henry James, it was his sense both of the gulf between human beings and the difficulty of bridging it which made him abound in such reassurances. Like many remarkable men, while drawn towards others, he was conscious also of his own aloofness. There is a kind of detachment (it is to be felt in the deeply religious, in some artists, in some imaginative men of action), which seems to bring the possessor of it at once nearer to his fellow beings than others get, and at the same time to remove him into a kind of solitude. I think Henry James was aware of that solitude to an extraordinary degree.

His manner of receiving you expressed an anxiety (sometimes comic in desperate thoroughness of intention) to show you that whatever might have happened in the interval, on his side, at least, the splinters had kept new and fine; so that if your half of the tally was in a similar condition, the two would dovetail at touch. I have seen him keep a lady in a paralysed condition for five minutes while he slowly recalled everything about her. And if your talk with him had been something of a failure, his farewell expressed that what you had wanted, yet failed to get, he had also wanted, and that nothing must blind you to his recognition of any affection or admiration you might be so generous as to feel for " your old Henry James."

I imagine being interrupted here by a pointed question, " But did not this agitated anxiety to signal, defeat its own end and make complications? " It often did so, just as some of his letters, long as they are, were sometimes almost entirely composed of signals and gestures. But to many sensitive natures who find the world only too full of callous, off-hand people, this exquisite and agitated recognition of their own identity and of their relation to himself was a delightful refreshment. To say that he was a magnet to muffs would be a grievous injustice to his friends, but certainly those who were most easily attracted to him were the sort who are excoriated by the rough contacts of life. He himself was clearly one of the most sensitive of men. The importance to him of urbanity, money, privacy, lay in the fact that they were salves. His art was a refuge to him as well as the purpose of his life. He was horrified by the brutality and rushing confusion of the world, where the dead are forgotten, old ties cynically snapped, old associations disregarded, where one generation tramples down the other, where the passions are blind, and men and women are satisfied with loves and friendships which are short, common and empty. I picture him as flying with frightened eyes and stopped ears from that City of Destruction, till the terrified bang of his sanctuary door leaves him palpitating but safe; free to create a world which he could people with beings who had leisure and the finest faculties for comprehending and appreciating each other, where the reward of goodness was the recognition of its beauty, and where the past was not forgotten. His sense of the past—of the social world's, of his own—which he recorded with a subtlety and piety never excelled in autobiography, was almost the deepest sense in him. Such reverence for human emotions is usually associated with the religious sense; yet that, as I have said, is singularly absent from his work. While we read his books, only the great dome of civilization is above our heads— never the sky; and under our feet is its particoloured mosaic—never the earth. All that those two words " sky " and " earth " stand for in metaphor is absent.

One word on the style and method of Henry James's stories. He is the most metaphorical of writers and " metaphysical " in the sense in which that term was applied to Cowley and Donne. He abounds in " conceits," that is to say, he often follows a metaphor or verbal association to its furthest ramifications, and ingeniously forces them to help him carry on his thought, which in this way takes many turns and twists in approaching a particular point. The characteristic of his later style is a spontaneous complexity. The sentences are often cumbrous and difficult, struggling through a press of hints and ideas which gather round every word and are carried on to help elucidating the situation; this end, however, they only achieve for those who take the trouble to see their bearing; and this requires close attention. But apart from the frequency of happy and beautiful phrases, both his style and his method of telling a story have often a charm usually associated with a very different kind of imaginative work. The charm of all writing which has the quality of improvisation is that, in such writing, the reader catches the author's own excitement in the development of his idea, shares his delight in dallying with it, in turning it round and round, or if it is a simple story, he feels it growing at the same time as he enjoys the tale. It is a quality which cannot be illustrated by extracts; but that much of Henry James's writing has this charm and merit, which usually accompanies simplicity of thought, is clear to anyone who analyses the pleasure he gets from reading him. He does not clip his ideas or cut his coat according to his cloth, but he weaves it as he goes along. As he follows this idea wherever it leads him, his readers are sometimes landed in strange places, and those who are capable of a psychological glow, experience again something like the thrill with which they used in their childhood to read such phrases as " as soon as his eyes grew accustomed to the darkness . . . " what on earth is he going to see next!

When I look up and see the long line of his books, the thought that it will grow no longer is not so distressing (he has expressed himself) as the thought that so many rare things in the world must now go without an appreciator, so many fine vibrations of life lose themselves in vacancy.

## THE QUEERNESS OF HENRY JAMES

A year ago, when Henry James wrote an essay on women that brought to our cheek the hot, rebellious blush, we said nothing about it, thinking that perhaps, after all, the man's style was his sufficient fig-leaf, and that few would see how shocking he really was. And, indeed, it has been a long time since the public knew what Henry James was up to behind that verbal hedge of his, though half-suspecting that he meant no good, because a style like that seemed just the place for guilty secrets. But those of us who formed the habit of him early can make him out even now, our eyes having grown so used to the deepening shadows of his later language that they can see in the dark, as you might say. We say this not to brag of it, but merely to show that there are people who partly understand him even in *The Sacred Fount*, and he is clearer in his essays, especially in this last wicked one on "George Sand: The New Life," published in the April *North American*.

Here he is as bold as brass, telling women to go ahead and do and dare, and praising the fine old hearty goings-on at the court of Augustus the Strong, and showing how they can be brought back again if women will only try. His impunity is due to the sheer laziness of the expurgators. They will not read him, and they do not believe anybody else can. They justify themselves, perhaps, by recalling passages like these in the *Awkward Age:*

"What did this feeling wonderfully appear unless strangely irrelevant."

"But she fixed him with her weary penetration."

"He jumped up at this, as if he couldn't bear it, presenting as he walked across the room a large, foolish, fugitive back, on which her eyes rested as on a proof of her penetration."

"My poor child, you're of a profundity."

"He spoke almost uneasily, but she was not too much alarmed to continue lucid"

"You're of a limpidity, dear man!"

"Don't you think that's rather a back seat for one's best?"

"'A back seat?'" she wondered, with a purity.

"Your aunt didn't leave me with you to teach you the slang of the day."

"'The slang?' she spotlessly speculated."

Arguing from this that he was bent more on eluding pursuit than on making converts, they have let things pass that in other writers would have been immediately rebuked. He has, in fact, written furiously against the proprieties for several years. "There is only one propriety," he says, "that the painter of life can ask of a subject: Does it or does it not belong to life?" He has charged our Anglo-Saxon writers with "a conspiracy of silence," and taunted them with the fact that the women are more improper than the men. "Emancipations are in the air," says he, "but it is to women writers that we owe them. The men are cowards, rarely venturing a single coarse expression, but already in England there are pages upon pages of women's work so strong and rich and horrifying and free that a man can hardly read them. Halcyon days, they seem to him, and woman the harbinger of a powerful Babylonish time when the improprieties shall sing together like the morning stars. Not an enthusiastic person generally, he always warms to this particular theme with generous emotion.

His latest essay, discussing what he calls the "new life," cites the heart history of George Sand as "having given her sex for its new evolution and transformation the real standard and measure of change." It is all recorded in Mme. Karénine's biography, and Mme. Karénine, being a Russian with an "admirable Slav superiority to prejudice," is able to treat the matter in a "large, free way." A life so amorously profuse is sure to set an encouraging example, he thinks Her heart was like an hotel, occupied, he says, by "many more or less greasy males" in quick succession. He hopes the time will come when other women's hearts will be as miscellaneous:

"In this direction their aim has been, as yet, comparatively modest and their emulation low; the challenge they have hitherto picked up is but the challenge of the average male. The approximation of the extraordinary woman has been, practically, in other words, to the ordinary man. Madame Sand's service is that she planted the flag much higher; her own approximation, at least, was to the extraordinary. She reached him, she surpassed him, and she showed how, with native dispositions, the thing could be done. These new records will live as the precious text-book, so far as we have got, of the business."

This is plain enough. Any other man would be suppressed. In a literature so well policed as ours, the position of Henry James is anomalous. He is the only writer of the day whose moral notions do not seem to matter. His dissolute and complicated Muse may say just what she chooses. This may be because it would be so difficult to expose him. Never did so much vice go with such sheltering vagueness. Whatever else may be said of James, he is no tempter, and though his later novels deal only with unlawful passions, they make but chilly reading on the whole. It is a land where the vices have no bodies and the passions no blood, where nobody sins because nobody has anything to sin with. Why should we worry when a spook goes wrong? For years James has not made one shadow-casting character. His love affairs, illicit though they be, are so stripped to their motives that they seem no more enticing than a diagram. A wraith proves faithless to her marriage vow, elopes with a bogie in a cloud of words. Six phantoms meet and dine, three male, three female, with two thoughts apiece, and, after elaborate geometry of the heart, adultery follows like a Q. E. D. Shocking it ought to be, but yet it is not. Ghastly, tantalising, queer, but never near enough human to be either good or bad. To be a sinner, even in the books you need some carnal attributes—lungs, liver, tastes, at least a pair of legs. Even the fiends have palpable tails; wise men have so depicted them. No flesh, no frailty; that may be why our sternest moralists have licensed Henry James to write his wickedest. Whatever the moral purport of these books, they may be left wide open in the nursery.

To those who never liked him he is the same in his later writings as in his earlier. There were always mannerisms in his work, and his hunt for the distinguished phrase was always evident. His characters never would do enough things, and he was too apt to make them stand stock-still while he chopped them up. He was too apt, also, to think that when he had made a motive he had made a man And there were many then, as now, who loathed his little cobweb plots and finical analyses. He often hovered very near the outer boundary of common sense, and it was a wonder sometimes how he escaped burlesque; but, still, he did it. His world was small, but it was credible—humanity run through a sieve, but still humanity. Since then his interests have dropped off one by one, leaving him shut in with his single theme—the rag, the bone and the hank of hair, the discreditable amours of skeletons. They call it his later manner, but the truth is, it is a change in the man himself He sees fewer things in this spacious world than he used to see, and the people are growing more meagre and queer and monotonous, and it is harder and harder to break away from the stump his fancy is tied to.

*Frank Moore Colby.*

# Mrs Humphrey Ward, *A Writer's Recollections* (London: W Collins & Co. Ltd, 1918)

A friend of James for many years, Mary Augusta Arnold (1851–1920), better known as Mrs Humphrey Ward, offers an affectionate and admiring tribute in *A Writer's Recollections*. Ward was an extremely successful and well-regarded novelist, the niece of Matthew Arnold and the granddaughter of Thomas Arnold, the celebrated headmaster of Rugby. She was born in Tasmania but her family moved to Oxford when she was a child. Here her father worked with John Henry Newman, a major figure in the Oxford movement. Ward was herself greatly interested in theological and philosophical issues, and the theme of religious controversy is the focus of two of her most famous novels, *Robert Elsmere* (1888) and *Helbeck of Bannisdale* (1898). Her husband, Humphrey Ward, worked at *The Times* as an art critic and editorial writer. Although an advocate of higher education for women, Mrs Ward was strongly opposed to women's suffrage.

She and James met in London in November 1882 and the two novelists became good friends. He did not hesitate to criticise her novels in his letters, and remarked caustically of *Robert Elsmere*: 'One fears a little sometimes that he may suffer a sunstroke, damaging if not fatal, from the high, oblique light of your admiration for him' (*Letters*, iii, p. 235). In print he was more circumspect, though in a short essay on Ward written in 1891 he focuses on her undoubted success and popularity, and on her moral and intellectual qualities, skirting round the question of her novels' literary artistry.

In *A Writer's Recollections*, she describes a visit paid by James to the Wards in 1899. They were staying in the Villa Barberini which Ward had hired in order to soak up local colour for *Eleanor* (1900), a novel set in Italy. James was rather critical of this novel, in particular of its young American heroine Lucy whom he considered unconvincing, more like an English girl. He suspected that a minor character in the novel, a self-important novelist named Mr Bellasis who insisted that his books could not be appreciated except on a rereading, was based on himself (Edel, iv, p. 285). If his suspicions were justified Ward was perhaps getting her own back on James who had a few years earlier painted a satirical portrait of her in 'The Next Time' (1895) as Mrs Highmore, a popular novelist who longs to be taken seriously as a literary artist (Edel, iv, p. 277). For, despite their friendship, James felt some ambivalence towards this comparatively conventional novelist who was so much more popular (and wealthy) than himself.

Ward provides some fuel here for commentators trying to uncover evidence of James's attraction to young men (see the Introduction to this volume, p. xv). The timing is perhaps significant for it was at this stage in his life that James 'established intimate relationships, beyond his usual friendships, that for the first time provided him with the feeling of being in love' (Kaplan, p. 401). During this same trip to Italy James made an important new friend, an American sculptor of Norwegian birth named Hendrik Andersen. James was immediately drawn to the good-looking Andersen and spent fifty pounds on one of his sculptures. Andersen was the first (and one of the least satisfactory) of the many young men with whom James forged passionate friendships in his later life. The strength of his feelings towards Andersen is revealed in the tactile intensity of his letters: 'The sense that I can't *help* you, see you, talk to you, touch you, hold you close and long, or do anything to make you rest on me, and feel my participation – this torments me, dearest boy, makes me ache for you ...', he wrote after the death of Andersen's brother in 1902 (*Letters*, iv, p. 226). Perhaps James's rapturous response to the 'beautiful youth', Aristodemo, described here by Ward, was another reflection of this apparent fresh receptiveness to masculine beauty in middle age.

## CHAPTER XVI

### THE VILLA BARBERINI. HENRY JAMES

IT was in the summer of 1898, that some suggestions gathered from the love-story of Chateaubriand and Madame de Beaumont, and jotted down on a sheet of notepaper led to the writing of 'Eleanor.' Madame de Beaumont's melancholy life came to an end in Rome, and the Roman setting imposed itself, so to speak, at once. But to write in Rome itself, played upon by all the influences of a place where the currents of life and thought, so far as those currents are political, historical or artistic, seem to be running at double tides, would be, I knew, impossible, and we began to make enquiries for a place outside Rome, yet not too far away, where we might spend the spring. We tried to get an apartment at Frascati, but in vain. Then some friend suggested an apartment in the old Villa Barberini at Castel Gandolfo, well known to many an English and French diplomat, especially to the diplomat's wife and children, flying to the hills to escape the summer heat of Rome. We found by correspondence two kind little ladies living in Rome, who agreed to make all the preparations for us, find servants, and provide against a possibly cold spring to be spent in rooms meant only for *villegiatura* in the summer. We were to go early in March, and fires or stoves must be obtainable, if the weather pinched.

The little ladies did everything, engaged servants, and bargained with the Barberini Steward, but they could not bargain with the weather! On a certain March day when the snow lay thick on the olives, and all the furies were wailing round the Alban hills —we arrived. My husband, who had journeyed out with us to settle us in, and was then returning to his London work, was inclined to mocking prophecies that I should soon be back in Rome at a comfortable Hotel. Oh, how cold it was that first night!—how dreary on the great stone staircase, and in the bare comfortless rooms! We looked out over a grey storm-swept Campagna, to distant line of surf-beaten coast; the kitchen was fifty-two steps below the dining-room; the Neapolitan cook seemed to us a most formidable gentleman, suggesting stilettos, and we sat down to our first meal, wondering whether we could possibly stay it out.

But with the night (as I wrote some years ago) the snow vanished, and the sun emerged. We ran east to one balcony, and saw the light blazing on the Alban Lake, and had but to cross the apartment to find ourselves, on the other side, with all the Campagna at our feet, sparkling in a thousand colours to the sea. And outside was the garden, with its lemon trees growing in vast jars—like the jars of Knossos—but marked with Barberini bees; its white and red camellias be-carpeting the soft grass with their fallen petals; its dark and tragic recesses where melancholy trees hung above piled fragments of the great Domitian villa whose ruins lay everywhere beneath our feet; its olive gardens sloping to the west, and open to the sun, open too to white, nibbling goats, and wandering *bambini*;

its magical glimpse of St. Peter's to the north, through a notch in a group of stone-pines ; and, last and best, its marvellous terrace that roofed a crypto-porticus of the old villa, whence the whole vast landscape, from Ostia and the mountains of Viterbo to the Circæan promontory, might be discerned, where one might sit and watch the sunsets burn in scarlet and purple down through the wide west into the shining bosom of the Tyrrhenian sea.

And in one day we had made a home out of what seemed a desert. Books had been unpacked, flowers had been brought in, the stoves were made to burn, the hard chairs and sofas had been twisted and turned into something more human and sociable, and we had began to realise that we were, after all, singularly fortunate mortals, put in possession for three months—at the most moderate of rents !—of as much Italian beauty, antiquity, and romance, as any covetous soul could hope for—with Rome at our gates, and leisurely time for quiet work.

Our earliest guest was Henry James, and never did I see Henry James in a happier light. A new light too. For here, in this Italian country, and in the Eternal City, the man whom I had so far mainly known as a Londoner was far more at home than I ; and I realised perhaps more fully than ever before the extraordinary range of his knowledge and sympathies.

Roman history and antiquities, Italian art, Renaissance sculpture, the personalities and events of the Risorgimento, all these solid *connaissances* and many more were to be recognised perpetually as rich elements in the general wealth of Mr. James's mind. That he had read immensely, observed immensely, talked immensely, became once more gradually and delightfully clear on this new field. That he spoke French to perfection was of course quickly evident to anyone who had even a slight acquaintance with him. M. Bourget once gave me a wonderful illustration of it. He said that Mr. James was staying with himself and Madame Bourget at their villa at Hyères, not long after the appearance of Kipling's ' Seven Seas.' M. Bourget, who by that time read and spoke English fluently, complained of Mr. Kipling's technicalities, and declared that he could not make head or tail of McAndrew's Hymn. Whereupon Mr. James took up the book, and standing by the fire, fronting his hosts, there and then put McAndrew's Hymn into vigorous idiomatic French —an extraordinary feat, as it seemed to M. Bourget. Something similar, it will be remembered, is told of Tennyson. ' One evening,' says F. T. Palgrave of the poet, ' he read out, off-hand, Pindar's great picture of the life of Heaven, in the Second Olympian, into pure modern prose splendidly lucid and musical.' Let who will decide which *tour de force* was the more difficult.

But Mr. James was also very much at home in Italian, while in the literature, history and art of both countries he moved with the well-earned sureness of foot of the student. Yet how little one ever thought of him as a student! That was the spell. He wore his learning—and in certain directions he was learned—' lightly, like a flower.' It was to him not a burden to be carried, not a possession to be proud of, but merely something that made life more thrilling, more full of emotions and sensations; emotions and sensations which he was always eager, without a touch of pedantry, to share with other people. His knowledge was conveyed by suggestion, by the adroitest of hints and indirect approaches. He was politely certain, to begin with, that you knew it all; then to walk *with you* round and round the subject, turning it inside out, playing with it, making mock of it, and catching it again with a sudden grip, or a momentary flash of eloquence, seemed to be for the moment his business in life. How the thing emerged, after a few minutes, from the long involved sentences! —only involved because the impressions of a man of genius are so many, and the resources of speech so limited. This involution, this deliberation in attack, this slowness of approach towards a point which in the end was generally triumphantly rushed, always seemed to me more effective as Mr. James used it in speech than as he employed it—some of us would say, to excess—in a few of his latest books. For, in talk, his own living personality—his flashes of fun—of courtesy—of ' chaff '—were always there, to do away with what in the written word, became a difficult strain on attention.

I remember an amusing instance of it, when my daughter D——, who was housekeeping for us at Castel Gandolfo, asked his opinion as to how to deal with the Neapolitan cook, who had been anything but satisfactory, in the case of a luncheon-party of friends from Rome. It was decided to write a letter to the ex-bandit in the kitchen, at the bottom of the fifty-two steps, requesting him to do his best, and pointing out recent short-comings. D——, whose Italian was then rudimentary, brought the letter to Mr. James, and he walked up and down the vast *salone* of the Villa, striking his forehead, correcting and improvising. ' A really nice pudding' was what we justly desired, since the Neapolitan genius for sweets is well known. Mr. James threw out half phrases—pursued them—improved upon them—withdrew them—till finally he rushed upon the magnificent bathos—'un dolce come si deve!'—which has ever since been the word with us for the tip-top thing.

With the country people he was simplicity and friendship itself. I recollect him in close talk with a brown-frocked bare-footed monk, coming from the monastery of Palazzuola on the farther side of the Alban lake, and how the super-subtle, super-sensitive cosmopolitan found not the smallest difficulty in drawing out the peasant, and getting at something real and vital in the ruder, simpler mind. And again, on a never to be forgotten evening on the Nemi lake, when on descending from Genzano to the strawberry farm that now holds the site of the famous temple of Diana Nemorensis, we found a beautiful youth at the *fattoria*, who for a few pence undertook to show us the fragments that remain. Mr. James asked his name. 'Aristodemo,' said the boy, looking as he spoke the Greek name, 'like to a god in form and stature.' Mr. James's face lit up; and he walked over the historic ground beside the lad, Aristodemo picking up for him fragments of terra-cotta from the furrows through which the plough had just passed, bits of the innumerable small *figurines* that used to crowd the temple walls as ex-votos, and are now mingled with the *fragole* in the rich alluvial earth. It was a wonderful evening; with a golden sun on the lake, on the wide stretches where the temple stood, and the niched wall where Lord Savile dug for treasure and found it; on the great ship-timbers also, beside the lake, wreckage from Caligula's galleys, which still lie buried in the deepest depth of the water; on the rock of Nemi, and the fortress-like Orsini villa; on the Alban Mount itself, where it cut the clear sky. I presently came up with Mr. James and Aristodemo, who led us on serenely, a young Hermes in the transfiguring light. One almost looked for the winged feet and helmet of the messenger god! Mr. James paused—his eyes first on the boy, then on the surrounding scene. 'Aristodemo!' he murmured smiling, and more to himself than me, his voice caressing the word—'what a name! what a place!'

On another occasion I recall him in company with the well-known antiquary, Signor Lanciani, who came over to lunch; amusing us all by the combination of learning with 'le sport' which he affected. Let me quote the account of it given by a girl of the party:

> Signor Lanciani is a great man who combines being *the* top authority in his profession, with a kindness and *bonhomie* which makes even an ignoramus feel happy with him—and with the frankest love for *flânerie* and 'sport.' We all fell in love with him. To hear him after lunch in his fluent but lisping English holding forth about the ruins of Domitian's villa—'what treasures are still to be found in ziz garden if somebody would only *dig*!'—and saying with excitement—'ziz town, ziz Castello Gandolfo was built upon the site of Alba Longa, not Palazzuola at all. *Here*, Madame, beneath our feet, is Alba Longa'—And then suddenly—a pause, a deep sigh from his ample breast, and a whisper on the summer air—'I vonder—vether—von could make a golf-links around ziz garden!'

And I see still Mr. James's figure strolling along the terrace which roofed the crypto-porticus of the Roman villa, beside the professor—the short coat, the summer hat, the smooth-shaven, finely-cut face, now alive with talk and laughter, now shrewdly, one might say coldly observant; the face of a satirist—but so human!—so alive to all that under-world of destiny through which move the weaknesses of men and women. We were sorry indeed when he left us. But there were many other happy meetings to come through the sixteen years that remained ; meetings at Stocks and in London; letters and talks that were landmarks in my literary life and in our friendship. Later on I shall quote from his ' Eleanor ' letter, the best perhaps of all his critical letters to me, though the ' Robert Elsmere ' letters, already published, run it hard. That, too, was followed by many more. But as I do not intend to give more than a general outline of the years that followed on 1900, I will record here the last time but one that I ever saw Henry James—a vision, an impression, which the retina of memory will surely keep to the end. It was at Grosvenor Place in the autumn of 1915, the second year of the war. How doubly close by then he had grown to all our hearts ! His passionate sympathy for England and France, his English naturalisation—a *beau geste* indeed, but so sincere, so moving—the pity and wrath that carried him to sit by wounded soldiers, and made him put all literary work aside as something not worth doing, so that he might spend time and thought on helping the American ambulance in France :—one must supply all this as the background of the scene.

It was a Sunday afternoon. Our London house had been let for a time, but we were in it again for a few weeks, drawn into the rushing tide of war-talk and war anxieties. The room was full when Henry James came in. I saw that he was in a stirred, excited mood, and the key to it was soon found. He began to repeat the conversation of an American envoy to Berlin—a well-known man—to whom he had just been listening. He described first the envoy's impression of the German leaders, political and military, of Berlin. 'They seemed to him like men waiting in a room from which the air is being slowly exhausted. They *know* they can't win! It is only a question of how long, and how much damage they can do.' The American further reported that after his formal business had been done with the Prussian Foreign Minister, the Prussian—relaxing his whole attitude and offering a cigarette—said—'Now then let me talk to you frankly, as man to man!'—and began a bitter attack on the attitude of President Wilson. Colonel —— listened, and when the outburst was done, said—'Very well! Then I too will speak frankly. I have known President Wilson for many years. He is a very strong man, physically and morally. You can neither frighten him, nor bluff him—'

And then—springing up in his seat—'And, by Heaven, if you want war with America, you can have it to-morrow!'

Mr. James's dramatic repetition of this story, his eyes on fire, his hand striking the arm of his chair, remains with me as my last sight of him in a typical representative moment.

Six months later, on March 6, 1916, my daughter and I were guests at the British Headquarters in France. I was there at the suggestion of Mr. Roosevelt and by the wish of our Foreign Office, in order to collect the impressions and information that were afterwards embodied in 'England's Effort.' We came down ready to start for the front, in a military motor, when our kind officer escort handed us some English telegrams which had just come in. One of them announced the death of Henry James; and all through that wonderful day, when we watched a German counter-attack in the Ypres salient from one of the hills south-east of Poperinghe, the ruined tower of Ypres rising from the mists of the horizon, the news was intermittently with me as a dull pain, breaking in upon the excitement and novelty of the great spectacle around us.

'*A mortal, a mortal is dead!*'

I was looking over ground where every inch was consecrate to the dead sons of England, dead for her; but even through their ghostly voices came the voice of Henry James, who, spiritually, had fought in their fight and suffered in their pain.

One year and a month before the American declaration of war. What he would have given to see it—my dear old friend—whose life and genius will enter for ever into the bonds uniting England and Amercia!

. . . . . . .

Yes!—

> . . . He was a priest to us all
> Of the wonder and bloom of the world,
> Which we saw with his eyes and were glad.

For that was indeed true of Henry James, as of Wordsworth. The 'wonder and bloom,' no less than the ugly or heart-breaking things, which like the disfiguring rags of old Laertes, hide them from us—he could weave them all, with an untiring hand, into the many-coloured web of his art. Olive Chancellor, Madame Mauve, Milly, in 'The Wings of a Dove'—the most exquisite in some ways of all his women—Roderick Hudson, St. George, the woman doctor in the 'Bostonians,' the French family in the 'Reverberation,' Brooksmith—and innumerable others :—it was the wealth and facility of it all that was so amazing! There is enough observation of character in a chapter of the 'Bostonians,' a story he thought little of, and did not include in his collected edition, to shame a Wells novel of the newer sort, with its floods of clever half-considered journalism in the guise of conversation, hiding an essential poverty of creation. 'Ann Veronica' and the 'New Machiavelli,' and several other tales by the same writer, set practically the same scene, and handle the same characters under different names. Of an art so false and confused, Henry James could never have been capable. His people, his situations, have the sharp separateness—and something of the inexhaustibleness —of nature, which does not mix her moulds.

As to method, naturally I often discussed with him some of the difficult problems of presentation. The posthumous sketches of work in progress, published since his death, show how he delighted in these problems, in their very difficulties, in their endless opportunities. As he often said to me, he could never read a novel that interested him without taking it mentally to pieces, and re-writing it in his own way. Some of his letters to me are brilliant examples of this habit of his. Technique—presentation —were then immensely important to him; important as they never could have been to Tolstoy, who probably thought very little consciously about them. Mr. James, as we all know, thought a great deal about them, sometimes, I venture to think, too much. In 'The Wings of a Dove,' for instance, a subject full of beauty and tragedy is almost spoilt by an artificial technique, which is responsible for a scene on which, as it seems to me, the whole illusion of the book is shattered. The conversation in the Venice apartment where the two *fiancés*—one of whom at least, the man, is commended to our sympathy as a decent and probable human being—make their cynical bargain in the very presence of the dying Milly, for whose money they are plotting, is in some ways a *tour de force* of construction. It is the central point on which many threads converge, and from which many depart. But to my mind, as I have said, it invalidates the story. Mr. James is here writing as a *virtuoso*, and not as the great artist we know him to be. And the same, I think, is true of ' The Golden Bowl.' That again is a wonderful exercise in virtuosity; but a score of his slighter sketches seem to me infinitely nearer to the truth and vitality of great art. The book, in which perhaps technique and life are most perfectly blended—at any rate among the later novels—is ' The Ambassador.' There, the skill with which a deeply interesting subject is focussed from many points of view, but always with the fascinating unity given to it, both by the personality of the ' Ambassador,' and by the mystery to which every character in the book is related, is kept in its place, the servant, not the master, of the theme. And the climax—which is the river scene, when the ' Ambassador' penetrates at last the long kept secret of the lovers—is as right as it is surprising, and sinks away through admirable modulations to the necessary close. And what beautiful things in the course of the handling!—the old French Academician and his garden, on the *rive gauche*, for example ; or the summer afternoon on the upper Seine, with its pleasure-boats, and the red parasol which finally tells all—a picture drawn with the sparkle and truth of a Daubigny, only the better to bring out the unwelcome fact which is its centre. 'The Ambassador' is the master-piece of Mr. James's later work and manner, just as 'The Portrait of a Lady' is the masterpiece of the earlier.

And the whole?—his final place?—when the stars of his generation rise into their place above the spent field? I, at least, have no doubt whatever about his security of fame; though very possibly he may be no more generally read in the time to come than are most of the other great masters of literature. Personally, I regret that, from 'What Maisie Knew' onwards, he adopted the method of dictation. A mind so teeming, and an art so flexible, were surely the better for the slight curb imposed by the physical toil of writing. I remember how and when we first discussed the *pros* and *cons* of dictation, on the fell above Cartmel Chapel, when he was with us at Levens in 1887. He was then enchanted by the endless vistas of work and achievement which the new method seemed to open out. And indeed it is plain that he produced more with it than he could have produced without it. Also, that in the use of dictation as in everything else, he showed himself the extraordinary craftsman that he was, to whom all difficulty was a challenge, and the conquest of it a delight. Still, the diffuseness and over-elaboration which were the natural snares of his astonishing gifts were encouraged rather than checked by the new method; and one is jealous of anything whatever that may tend to stand between him and the unstinted pleasure of those to come after.

But when these small cavils are done, one returns

in delight and wonder to the accomplished work. To the *wealth* of it above all—the deep draughts from human life that it represents. It is true indeed that there are large tracts of modern existence which Mr. James scarcely touches, the peasant life, the industrial life, the small trading life, the political life; though it is clear that he divined them all, enough at least for his purposes. But in his vast, indeterminate range of busy or leisured folk, men and women with breeding and without it, backed with ancestors or merely the active ' sons of their works,' young girls and youths and children, he is a master indeed, and there is scarcely anything in human feeling, normal or strange, that he cannot describe or suggest. If he is without passion, as some are ready to declare, so are Stendhal and Turguéniev, and half the great masters of the novel; and if he seems sometimes to evade the tragic or rapturous moments, it is perhaps only that he may make his reader his co-partner, that he may evoke from us that heat of sympathy and intelligence which supplies the necessary atmosphere for the subtler and greater kinds of art.

And all through, the dominating fact is that it is ' Henry James ' speaking—Henry James, with whose delicate, ironic mind and most human heart we are in contact. There is much that can be *learnt* in fiction; the resources of mere imitation, which we are pleased to call realism, are endless; we see them in scores of modern books. But at the root of every book is the personality of the man who wrote it. And in the end, that decides.

# Compton Mackenzie, 'Henry James', *Life and Letters Today* (1943)

Much has been written about Henry James's unsatisfactory and ultimately traumatic relationship with the theatre. It was during this period of his life that he first became acquainted with the young Compton Mackenzie (1883–1972). In later life Mackenzie became a writer whose output was astonishingly varied, and included essays, novels, drama and music criticism. He is now best known for his comic novel *Whisky Galore* (1947). In 1889 his father, the actor and theatre manager Edward Compton, encouraged Henry James to embark on an ultimately unsuccessful experiment in drama when he wrote to suggest that James adapt *The American* for the stage. Compton's approach to James was made at the instigation of his wife, the American actress Virginia Bateman, who later acted the part of Claire de Cintré opposite Compton's Newman. James's excited note on his new project reveals that Compton was encouraging a long-standing ambition:

> I had practically given up my old, valued, long cherished dream of doing something for the stage, for fame's sake, and art's, and fortune's: overcome by the vulgarity, the brutality, the baseness of the condition of the English-speaking theatre today. But after an interval, a long one, the vision has revived, on a new and a very much humbler basis, and especially under the lash of necessity. (*Notebooks*, p. 52)

In her reminiscences, James's secretary Theodora Bosanquet describes Henry James's attraction to the theatre, and his mixed motives for seeking success as a playwright:

> The theatre had both allured and repelled him for many years, and he had already been the victim of a theatrical misadventure. His assertions that he wrote plays solely in the hope of making money should not, I think, be taken as the complete explanation of his dramas. It is pretty clear that he wrote plays because he wanted to write them, because he was convinced that his instinct for dramatic situations could find a happy outlet in plays, because writing for the stage is a game rich in precise rules and he delighted in the multiplication of

technical difficulties, and because he lived in circles more addicted to the intelligent criticism of plays than to the intelligent criticism of novels. (Theodora Bosanquet, *Henry James at Work* (London: Hogarth Press, 1924), p. 20)

For the next six years James was intensely preoccupied with the theatre. Although his motives for this ultimately ill-judged move were indeed partly financial it is clear that Bosanquet was right to insist that he was actively drawn to the stage – in the spring of 1888 he had begun to write his novel, *The Tragic Muse*, whose heroine, Miriam Rooth, is a dedicated actress. He seems in particular to have enjoyed the camaraderie of rehearsals. The actress Elizabeth Robins, who played Claire de Cintré in the London production of *The American*, records his attentive concern for the wellbeing of his cast:

> I do not think any of us could forget his concern for everyone's comfort. Apart from his brief experience of provincial rehearsals he of course realized that actors must keep different hours from other people. But, as much as other people, if not more abundantly, actors must, he clearly felt, need to *be fed* … Somewhere, off-stage, there used to appear a large hamper of delicacies, to which with some ceremony Mr. James would conduct us in two's or three's, as we happened also to be 'off'. He himself, sandwich in hand, would return to the fray with obvious relief and satisfaction, leaving us to make our more serious inroads. No other playwright in my tolerably wide experience ever thought of feeding his company! (Robins, pp. 50–1)

James achieved some success with *The American*, but went on to produce a succession of comparative failures, culminating in the disastrous opening night of *Guy Domville* in 1895. The play's failure was made still more painful by the tremendous success of Oscar Wilde's *An Ideal Husband* which opened on the same night. H. G. Wells offers a vivid account of the fiasco and of the response of the lead actor, George Alexander, to his own failure:

> Disaster was too much for Alexander that night. A spasm of hate for the writer of these fatal lines must surely have seized him. With incredible cruelty he led the doomed James, still not understanding clearly how things were with him, to the middle of the stage, and there the pit and the gallery had him. James bowed; he knew it was the proper thing to bow. Perhaps he had selected a few words to say, but if so they went unsaid. I have never heard any sound more devastating than the crescendo of booing that ensued. The gentle applause of the stalls was altogether overwhelmed. For a moment or so James

faced the storm, his round face white, his mouth opening and shutting and then Alexander, I hope in a contrite mood, snatched him back into the wings. (H. G. Wells, *Experiment in Autobiography*, 2 vols (London: Faber & Faber, 1934), vol. ii, p. 536)

But in 1889 James's hopes were still high and it was at this period, during discussions of the first draft of *The American,* that the seven-year-old Compton Mackenzie met the novelist and asked him to sign his birthday book. Much later, in 1914, James wrote to Mackenzie, reminiscing about their first encounters, and praising the young writer's works:

> [Your talent] strikes me as very living and real and sincere, making me care for it – to anxiety – care above all for what shall become of it. You ought, you know, to do only some very fine and ripe things, really solid and serious and charming ones; but your dangers are almost as many as your aspects, and as I am a mere monster of *appreciation* when I read – by which I mean of the critical passion – I would fain lay an earnest and communicative hand on you and hypnotize or otherwise bedevil you into proceeding as I feel you most *ought* to, you know. (*Letters*, iv, p. 697)

Later that year James included Compton Mackenzie in an article, 'The Younger Generation' which appeared in two installments in the *Times Literary Supplement.* This was thought by many to be an ill-judged piece. Certainly some of James's preferences – for Mackenzie's own *Sinister Street* (1913–14) over D. H. Lawrence's *Sons and Lovers* (1913) for example – have not stood the test of time.

# HENRY JAMES
## By COMPTON MACKENZIE

THE OTHER DAY in clearing out an old chest I came across a small volume bound in crushed morocco—*The Tennyson Birthday Book* presented to myself in 1886—of the existence of which I had been oblivious for at least fifty years. I turned the pages to see what names my youthful enterprise had managed to secure for what was, as I think, a much more practical kind of nominal reliquary than the polychromatic autograph albums of to-day.

Sarasate, Charles Hallé, Wilson Barrett, W. G. Wills, Thomas Hughes, Henry James ... Henry James? The occasions when I begged those other names for the book have vanished from my memory, but that first far away meeting with Henry James remains vivid. The very day can be fixed because Henry James himself noted it in the space for his birthday signature on 15th April. It was 5th May, 1890. Henry James was just forty-seven : I was a few weeks over seven.

As my father and I walked along by Kensington Gardens I was told how he when a boy at school had met Thackeray walking along this same stretch of pavement with *his* father and how the great man had tipped him handsomely. Not yet being at school myself, I did not regard middle-aged gentlemen as milch cows and therefore did not cross the road to De Vere Gardens with the smallest expectations from Henry James. At that date he wore a beard, and I remember the almost ritualistic courtesy of his welcome to what he once called his " chaste and secluded Kensington quatrième ... flooded with light like a photographer's studio ". He was, it might have seemed, absurdly solicitous for the comfort of the seven-year-old visitor before he immersed himself with its father in the mysterious deeps of the theatre. I was warned by the paternal finger on the paternal lips not to interrupt the colloquy. Not that I was remotely planning such a sacrilege. My attention was preoccupied by the variety of desks of different heights and by a kind of day-bed along the wall to which a reading-desk was attached. Finally I was bidden to produce my birthday book, and I had the gratification of seeing Henry James take it to the tallest and to me the most puzzling desk in a corner beside the windows and inscribe his name, standing. That anybody should stand at a desk to write cut sharply for my childish fancy a difference between authors and the rest of mankind.

Probably in the course of this visit to 34 De Vere Gardens it was more or less settled that my father should produce James's dramatized version of his novel *The American*. The author would be writing to his sister from Venice two months later to say how " ravished " he was by her letter after reading the play, which was to be produced first in the provinces and next year in London. He would be congratulating himself upon the technical experience he had gained from writing a play that would act in " to a minute, including entr'actes 2 hours and $\frac{3}{4}$ ". Here Henry James was premature. In the autumn he went to Sheffield to read the play before it was put into rehearsal to the company that would perform it. The reading began at eleven o'clock and finished at a quarter to three.

" Well ? " the author asked anxiously, when he and the actor-manager came out of the stage-door to take a short walk before dining together at half-past three, " What was your impression, Compton ? "

" It's too long," said my father.

" Too long ? " James repeated in courteous but distressed amazement.

" It took you three hours and three-quarters to read it and there are three intervals to allow for."

" What shall we do ? "

" We shall have to cut it."

Henry James stopped dead and gazed at my father in agony.

" Cut it ? " he gasped. " Did you say ' cut it ' ? But when we discussed the play you did not suggest it was too long."

" No, it was not too long then. You've added at least forty pages to the script."

" But here and there additions and modifications were necessary," the author insisted.

Later on that afternoon my mother was able to prevail on Henry James to allow her to make suggestions for cuts, and that led to a formidable correspondence between them, much of it carried on by James in very long and elaborate telegrams offering to sacrifice a couple of " that's " on one page. Fifteen years earlier Tennyson had handed over *Queen Mary* to be cut by my grandmother for production on the stage. I have a letter to her in which the poet's depression is revealed in a postscript; " Do you think *all* the changes good ? "

On the evening of that day in Sheffield when Henry James read *The American* to the company he saw a performance of *The School for Scandal*. After the curtain had fallen he went round to my father's dressing-room. For some minutes James sat in a contemplative silence. At last my father, in the way of the actor-manager, asked him how he had enjoyed Sheridan's comedy.

" A curious old play," said Henry James slowly. " A very curious old play," he repeated in a tone that revealed his astonishment that such a play could still be put on the stage. And that was the only comment he made.

*The American* was produced at Southport on 3rd January, 1891. I attended the first night, and my distress over the unhappy ending might have warned the author and the actor that they were taking a risk with the audiences of that date, which were on a level with an intelligent child on the edge of his eighth birthday. Nevertheless, both Henry James and my father began to dream of a London success. James's letters at that time were full of his golden prospects. They were also full of apologies for what he called in a letter to Robert Louis Stevenson his "tribute to the vulgarest of the muses". He would not pay it, he protested, if he were not driven to it by the need of money. In fact he was really in no need of money, and it was poetic justice that Melpomene and Thalia should both desert him after that insult.

*The American* was performed for the first time in London at the Opéra Comique on 26th September, 1891, and ran for about two months. His only other acted play, *Guy Domville*, was produced at the St. James's Theatre on 5th January, 1895, and, after a painful scene on the first night when poor Henry James was hooted by the gallery on taking his call, a month later it was "whisked away to make room for the triumphant Oscar" and *The Importance of Being Earnest*. On the night of the production of *Guy Domville* Henry James, anxious to be "coerced into quietness" but too nervous to watch the first performance of his own play, had been to see *An Ideal Husband* at the Haymarket, and it had seemed to him "so helpless, so crude, so bad, so clumsy, feeble, and vulgar" that on his way across St. James's Square to learn the fate of his own play he had stopped short in a sudden apprehension for the future of *Guy Domville* if this "thing" was, as it seemed to be, a success.

The general feeling among Henry James's friends was one of relief that he would never again be beguiled into writing for the theatre. Nevertheless, I think the English theatre lost something. I have just read *The American* again after many years, and although it bears some of the marks of now being itself " a curious old play ", there are indications of dramatic potentiality which might one day have produced a masterpiece.

In 1908 my mother wrote to ask Henry James if he would enlist William Heinemann's personal interest in the MS. of a novel I was proposing to send him. This was *The Passionate Elopement*, which had already been returned by three publishers with unusual promptitude.

James wrote back to say that he would ask Heinemann to give it his personal attention but warned her that nothing he could say would have the slightest influence on his decision as a publisher, and, probably in dread of a request to read the MS. himself, he added that the thought of a novel about the eighteenth century filled him with misgivings. My mother then sent him a copy of some poems I had published the previous year and she received a kind letter from Henry James, the full measure of the astonishing encouragement of which I, with the arrogant ignorance of youth, did not appreciate at the time. Now, thirty-five years later, I feel embarrassed by the idea of printing it.

In the winter of 1913–14 J. B. Pinker sent me a letter he had had from Henry James to thank him for drawing his attention to the first volume of *Sinister Street*, and, already humbler and wiser, I wrote to express a hope that I might meet him again and profit by his counsel.

I was in Capri at the time, and it was not until the late summer of 1914 that I saw Henry James for the first time since 1891. He had forgotten the visit to De Vere Gardens, but remembered what I had quite forgotten and that was his presiding at a birthday party of mine and blessing a book which one of the ladies of the company had presented to me.

Henry James had just laid on me what in a previous letter he had called " an earnest and communicative hand " in order to " hypnotize or otherwise bedevil " me into proceeding on the right lines for my future as a writer, when his housekeeper came in to ask if he had written to the Army and Navy Stores about the marmalade. Henry James was like a porpoise arrested in mid-leap and prevented by some mischievous sea-god from plunging back to gambol in its element.

" The marmalade, Mrs X ? " he repeated.

" Because if you haven't, Mr. James," the inexorable woman continued, " it would be as well if you wrote the order for six pots now and I'll give it to the man, who is waiting."

James looked toward the Thames as if he contemplated a plunge through the window of 21 Carlyle Mansions to escape from this domestic exigency. Then he turned to me. " Will you forgive me, my dear boy, if I interrupt this so absorbing . . . this so delightful colloquy the pleasure of which has . . . "

" Mr. James, please, the man is waiting."

" Yes, yes, Mrs. X." Then he was brooding over me again. " Now can you, do you think, engage your attention for a few minutes while I attempt to confront this hideous problem which has . . . "

" Mr. James, please ! "

And this time the housekeeper tapped her foot with a hint of impatience.

" In one moment, Mrs. X." He turned back to me in anxious hospitality and then picked up a volume from the table.

" Here is kind Arnold Bennett's last book. I have not yet had the time to savour it myself, but you may find . . . or here is dear H. G. Wells. He is always at once so . . . so . . . " He clutched at the air for what H. G. Wells was.

" Mr. James ! Mr. James ! Please ! This marmalade," Mrs. X interjected sharply, squashing the uncaught epithet like a clothes-moth.

Henry James made an ample gesture of despair over his thwarted solicitude for a guest's entertainment. Then unlading words from the rich cargo of his mind to pack into his theme, he began to discourse of the intrusion of the world upon the holy fane of art. I listened, with half an eye on Mrs. X who I feared would presently nip the Master's ear between an exasperated finger and thumb and lead him like a schoolboy to his desk.

" The man is waiting for the order, Mr. James. You were going to order six 2 lb. pots of marmalade."

Henry James extricated himself from his discourse and sat down at the desk. He raised his pen, looked round over a reproachful shoulder at the housekeeper, and in the hollow voice of a ghost, " Marmalade ? " he asked.

" Marmalade," she replied firmly. " Six 2 lb. pots of the marmalade we always have."

Henry James poised his pen above the notepaper. He was obviously searching for the phrase which would express at once with the utmost accuracy and beauty the demand he was making upon the Army and Navy Stores. It evaded him. He turned round to me.

" I hope you are continuing to beguile this unavoidable but not therefore less deplorable . . . " the left arm was raised and the hand plucking at the air was seeking a word more richly equipped than " interruption " ; but it evaded him, and he had to make the best of " interruption " by stressing " rup " at the expense of the other syllables, with a glance of stern reproach at Mrs. X. She was unimpressed.

" Six 2 lb. pots of the marmalade we always have," she repeated coldly.

Henry James bent over the desk and wrote fast. Then he thrust the missive into the hands of his housekeeper, and sighed forth as she retired an elaborate polyepithetic lament for these monstrous co-operative stores which our Frankenstein of a civilization had created to destroy the amenity of existence.

I hesitate to set down on paper *obiter dicta* of all but thirty years ago, because to those who never heard Henry James speak the experience is incommunicable, and if I yield to temptation and record one or two it must be without any attempt to involve myself in what would at best be mere parody.

Speaking of my novel *Carnival*, James said that the chief character by the limitation of her life as a ballet-girl was not capable of sustaining so large a story. He added quickly that he should say as much of *Madame Bovary*. Presently I was telling him that it was my intention to rewrite *Carnival* and get rid of what I now thought were mistakes of treatment. The massive face of Henry James looked what must be called horror-stricken. He laid a deterrent hand upon my shoulder and bade me banish for ever from my fancy a project so . . . would that I could recall the very adjective he at last conjured from the air, an adjective so decisive in its condemnation.

" I wasted months of labour upon the thankless, the sterile, the preposterous, the monstrous task of revision. There is not an hour of such labour that I have not regretted since. You have been granted the most precious gift that can be granted to a young writer—the ability to toss up a ball against the wall of life and catch it securely at the first rebound. You have that ability to an altogether unusual extent. None of your contemporaries, so far as I have knowledge of their work, enjoys such an immediate and direct impact, and of those in the generation before you only H. G. Wells. It is a wonderful gift but it is a dangerous gift, and I entreat you, my dear boy, to beware of that immediate and direct return of the ball into your hands, while at the same time you rejoice in it. I, on the contrary, am compelled to toss the ball so that it travels from wall to wall..." here with a gesture he seemed to indicate that he was standing in a titanic fives-court, following with anxious eyes the ball he had just tossed against the wall of life... "from wall to wall until at last, losing momentum with every new angle from which it rebounds, the ball returns to earth and dribbles slowly to my feet when I arduously bend over, all my bones creaking, and with infinite difficulty manage to reach it and pick it up."

On another occasion we were talking about his *Notes on Novelists* and I ventured to say that some of the confidence he had inspired in me by the attention he had accorded to my work had been shaken by what seemed the equal approval he had accorded to a contemporary, Y.Z.

Again that horror-stricken expression pervaded the massive face, and the arms were raised in astonishment.

"You alarm me... you startle... you... all that I supposed I had indicated, however kindly, for kindness was imperative—yet, as I perhaps all too rashly supposed, with firmness and with the sharpest and most unmistakable clarity, was that so far our excellent, our greatly loved, our dear young friend Y. had written precisely nothing."

But after all I have been led into trying to present Henry James dramatically, and that is to invite disaster.

Edmund Gosse came nearer than anybody to expressing that abundant personality within the confines of the printed page. I commend what he has written about Henry James to disciples who never heard the master.

And now I have just been assailed by the disturbing reflection that $53\frac{1}{2}$ years subtracted from 5th May, 1890, would land me in the last year of King William the Fourth's reign, but that when I add them to the same date they seem at the most a couple of swift decades. The shrivelled face of dotage smiles fatuously over my shoulder.

I shall babble no more.

# Henry James and the Theatre

a) W. Graham Robertson, *Time Was* (London: Hamish Hamilton, 1931)
b) Henry Mackinnon Walbrook, 'Henry James and the English Theatre', *Nineteenth Century* (1916)

Walford Graham Robertson (1866–1948) was a painter, theatre designer and Blake scholar. As a young man Robertson became acquainted with several of the older generation of Pre-Raphaelite artists, including Walter Crane and George Moore. He was handsome as well as talented and Sargent (who accompanied Robertson to the ill-fated opening night of *Guy Domville*) painted a striking portrait of him in 1894. Robertson designed costumes for Wilde's *Salome* as well for a number of Shakespearean productions and he is particularly alert to the design qualities of *Guy Domville*, praising its striking sets but deprecating the over elaborate and distracting costumes.

Henry Mackinnon Walbrook (1865–1941) was a theatre critic and writer whose works include *Gilbert and Sullivan Opera: A History and a Comment* (1922). He wrote a review of *The Saloon*, a one-act play adapted from one of James's own short stories, 'Owen Wingrove', which James himself, according to the diarist Sydney Waterlow, described as 'a gloomy, sinister little thing' (Hyde, p. 124). *The Saloon* was written in 1908 but was not produced until 1911 when it appeared as a 'curtain raiser' at the Little Theatre in 1911. Walbrook's review praised the play's capacity to make its audience's nerves tingle with terror. He concluded '"The Saloon" is, beyond doubt, one of the most thrilling one-act plays produced in London of late years' (H. M. Walbrook, *Nights at the Play* (London: W. J. Ham-Smith, 1911), p. 116). As Walbrook recalls in the essay reprinted below, James wrote to the critic after reading this piece. His letter, in which he asserts that the play as a text must be privileged above its performance on stage, perhaps helps suggest why James ultimately failed as a dramatist:

*And*, dear young man, you will thereby nobly *help the great cause* – that of righting and overhauling the monstrous disproportion, *false* proportion, that has come, in this country, to get established between the drama itself, the responsible originating sources of it, the matters at issue in the play, the authority of the author &c, and the wretched ruck of the interpretation. That has produced the state of things in which the actor-manager is so grotesquely possible, and in which he and his train are so tremendously cocks of the walk. America makes it still worse – in America no one but the actor is regarded as the theatre at all; with results of a colossal vulgarity. (Horne, pp. 507–8)

In his essay, Walbrook responds to the frustrations voiced by James, exploring the tensions between art and commerce within the world of the theatre.

'Guy Domville.' That recalls another beautiful production at the St. James's. I had nothing to do with it, I am sorry to say—I should like to have been responsible for the White Parlour—but I was present on the first night, and that is not a happy memory.

The play was by Henry James. He had tempted fortune on the stage on one or two former occasions but with small success; now, with the Company and resources of the St. James's Theatre at his back, all would surely be well.

His old friend, John Sargent, and I had dined together quietly and we set out for the first night with high hopes.

The opening act delighted the audience; all the delicate charm of the dialogue was brought out by careful acting and stage management.

Marion Terry at her enchanting best was an ideal 'Mrs. Peveril' and Alexander played 'Guy Domville' with quiet grace, though Sargent, always on the look-out for 'bad drawing,' kept whispering to me, " Why does he open his mouth on one side like that? It makes his face all crooked."

The curtain fell to general applause and the play seemed safe.

But with the next act came a change. The author had done a dangerous thing in dropping most of the first-act characters and introducing a new set in whom little interest was taken. The excellence of the opening was now a drawback, the audience wanted more of it; they longed to follow the fortunes of Marion Terry and sulkily refused to be interested in the doings of Miss Millard. An elderly actress entered in a costume which struck them as grotesque.

As a fact, the dress was a particularly fine one, but it wanted wearing; the huge hoop and great black hat perched upon a little frilled under-cap should have been carried by one filled with the pride of them and the consciousness of their beauty.

But at the unexpected laughter the actress took fright, she became timid, apologetic, she tried to efface herself. Now the spectacle of a stately dame whose balloon-like skirts half filled the stage and whose plumes smote the heavens trying to efface herself was genuinely ludicrous and the laugh became a roar. After this the audience got out of hand; they grew silly and cruel and ready to jeer at everything.

The last act, with its lovely White Parlour and the longed-for return of Marion Terry, almost pulled things together again, but by this time the hero's continual vacillations between his lady-loves had struck the demoralised house as comic, and when he changed his mind for the last time the irreverent let themselves go. The play ended in a storm of laughter and hisses, during which Alexander led on the unhappy Henry James and held him there in the middle of the stage confronting the jeering and booing house. Why he did this I cannot imagine. Possibly he thought that the appearance of a man of letters, an artist of great and acknowledged reputation, would silence the mockers, but alas, the bewildered and terrified face of poor Mr. James only gave them new delight. It seemed to me that the two stood there for hours—to Henry James it must have been a lifetime—and my discomfort was not allayed by the violent eruption at my side of John Sargent, who had one of his rare attacks of fury and seemed about to hurl his hat at Alexander and leap upon the stage to rescue his friend.

It was a miserable evening, but I think the most acute impression left upon me as I staggered homewards was amazement and admiration at Sargent's eloquent summing up. To think that I had denied to this Lord of Language the gift of self-expression in picturesque and impassioned speech! He expressed himself for upwards of half an hour without repeating a phrase or an epithet. It was colossal —I never heard anything like it.

★ ★ ★ ★ ★

The Henry James of those days was strangely unlike the remarkable-looking man of almost twenty years later, who was then himself painted by Sargent.

In the 'nineties he was in appearance almost remarkably unremarkable ; his face might have been anybody's face ; it was as though, when looking round for a face, he had been able to find nothing to his taste and had been obliged to put up with a ready-made ' stock ' article until something more suitable could be made to order expressly for him.

This special and only genuine Henry James's face was not ' delivered ' until he was a comparatively old man, so that for the greater part of his life he went about in disguise.

My mother, who was devoted to his works, used to be especially annoyed by this elusive personality.

" I always want so much to talk with him," she complained, " yet when I meet him I never can remember who he is."

Perhaps to make up for this indistinguishable presence he cultivated impressiveness of manner and great preciosity of speech.

He had a way of leaving a dinner-party early with an air of preoccupation that was very intriguing.

"He always does it," untruthfully exclaimed a deserted and slightly piqued hostess. "It is to convey the suggestion that he has an appointment with a Russian princess."

In later life both the impressive manner and fastidious speech became intensified: what he said was always interesting, but he took so long to say it that one felt a growing conviction that he was not for a moment, but for all time. With him it was a moral obligation to find the *mot juste*, and if it had got mislaid or was far to seek, the world had to stand still until it turned up.

Sometimes when it arrived it was delightfully unexpected. I remember in later years walking with him round my little Surrey garden and manœuvring him to a spot where a rather wonderful view suddenly revealed itself.

"My dear boy," exclaimed Henry James, grasping my arm. "How—er—how——" I waited breathless: the *mot juste* was on its way; at least I should hear the perfect and final summing up of my countryside's loveliness. "How—er—how——" still said Mr. James, until at long last the golden sentence sprang complete from his lips. "My dear boy, how awfully jolly!"

I also recall his telling of a tale about an American business man who had bought a large picture.

"And when he got it home," continued Mr. James, "he did not know what—er—what——"

"What to do with it," prompted some impatient and irreverent person.

Henry James silently rejected the suggestion. "He **did** not know what—er—what—well, in point of fact, the *hell* to do with it."

When, quite towards the end of his life, his new face

was evolved, it was a very wonderful one and well worth waiting for. Sargent's painting of it is fine, but lacks a certain something.

"It is the sort of portrait one would paint of Henry James if one had sat opposite to him twice in a bus," said a disappointed admirer, and the statement, though untrue, had some grains of truth in it.

Yet this should not have been so. Sargent and Henry James were real friends, they understood each other perfectly and their points of view were in many ways identical.

Renegade Americans both, each did his best to love his country and failed far more signally than does the average Englishman: they were *plus Anglais que les Anglais* with an added fastidiousness, a mental remoteness that was not English.

Both were fond of society, though neither seemed altogether at one with it: Henry James, an artist in words, liked to talk and in order to talk there must be someone to talk to, but Sargent talked little and with an effort; why he 'went everywhere' night after night often puzzled me.

I saw a good deal of Henry James at about this time, then we lost sight of each other for many years. When I next met him, almost unrecognisable in his new face, he seemed much aged and broken. His ever troublesome nerves had now made him more dependent upon companionship; some of the mystery and remoteness had disappeared.

His final nationalisation as an Englishman came as a surprise to many. His liaison with Britannia was then such an old story, both had completely lived down any scandal, and that he should wish at the eleventh hour to make an honest woman of her seemed almost unnecessary.

His portrait by Sargent, one of the few men who really knew him, should have supplied a clue to the true Henry James that no one else could have found: perhaps the artist intentionally withheld it.

## HENRY JAMES AND THE ENGLISH THEATRE

ON the night of the 17th of January 1911 a play in one act by Mr. Henry James called *The Saloon* was presented for the first time at the Little Theatre in John Street, Adelphi; and an appreciation of it which I had the pleasure of writing for the next day's *Pall Mall Gazette* was sent on to him (he was on his last visit to New York at the time) by one of his friends in London. Three weeks later I received a letter from him touching upon so many points in so frank and interesting a way that the impulse to reply was irresistible; and on his return to England a few months later the correspondence was resumed, and presently developed into the privilege of meeting. During the remaining years of his life he was good enough to make frequent opportunities of giving me his views on the English Theatre in general; and it is from my memory, and my written notes of these conversations, that most of what briefly follows will flow.

Like a good many other men and women of letters in this country who had been witnesses of some of the latter-day processes and tendencies of the English Theatre, Henry James may, I think, be said to have loved the Drama but very nearly hated the Theatre. It was difficult in those concluding years of his strenuous life to draw him from his 'lately plotted fireside' in Chelsea for an evening at the play, and when at last he would be persuaded to such a relaxation he was quite as likely to become almost as much of an anxiety to his companions as a joy. There he would sit, deep down in his stall, with his shoulders hunched up to his ears, and his eyes firmly bent upon the scene and its inhabitants, following the 'traffic of the stage,' if he disapproved of it, with ominous murmurings, threatening at any moment to become a storm; and there are several cases on record of his rising at last, half-way through the entertainment, and with a perfectly audible 'I can't bear it any longer' walking out. In his whimsical way he even attributed the very trying illness which laid him low at Rye in the autumn and winter of 1912 to an evening spent at a West End theatre! His face when watching a dramatic entertainment which was not in accordance with his very positive and exacting sense of 'how the thing should be done' was indeed a masterpiece of the inscrutable. I once heard a dramatist expatiating with satisfied wonder upon the 'remarkable expression of countenance' with which Henry James had sat through two acts of a play of which the narrator was the author, and I listened to the narrative with a self-repression that was nearly a pain, for I happened to know what he had suffered on that occasion, and the mental and spiritual torment which that 'remarkable expression of countenance' had so benignantly concealed.

Many things in the Theatre depressed this fastidious idealist, among them the large commercialism of the institution and the comparative absence of the spirit of art for art's sake. Needless to say, he was the very reverse of being, in any way, *blasé*. I have seen him deriving a great deal of pleasure from some quite untrumpeted but sincere and highly-motived dramatic entertainment; and I have seen him irritated nearly beyond bearing by a 'star' actor in a 'play of the day.' In the one case, possibly, his ideals were not too cocksurely challenged; in the other, perhaps, they were appealed to with what he felt to be a multiform brazen incompetence, against which he would rebel with an immediate 'remarkable expression of countenance,' and a subsequent immense flow of epistolary and conversational denunciation for the benefit and amusement of his friends.

It is not to be wondered at that the long dissociation between the English Theatre and the intellectual life of the country, which the Vedrenne-Barker management at the Court Theatre was the first real effort to heal, weighed heavily on him. He attributed it not only to the domination of what we may call the box-office spirit but also to the timidity of the dramatists themselves. In talking over instances of playwrights consenting to the violent misrepresentation of their intentions by actors, and even the free alteration of their carefully composed dialogue, he would rise to impressive heights of indignation. 'Until our dramatists respect their craft a good deal more than, as a rule, they do to-day,' he once said to me, 'there will be no hope for the English Theatre. It is, indeed, in very plain danger of becoming a colossal vulgarity.' It positively enraged him to hear of a dramatist signing a contract—as so many have disastrously done—giving a manager power to alter his manuscript without his consent. Who can wonder? As that admirable lady, Miss Horniman of Manchester, once said: 'There should be but one authority in the "production" and rehearsal of a play—the author.' Only last year a play was produced in London of which the first half proved in performance quite strikingly sincere and original, and the second half as conspicuously artificial and bad. The first half had been left as the author had written it; the second had been freely altered to suit the demands of a popular actor!

Another topic upon which Henry James would declaim with overwhelming tragi-comic energy was the extravagant interest taken by the play-going public of London in the histrionic *personalia* of the stage—what Mr. George Moore in one of the most amusing of his *Impressions and Opinions* called Mummer-worship. 'These hungry histrions!' he would exclaim, 'carrying on their most self-exhibitional of trades, in which the men become as vain and jealous and touchy as the women, and the women still more of all these things than Nature had already made them! These intense, importunate, irritable persons! Oh, it is preposterous that they should be commemorated as they are!' And then he would turn and rend the dramatic critics for giving so much space in their articles to these 'inefficient hungerers after adulation,' and would cite the better way of the French critics, Jules Lemaître and Emile Faguet, who when they reprinted their *Impressions* and *Propos de Théâtre* did so with the actors and their work left out, and the analysis concentrated upon the intentions and processes of the dramatist. 'There,' Mr. James would say, 'there lies your work! The play's the thing! Never mind the players. Find out what the dramatist has to say, and follow it up! And do it all with the ferocious seriousness and courage with which the grand old Sarcey did it for forty years, without fear or favour, and heedless of everything save Truth and the High Standard!' And then he would throw himself back in his chair and add, with that upliftment of his outstretched right hand which was one of his characteristic gestures, 'And yet, I suppose, writing for a newspaper in this country, you cannot leave them out. But oh! the task of the dramatic critic is horrific. I wouldn't be one for anything in the world. Indeed, no gentleman can be one for long, for in that office there is literally no satisfying other people and oneself at the same time!'

In the essay just referred to, Mr. George Moore used the oft-quoted words 'Acting is the lowest of the arts, if it is an art at all,' and Henry James always seemed to me to be of the same opinion, although of course he made many friends in the acting world of the theatre, to whom, on personal grounds, he was very sincerely attached. My suggestion to him of Coquelin as 'a great actor' in such parts as Tartuffe and Cyrano de Bergerac he waved aside with a 'Not at all! A fine *diseur*, nothing more!' And when I quoted to him Tennyson's superb compliment to Henry Irving's Hamlet—'I have seen it again after five years: it has improved five degrees, and those five degrees have lifted it to Heaven!'—he just assumed that 'remarkable expression of countenance' and exclaimed 'My dear boy, you are detestably young!' and went on, 'It is all wrong, this worship of the actor in England and America—the two countries, too, in which they exhibit least training, least talent, least temperament : the two countries in which they do nothing at all, or as little as possible, for the Drama ; in which they have no *action* to speak of, or only a discouraging one, and no vision of anything save the vulgarer aspects of the theatre ! '

From these recollections it will be seen that his counsels to a dramatic critic were somewhat austere, and the path he pointed not an easy one to follow without plenty of company, though it was undoubtedly the right one to take in the best interests both of criticism and of the stage.

Another point, too, which comes back to me, as I recall these interchanges with the great man now dead, was his view of the uncritical attitude of the average theatrical audience of his later years, and particularly of the depressing proneness to untimely laughter which has grown so fast in London theatres during the past ten years. I remember talking with him one afternoon at the Reform Club, when he had been overnight to see Miss Githa Sowerby's fine play, *Rutherford and Son*, at the Vaudeville. The laughter, or rather the audible giggling, of a section of the audience during the serious scenes had struck him most painfully. He ended his account of it with these words, which I shall never forget : ' I scarcely ever take a foreign friend to see a serious play in London without being made to feel ashamed by this extraordinary behaviour.' A good many playgoers have gone through that humiliation. And the huge tragedy of the War seems to have left the gigglers more giggly than ever.

Of course Mr. James realised—no one more clearly—the advantages of success as a dramatist, and no small part of his tireless work was done for the Theatre. He strove hard to adapt his subtle and exquisite art as a writer to the imperatively demanded bold and broad effects of the dramatist; and as long as seventeen years after the failure of his comedy, *Guy Domville*, at the St. James's Theatre, he acknowledged to me that there was a certain justice in the adverse verdict originally pronounced upon that work. ' Instead of making the dramatic interest my sole or even my chief consideration,' he said, ' I aimed at a supreme technical victory in observing a unity for unity's sake. Consequently it was too compressed ; and I now have dreams of re-writing it in four acts instead of the original three.' Another of his plays, *The High Bid*, presented at a series of matinées at His Majesty's Theatre in February 1909 by a society which called itself ' The Afternoon Theatre,' was in every way more satisfactory. Its chief characters, an American girl, with a passion for medieval things, and an English aristocrat indifferent to them and living mainly to promote Socialism, provided a clash of ideals, and played a duel of wits through the three acts, which was truly exhilarating ; and the general setting of the story in the most exquisite elements of conversation was a continual delight. Even this enjoyable piece, however, in which Sir J. Forbes-Robertson and his wife found quite memorable characters in which to display their art and charm, has since been seen but little, and that only in a provincial city or two; and here, as in so many cases and ways, the commercialisation of our Theatre seems to come in. Broadly composed as was *The High Bid*, its appeal was still chiefly to the fastidious—to those who could enjoy not only, for its own sake, a duel of ideals, but also those soft rhythms of prose and delicate economies of expression in which Mr. James's plays, no less than his novels, are so richly charged. As a result it has, up to the present, been virtually shelved. Perhaps one day London will be allowed to see it again. Perhaps when their bravely borne sacrifices in the War have purged the nation, the nation will proceed to the purging of the Theatre. Perhaps—perhaps—perhaps. Yet, even as I write, I remember that there is at this moment in existence a dramatisation of *The Egoist* in which George Meredith himself collaborated and put splendid things—as, for instance, when Harry de Craye, summarising in a single sentence his attitude of wanting more than the 'friendship' Clara offers him, is made to say to her 'Am I to banquet on that wafer?'—which has never yet been acted, for the reason that, in the opinion of those who were commercially concerned, it would not have 'paid.'

It is interesting to recall that the other contemporary English writer with whom Henry James was most often coupled as a craftsman, George Meredith, shared his general opinion of the Theatre. Again and again in his letters we find him taking with him to the playhouse ideals which were almost incapable of satisfaction. So it will be to the end of the chapter. Books are only read by one person at a time, and an author can, with an easy mind, write up or down to a particular type of reader. A play, on the other hand, is read by two thousand together at a sitting, and therefore dare not appeal to only one sort of artistic ideal. But to admit this is not to declare that literary and interpretative perfection are outside the scope even of the contemporary Theatre. Indeed, both have been seen more than once in a London playhouse within the last dozen years, and the public who wanted them duly found them. It is the ignorance of the existence of such a public, or the deafness to its entreaties, on the part of much of the official headship of the English stage that has wearied so many cultured Englishmen and Englishwomen out of the habit of playgoing, and has left them crying 'I love the Drama but hate the Theatre.'

H. M. WALBROOK.

# Hamlin Garland, *Roadside Meetings* (London: John Lane, 1931)

Here we see that American resentment of the expatriate Henry James, expressed so clearly by Nadal (in section 2), was still felt even towards the end of the novelist's life, long after his initial defection. Hamlin Garland (1860–1940) was an American writer of essays, short stories and novels. His volumes of autobiography and family history, including *A Son of the Middle Border* (1917) were particularly successful, and he was awarded the Pulitzer Prize for biography in 1921. *Roadside Meetings* (1931) is one of several volumes of reminiscences written by Garland in later life. In 1904, during James's tour of the United States, Garland attended a dinner in honour of Henry James held at New York's Metropolitan Club. He subsequently invited James to dine in his studio when James visited Chicago in 1905. According to Edel, James found Garland dull (Edel, v, p. 319). He certainly emerges as a self-important figure in Elizabeth Jordan's account of the two men's first meeting:

> While he was here I gave a reception for him, to which I invited his available old friends, as well as our best group of up-and-coming young writers. The names of the latter meant nothing to him, and his hearty handclasps did not comfort them for the revelation conveyed by his vague smile. Some of the writers, both old and young, resented this. In presenting them to the Master I pronounced each name with almost piercing distinctness, but usually in vain. Hamlin Garland was so affected by the unbroken calm with which his name was received that he broke out earnestly, 'I'm *Hamlin* Garland, Mr. James!'
> 
> 'A-h–h,' said Mr. James, and shook hands all over again, smiling cherubically. (Elizabeth Jordan, *Three Rousing Cheers* (New York: D. Appleton-Century Company, Inc., 1938), pp. 217–18)

The extract printed below was written after Garland had visited James in Rye in 1906. He was clearly charmed by the Sussex countryside and particularly by Lamb House. Perhaps because James never married, never had children, and seemed to repress any sexual feelings he may have experienced (except to some degree in his relationships with young men towards the end of his life) James's biography seems to structure itself less around interpersonal relationships than do most life stories. One milestone in his life was his disastrous relationship with the theatre. Another was his far happier relationship with Lamb House, his principal home after 1897. As described by Theodora Bosanquet, James's secretary, his purchase of Rye reads like an account of an old fashioned courtship.

> It must have been ten years since he had settled into Lamb House, the place he had lost his heart to one summer when he was staying near Rye and used to walk over 'to make sheep's eyes at it', charmed by the beauty of its tone and proportions. He had talked freely of his feelings and one of the people he had talked to, the local ironmonger, wrote to him when the owner died. He thought the house might be let as the heir had no wish to live there. Henry James lost no time about taking a lease which was converted later into purchase. (Theodora Bosanquet, 'As I Remember – Henry James', *Time and Tide* (3 July 1954), 875)

The story of James's very first encounter with Lamb House reinforces these strange parallels with a courtship narrative, for he saw it first as a painting in the house of his friend Edward Warren, the architect (Edel, iv, p. 185). Like a fairy-tale prince confronted with a portrait of a beautiful princess, he seems to have fallen in love at first sight.

A great many of James's friends and acquaintances have left accounts of visits to Lamb House, of James's travails with his servants, of his anxious frugality, of his daily routine in which guests and dictation sessions each had their allotted place, of his affable relations with the people of Rye. His great friend the American novelist Edith Wharton writes particularly warmly of his hospitality:

> From the moment when I turned the corner of the grass-grown street mounting steeply between squat brick houses, and caught sight, at its upper end, of the wide Palladian window and the garden-room, a sense of joyous liberation bore me on. There *he* stood on the doorstep, the white-panelled hall with its old prints and crowded book-cases forming a background to his heavy loosely-clothed figure. Arms outstretched, lips and eyes twinkling, he came down to the car, uttering cries of mock amazement and mock humility at the undeserved honour of my visit. (Wharton, p. 245)

Garland was similarly disarmed by the warmth of James's welcome and the charm of his surroundings, even though he conveys a (possibly exaggerated) sense of James as a lonely man who wishes to return home to America. The piece is very clearly written with an eye to his American readers – the 'quaint' charm of English life appeals to Garland but we constantly sense his partisan attachment to the States. Another patriotic American journalist simultaneously attracted to and repelled by the English way of life, Henrietta Stackpole, might have composed a rather similar portrait of James.

## CHAPTER THIRTY-SIX

### HENRY JAMES AT RYE

ALL through the early years of my stay in Boston, the critics and James reviewers invariably alluded to "Howells and James" as if they were a literary firm or literary twins. Usually they were thus named in a tone of resentment, as if representing a school of fiction unjustly in the ascendant. For no reason at all I had begun by sharing this resentment, but after I had read "The Minister's Charge" and "The Bostonians," I developed sincere admiration for them both.

It amused me then to wonder why they were thus bracketed, for they were not in the least alike, except in the broad sense of being students of manners rather than writers of romance. James was even then rather difficult to read, whereas Howells' pages were as limpid and flexible in flow as a brook. James concerned himself with stories of extraordinarily intellectual characters, people of the upper class, men and women whose deeds hinged on some psychologic subtlety, whereas Howells dealt with those of ordinary life—editors, business men, ministers, lawyers—reporting and analyzing their doings with such humor and insight that they are to-day exponents of New England social history. Nevertheless, people persisted in naming him and James in one breath as engaged in a combined assault on something which should be revered, not destroyed.

Howells often talked of James to me, quoting some of his

opinions with approval, and speaking of his books with delight. "We are friends of long standing," he said, "and when next he comes to New York, I shall contrive to have you meet him."

The opportunity did not offer during my life in Boston, and James remained a remote and rather awesome personality till in 1895, when he reviewed my "Rose of Dutcher's Coulée" in *Harper's Weekly*, speaking of it with surprising warmth of interest. Very naturally I wrote to thank him, and thus began a correspondence which continued at long intervals for three years.

His missives were hard to decipher, for he had the habit of writing completely to the bottom of the fourth page of his sheet and then criss-crossing it with diagonal lines, ending in some cases on the first page, thus bringing the signature and the salutation side by side. At other times he still further complicated his page by writing backward along the margins. Notwithstanding these complications, I enjoyed the matter of his notes so thoroughly that their illegibility was ignored, or rated only as an added interest. He never wrote aimlessly.

In one of these cryptograms, or palimpsests, he expressed a desire to have me visit him if I should ever come to England, and when I replied that I never expected to have money enough to cross the ocean, and asked in return, "Are you never coming to America?" he responded rather sadly, "I have no intention of doing so."

Now here I was leaving London with a letter of invitation in my pocket and Rye less than two hours away! "Come down on Saturday and spend Sunday with me," he had written, giving me the most minute directions as to trains.

As I looked back on the South Side of London that June

afternoon, it all seemed ugly, commonplace, and depressing. The railway ran to the southeast, bringing miles and miles of characterless streets into view, with acres of grimy roofs bristling with rectangular chimneys. It was about as inspiring as the West Side of Chicago, a wilderness of drab human dens and angular plots of verdureless ground.

The tragic significance of this congestion appeared as we came into the green countryside, overhung by a gray sky and swept by a clean wind from the east. Here was the real England, the England of our novels. While white uniformed cricketers were at play, girls lithely contended at tennis. Scullers were moving briskly along sluggish rivers thick with boats and crowded with gay young life. It appeared that all Surrey was out for a holiday, in a fresh, finished, unsoiled land, and yet the train was only a few miles out of the ugly, huge, and smoky town.

Glorious curving roads ran past embowered cottages. Wooded hills succeeded with comfortable farmsteads set among green pastures, while gray towers rising out of deep groves of elms and oaks suggested feudal manors. Tall roofs, lichen-spotted and black with immemorial soot, gave picturesque chimneys to the sky like clustered boles of close-growing trees. For an hour or more my ride through the country was a delight.

At Ashford I deflected to the south, and almost at once the land dipped into a succession of smooth, suave, coast-sloping meadows. Long-armed windmills peered over the hills. Sheep fed everywhere—sheep lately sheared and looking shivery and thin by reason of it. Thatched roofs, the kind I had seen in illustrations of old-time English novels, covered ancient homesteads very beautiful to look at, but very unsanitary to live in, I am told. The railway hedges were nicely trimmed. Faggots in bundles lay beside the cottages. Climbing roses covered the porches.

Soon all the meadows visibly descended to the sea beach, each slope covered with sheep. I could see the tidewater running in snakelike canals amid the flocks. Bent, sunburned shepherds were tending the lambs, each man in the immemorial English yeoman's smock.

Then came Rye, a town set on a height overlooking the ocean. The railway wound around the foot of this hill and stopped at a little depot on the west side. As I stepped from the car a portly, brisk, and smiling man met me—Henry James himself!

After a hearty handclasp he said, "It is only a short walk to my house and, if you don't mind, we'll make our way there on foot. My man will carry your bag."

As he led the way up a steep, narrow, cobble-paved street toward a compact, bristling cluster of old roofs and chimneys, I had a feeling that I was living a story. He was not in the least as I had expected him to be. He was cordial, hearty, almost commonplace.

The way became narrower until it was hardly more than an alley, walled by the most satisfyingly ancient brick dwellings and then, suddenly, the walk made a turn and left me facing an open white doorway and huge brass knocker. "Here it is," said James, "this is my house. It is a very small one, as you see, but of rather fine Georgian type. It is old. It dates from 1716."

It was indeed small, but in perfect taste. The hall was paneled in oak, but the rooms above were furnished in white. Many rare engravings hung on the walls, portraits of England's worthies, classical subjects, Italian scenes, and the like. The furniture was in keeping, and the entire effect charming and restful.

When I came downstairs James met me and led the way to his garden, which was spacious and surrounded by a high wall. A few trees shaded one corner, and roofs with odd angles overpeered on two sides. A steeple rose not far away and a little, cracked bell sounded. It was all so English, so remote that I can not do justice to it. It was the place for a recluse—a dreamer such as I understood James had become.

Taking seats, we began to talk on subjects which mutually concerned us and for a time James was hesitant, distressingly so. He groped for just the right word, but as we proceeded he grew less constrained. He told me how, almost by accident, he had found this house and that from the first moment he saw it he wanted it. "It had been lived in by one continuous family since its erection till a few years ago, when it fell into the hands of an old gentleman, a resident of this town. Upon his death the widow offered it for sale and I bought it and moved my few possessions down from London. I bought it as a refuge from the city, and I now spend the larger part of my time here. It is my home."

He went on to say that he found London more and more of a distraction, a whirlpool. "As I grow older, I go to it reluctantly in January usually, but only for a short time. Most of the year I live in Rye. Since the death of my sister I live here alone, and work, work incessantly."

In answer to my questions he told me much that was of interest concerning the history of Rye and Wynchelsea, which stands on the next hill to the south. "Both were ports at one time," he explained, "and rivals of London, but now they are left high and dry by the recession of the sea, a strange phenomenon. Rye, as you will see, is only a sleepy, curious, decaying little town, neither farm village nor sea town, and yet it possesses some of the characteristics of both."

He was curious about conditions of authorship in America —wanted to know more of the men whose books sold so enormously. He was amazed at my statement of the money certain writers made by their writings. He had no understanding of the midland America. Chicago was almost as alien to him as a landscape on Mars. He resented the self-satisfaction of the novelists who sold their hundreds of thousands of copies of superficial fiction. "I have never even heard of them," he said when I named two of the most successful.

It was natural that he should resent such upstarts; for he, to my mind, represented something fought for, something attained with care. He stood for culture, workmanship, style. In a quiet way he was intellectually contemptuous of commercial America. In all that he said he remained very human, very judicial, and very kindly. His large, pellucid, rather prominent eyes studied me tranquilly.

When I asked him what he was doing at the time, he replied, "I am putting a selective edition of my books into form for an American publisher."

He spoke of the placid quiet of his little town, of his kindly neighbors. "They are a great comfort to me, for I am a lonely man," he said. He spoke rejoicingly of the fact that there were only three wheeled vehicles in the village. "You noticed, perhaps, that the streets are grass-grown between the cobbles? Only now and then do I hear a footfall pass my door."

He alluded gratefully to my letters of appreciation of his stories. "I have for many years discharged my books into

America as into a hollow void," he admitted with somber inflection; "no word but yours has lately come back to me."

No doubt this was an exaggeration, and yet he meant that I should remember it as a confession.

He spoke of Howells with sincere love and appreciation. "He is an artist—always—but he has written too much, and so have I."

I then quoted Howells' remark, apropos of this criticism: "But what else am I to do?"

James instantly agreed. "Yes, we writers are lost without our pens in our hands."

He praised Owen Wister's work and commended Mrs. Wharton's "Valley of Decision," and this led up to his own fervid enthusiasm for Italy. He advised my hastening there at once. "Why study France?" he demanded; "France is only an imitation of Italy. Why waste time on the imitation when you can see the real thing?"

Precisely what he meant by this I could not determine, but I took it to mean that the historical remains of France were Roman. He could not have meant that France was in any modern sense an imitation of Italy.

A little farther on he spoke of his novel. "The Ambassadors," as the best of all he had written. "I am rewriting, not merely revising, my earlier books," he explained, and to this I could not respond with any enthusiasm. To me such work was a kind of wholesale deception—as well as a doubtful improvement. To relanguage a "Portrait of a Lady" would be but to blur its clear, original outlines. However, I did not say so at the moment, for it would have been obvious disapproval, and if my silence gave him that impression he did not remark upon it.

He referred to Thomas Hardy as a man who had lost his

power. Of his brother William James he spoke with affection. Several other American writers came in for his comment, which was never bitter nor ironic. He had a certain straightforward glance which made his words sound less harsh than they would look if printed. As he described his New York ancestry, I perceived that he was less remote than he had seemed to me hitherto. "I still read the New York journals and keep informed of New World politics in the mass!" he said.

He became very much in earnest at last and said something which surprised and gratified me. It was an admission I had not expected him to make. "If I were to live my life over again," he said in a low voice, and fixing upon me a somber glance, "I would be an American. I would steep myself in America, I would know no other land. I would study its beautiful side. The mixture of Europe and America which you see in me has proved disastrous. It has made of me a man who is neither American nor European. I have lost touch with my own people, and I live here alone. My neighbors are friendly, but they are not of my blood, except remotely. As a man grows old he feels these conditions more than when he is young. I shall never return to the United States, but I wish I could."

This may have been but a mood induced by his talk with me, but it filled me with a profound pity for this man, who, in spite of his great fame, was old and lonely. It brought back to my mind the feeling I used to have as I read his novels filled with expatriates, a feeling of emptiness and futility, an ache of resentment which I could never quite put into words. I knew the characters he depicted were mongrels, but I was never quite sure of his own attitude with respect to those who transferred their loyalty to France or England.

Whatever his mind had been, he now made it plain that he still loved the land of his youth and wished himself back in it and at home in it.

After our tea, which was served on a little table out under the trees, he took me to see the town, pointing out the most ancient of the buildings, well knowing that as a man from the plains of Iowa I would be interested in age-worn walls and door sills. He took me to the Old Mermaid Tavern, in which was a marvelous fireplace, as wide as the end of the room itself, with benches at the corners. Everybody we met seemed to know and like him; whether they recognized in him a famous author or not I cannot tell, but they certainly regarded him as a good neighbor. He greeted every one we met most genially. He was on terms with the postman and the butcher's boy. There was nothing austere or remote in his bearing. On the contrary, he had the air of a curate making the rounds of his village.

How beautiful, how far, how peaceful seems that small, crowded, lichen-covered town, as I recall it to-day! Its streets were like grass-grown alleys, and the graveyard which surrounded the old church was as lovely as a garden, with its graveled walks and its shrubs and vines. Ancient gates opened upon green meadows down below, meadows on which the sheep fed. Exquisite colors and quaint forms abounded in every direction, and yet it was not mine and did not satisfy Henry James—at least he had moments when he longed for the land of his birth. I understood his enthusiasms of the moment, but I understood also the hunger which he had voiced as we sat in his garden.

At seven o'clock we dined in his exquisite little dining room, and the dinner, which came on quite formally, was delicious. He had no other guest, but he presided at the service end of the table with quiet formality. The mahogany glistened with the care which had been lavished upon it, the silver was interesting and beautiful, and the walls of the room tasteful and cheerful—and yet I could not keep out of my mind a picture of him sitting here alone, as he confessed he did on many, many nights. To grow old even with your children all about you is a sorrowful business, but to grow old in a land filled with strangers is sadder still.

It was late when I went to bed that night, my mind filled with literary and artistic problems called up by his profound comment. The questions of National art, of Realism and Idealism, of New World garishness and crudeness, of its growing power and complexity—these were among the matters we had discussed. That James lived on the highest plane of life and thought was evident. He had no distractions, no indulgences. He permitted himself no loafing, no relaxation. He had not even the comfort of a comic spirit such as Clemens had. He was in earnest all the time—a genial earnestness, but an earnestness which could not be diverted.

I put down this statement in my record: "This man lives on the highest plane. No man of his time is nobler in his aspirations as an artist. He has put the best of his life, and in a sense he has put all of his life, into his art. Although elusive in its expression, his work is original. No other writer or school of writers has had a share in it."

We breakfasted in such comfort, so simple but so perfect as to form the most delightful luxury. The sun shone in at our window, the silver gleamed cheerily, the coffee was delicious, and James, immaculately clad and fresh and rosy again, presided at the opposite side of the table while his miraculous servants attended us.

At the close of our meal I said, "It is your habit to work in the morning—that I know, and I want you to keep to your routine. Don't permit me to interrupt your morning task."

"Very well," he said. "I will take you at your word, but first I want you to see my workshop."

His "shop" was a small detached building standing in the corner of the garden, and in the large room littered with books and manuscripts I found a smart young woman stenographer at work. James showed me the changes he was making in his earlier books—work which I did not approve, for he was rewriting these stories. In my judgment he was not bettering them; on the contrary it seemed to me he was transforming them into something which was neither of the past nor of the present. I think he was now aware of my disapproval, for he went on to explain that he found in the early versions many crudities which he could not think of allowing the future to observe—"if people ever take the trouble to look into my books," he added, with a note of melancholy in his voice.

After giving me elaborate directions concerning other landmarks of the region, he suddenly said, "But why should I not be your guide again? You do not come often. My work can wait."

My protesting availed nothing. Putting his secretary at another task he told me to come with him. "There are some other houses which I must show you. They are owned by some friends of mine and they will be glad to let you have a glimpse of them."

As he led me about the town, discovering for me delightful Georgian types of dwellings, the people everywhere greeted him with smiling cordiality. They liked and honored him, that was evident, and it gave me a keen sense of satisfaction to find him more and more neighborly, taking an interest in what his fellow citizens were doing and thinking. This phase of him was as surprising as it was amusing. To hear him asking after a child's health, or inquiring when Mr. Brown would return from London, was a revelation of the fact that, after all, he was more than half New England.

He sped me on my way to France with a hearty invitation to come and see him on my return, and I particularly urged him to come again to America, in order that we might show him the honor which so many of us were eager to pay, and also in order that we might profit by his criticism. To this he replied very thoughtfully, "I may do so, but I fear I shall not get so far as Chicago."

With this he gave me his hand, and I went away down the cobbled street on my way to Carcassonne and Pisa.

# Ford Madox Ford, *Mightier than the Sword* (London: Allen & Unwin, 1938)

Ford Madox Ford (1873–1939) wrote extensively about Henry James; as well as reminiscences of their friendship he published *Henry James: A Critical Study* in 1913. However he is not thought to be uniformly reliable – Edel describes him as a 'literary Munchausen' (Edel, v, p. 39) – and many of his assertions, such as his claim to have provided the model for Merton Densher in *The Wings of the Dove* (1902), cannot be taken at face value. Although he implies that he and James were close friends James's secretary, Mary Weld, tells a different story:

> His favourite walk was the road to Winchelsea, but unfortunately his literary flatterer Ford Madox Hueffer who lived at Winchelsea used to waylay him, and this annoyed Mr James. Once we actually jumped a dike to avoid meeting Hueffer who was looking out for us. (Hyde, p. 154)

Ford was born Ford Hermann Hueffer but changed his name twice, first to Ford Madox Hueffer, incorporating 'Madox' as a tribute to his grandfather, the painter Ford Madox Brown, and then to Ford Madox Ford. After eloping with Elsie Martindale, a doctor's daughter whose family disapproved of him, Ford settled in Winchelsea where he met Stephen Crane, H. G. Wells and Henry James himself, all of whom lived nearby. He began to build a reputation as a novelist and founded the influential *English Review*. Here he published works by up and coming new writers, including Joseph Conrad, an important influence on his own writings, and Ezra Pound. Although excellent at backing literary winners Ford had no business sense and lost his position as editor after just fourteen monthly issues due to his financial mismanagement. He was also conspicuous as a womaniser, and his mistresses included his wife's own sister, Mary Martindale, and the novelist Violet Hunt (see section 5), also a friend of Henry James. Ford Madox Ford is now best know for *The Good Soldier* (1915) and the tetralogy *Parade's End* (1924–8).

Ford and James first met in 1896. The younger writer wrote to James at the suggestion of the novelist Lucy Clifford, a mutual friend, and was invited to lunch. In *Return to Yesterday* (1931) a volume of reminiscences, Ford paints a rather alarming picture of this first meeting:

> The whole meal was one long questionnaire. He demanded particulars as to my age, means of support, establishment, occupations, tastes in books, food, music, painting, scenery, politics. He sat sideways to me across the corner of the dining table, letting drop question after question. The answers he received with no show at all of either satisfaction or reproof. (Ford Madox Ford, *Return to Yesterday* (London: Victor Gollancz, 1931), p. 14)

In *Thus to Revisit* (1921) Ford betrays some uneasiness about the status of his friendship with James:

> I think I will, after reflection, lay claim to a very considerable degree of intimacy with Henry James. It was a winter, and wholly non-literary intimacy. That is to say, during the summers we saw little of each other. He had his friends and I mine. He was too often expecting 'my friend Lady Maude,' or some orthodox critic to tea and I, modern poets whom he could not abide. (Ford Madox Ford, *Thus to Revisit* (London: Chapman & Hall, 1921), p. 113)

Towards the end of this piece his ambivalence towards James is conveyed still less equivocally.

> It occurs to me that I have given a picture of Henry James in which small personal unkindlinesses may appear to sound too dominant a note. That is the misfortune of wishing to point a particular moral. I will not say that loveableness was the predominating feature of the Old Man: he was too intent on his own particular aims to be lavishly sentimental over surrounding humanity. (*Thus to Revisit*, pp. 120–1)

In *Mightier than the Sword*, as elsewhere, Ford makes several assertions about James which are almost certainly inaccurate. (In 'Henry James: A Reminiscence', reproduced below, Walpole describes Ford's own accounts of James as 'fairy-tales'.) For example, the claim that James never forgave Flaubert because he once received him in a dressing gown is at odds with James's many affectionate allusions to Flaubert. (S. P. Waterlow for example records that James said he 'always had a warm corner in his heart' for Flaubert (Hyde, p. 126).) Ford's final, self-regarding reference to his walks with James is amusingly contradicted by Mary Weld's version of their relationship – though Weld herself may have been exaggerating for comic effect. James, Ford likes to tell us, apparently referred to him as 'le jeune homme modeste'. One suspects he was being ironic.

# MIGHTIER THAN THE SWORD

## I

## HENRY JAMES

### THE MASTER

I WILL begin this work with a little romance in the style of the Master—for *what* an intrigue he would have made of it if he had heard it at one of the hospitable boards where he so continually picked up what "I have always recognized on the spot as 'germs'"—the central ideas from which sprang his innumerable stories. . . . And it is the innumerability of his stories rather than the involutions of his style and plots that most have struck me in re-reading the works of him who must, whether we like to acknowledge it or not, be called the great master of all us novelists of to-day.

I hasten to avert thunders from my head by saying that I know that there are thousands of novelists of to-day and here who will swear that they never read a word of Henry James—just as the first words that Mr. H. M. Tomlinson ever said to me were, "Never heard of the fellow!"—the "fellow" being Conrad. But one's master is far more an aura in the air than an admonitory gentleman with uplifted forefinger, and one learns as much by reacting against a prevailing tendency as by following in a father's footsteps. . . .

Well, then . . . I was sitting one day in my study in Winchelsea when, from beside the window, on the little verandah, I heard a male voice, softened by the intervening wall, going on and on interminably . . . with the effect of a long murmuring of bees. I had been lost in the search for one just word or other so that the gentle sound had only dreamily penetrated to my attention. When it did so penetrate and after the monologue had gone on much, much longer, a certain irritation took hold of me. Was I not the owner of the establishment? Was I not supposed by long pondering over just words and their subsequent transference to paper to add at least to the credit, if not to the resources of that establishment? Was it not, therefore, understood that chance visitors must *not* be entertained at the front door which was just beside my window? . . . The sound, however, was not harsh or disagreeable and I stood it for perhaps another ten minutes. But at last impatience overcame me and I sprang to my door.

Silhouetted against the light at the end of the little passage were the figures of one of the housemaids and of Mr. Henry James. And Mr. James was uttering the earth-shaking question:

"Would you then advise me . . . for I know that such an ornament decorates your master's establishment and you will therefore from your particular level be able to illuminate me as to the . . . ah . . . smooth functioning of such, if I may use the expression, a wheel in the domestic timepiece—always supposing that you will permit me the image, meaning that, as I am sure in this household is the case, the daily revolution of a really harmonious *chez soi* is as smooth as the passing of shadows over a dial . . . would you then advise me to have . . . in short to introduce into *my* household and employ . . . a . . . that is to say . . . a Lady Help?"

I advanced at that and, as the housemaid with a sigh of relief disappeared amongst the rustlings of her skirts, in the strongest and firmest possible terms assured Mr. James that such an adornment of the household of an illustrious and well-appointed bachelor was one that should very certainly not be employed. He sighed. He appeared worn, thin for him, dry-skinned, unspirited. His liquid and marvellous dark eyes were dulled, the skin over his aquiline nose was drawn tight. He was suffering from a domestic upheaval—his household, that for a generation had, indeed, revolved around him as quietly as the shadows on a dial, with housekeeper, butler, upper housemaid, lower housemaid, tweeny maid, knife-boy, gardener, had suddenly erupted all round him so that for some time he had been forced to content himself with the services of the knife-boy.

That meant that he had to eat in the ancient hostelry, called The Mermaid, that stood beside his door. And, his housekeeper having for thirty years and more sent up, by the imposing if bottle-nosed butler who was her husband, all Mr. James's meals without his ever having ordered a single one—being used to such a halcyon cuisine the Master had not the slightest idea of what foods agreed with him and which did not. So that everything disagreed with him and he had all the appearance of being really ill. . . . The cause of the bottle-nose had been also the occasion of the eruption, all the female servants having one day left in a body on account of the "carryings-on" of the butler, and the butler himself, together, alas, with his admirable wife, the housekeeper, having, twenty-four hours later, to be summarily and violently ejected by a sympathetic police sergeant.

So the poor Master was not only infinitely worried about finding an appropriate asylum for the butler and his wife, but had had to spend long mornings and afternoons on what he called "the benches of desolation in purgatorial, if I may allow myself the word, establishments, ill-named, since no one appeared there to register themselves . . . eminently ill-named: *registry-offices* . . ." And there would be a sound like the hiss of a snake as he uttered the compound word. . . .

He would pass his time, he said, interviewing ladies all of a certain age, all of haughty—the French would say *renfrognée*—expressions, all of whom would unanimously assure him that, if they demeaned themselves merely by for an instant considering the idea of entering the household of an untitled person like himself, in such a God-forsaken end of the world as the Ancient Town of Rye, they having passed their lives in the families of never anyone less than a belted earl in mansions on Constitution Hill in the shadow of Buckingham Palace . . . if they for a fleeting moment toyed with the idea, it was merely, they begged to assure him . . . "forthegoodoftheirhealths." Mr. James having dallied with this sentence would utter the last words with extreme rapidity, raising his eyebrows and his cane in the air and digging the ferrule suddenly into the surface of the road. . . .

How they come back to me after a quarter of a century . . . the savoured, half-humorous, half-deprecatory words, the ironically exaggerated gestures, the workings of the closely shaved lips, the halting to emphasize a point, the sudden scurryings forward, for all the world like the White Rabbit hurrying to the Queen's tea-party . . . along the Rye Road, through the marshes, from Winchelsea . . . I walking beside him and hardly ever speaking, in the guise of God's strong, silent Englishman—which he took me really to be. . . .

To give the romance, then, its happy ending. . . . One of the matrons of Rye had conceived the idea of lodging a dependent orphan niece in poor Mr. James's house and so had recommended him to employ a Lady Help, offering to supply herself that domestic functionary. He had consulted as to the advisability of this step all the doctors', lawyers', and parsons' wives of the neighbourhood, and in addition one of the local great ladies—I think it was Lady Maude Warrender. The commoners' ladies, loyal to the one who wanted to dispose of the dependent niece, had all said the idea was admirable. Her Ladyship was non-committal, going no further than to assure him that the great ladies of the neighbourhood would not refuse to come to tea with him in his garden—that being their, as well as his, favourite way of passing an afternoon—merely because he should shelter an unattached orphan beneath his roof. But she would go no further than that.

So, in his passion for getting, from every possible angle, light on every possible situation—including his own—he had walked over to Winchelsea to consult not only me, but any female member of my household upon whom he should chance, and had kept the appalled and agitated housemaid for a full half hour on the doorstep whilst he consulted her as to the advisability of the step he was contemplating. . . . But I soon put a stop to *that* idea. In practical matters Mr. James did me the honour to pay exact attention to my opinions—I was for him the strong, silent man of affairs.

How long his agony lasted after that I cannot say. His perturbations were so agonizing to witness that it seemed to be a matter of years. And then, one day, he turned up with a faint adumbration of jauntiness. At last he had heard of a lady who gave some promise of being satisfactory. . . . The only shadow appeared to be the nature of her present employment.

"Guess," he said, "under whose august roof she is at the moment sheltering? . . . *Je vous le donne en mille.* . . ." He started back dramatically, rolling his fine eyes, and with great speed he exclaimed:

"The Poet Laureate . . . no less a person!"

Now the Poet Laureate occupies in England a position that it is very difficult to explain. By his official situation he is something preposterous and eminent . . . and at the same time he is something obsolescent, harmless, and ridiculous. Southey, Tennyson, and Doctor Bridges have commanded personally a certain respect, but I cannot think of anyone else who was anything else than ridiculous . . . rendered ridiculous by his office. And at the time of which I am speaking the whole literary world felt outragedly that either Swinburne or Mr. Kipling ought to have been the laureate. As it was, the holder of the title was a Mr. Alfred Austin, an obscure, amiable, and harmless poetaster who wrote about manor-houses and gardens and lived in a very beautiful manor-house in a very beautiful garden.

And, two days later Mr. James turned up, radiant. He lifted both hands above his head and exclaimed:

"As the German Emperor is said to say about his moustache, '*it is accomplished.*' . . . Rejoice—as I am confident you will—with me, my young friend. All from now onwards shall, I am assured, be with me gas and gingerbread. . . . Halcyon, halcyon days. In short, ahem. . . ." And he tapped himself lightly on the breast and assumed the air of a traveller returned from the wintry seas. "I went," he continued, "to the house of the Poet Laureate . . . to the back door of course . . . and interviewed a Lady who, except for one trifling—let us not say defect but let us express it 'let or hindrance' to what I will permit myself to call the perfect union, the continuing *lune de miel* . . . except for that, then, she appeared the perfect, the incredible, the except for the pure-in-heart, unattainable She . . . But upon delicate inquiry . . . oh, I assure you, inquiry of the *most* delicate . . . for the obstacle was no less than that on reckoning up the tale of her previous 'situation' . . . as twenty years with the Earl of Breadalbane, thirty years with Sir Ponsonby Peregrine Perowne, forty with the Right Honourable the Lord Bishop of Tintagel and Camelot . . . on reckoning up the incredible tale of years it appeared that she must be of the combined ages of Methusaleh and the insupportable Mariner—not of your friend Conrad, but of the author of *Kubla Khan*. But upon investigation it appeared that this paragon and phoenix actually was and in consequence will, to the end of recorded time, remain, exactly the same age as" . . . and he took three precise, jaunty steps to rear, laid his hand over his heart and made a quick bow . . . "*myself*. . . ."

"And," he resumed, "an upper housemaid and her sister, the under housemaid, who had left me in circumstances that I was unable to fathom but that to-day are only too woefully apparent to me, having offered to return and to provide a what they call tweeny of their own choosing . . . all shall for the future be as I have already adumbrated, not only gas and gingerbread, but cloves and clothes pegs and beatitude and bliss and beauty. . . ." And so it proved.

I have taken some time over that Romance because the whole of James, the man, could be evolved from it—and a great deal of James, the writer. For me the strongest note of all in his character was expressed in his precautions. Not his cautions, for in action, as in writing, he was not in the least cautious.

Whether for his books or life he studied every aspect of the affair on which he was engaged with extraordinary elaboration—the elaboration which he gave to every speech that he uttered. And he was a man of the most amazing vitality, inexhaustible, indefatigable. He consulted everybody from the conductor of the tram from Rye Harbour to Rye golf links, to the chauffeur of a royal automobile who, having conveyed his august master to call on the local great lady, spent a disgusted afternoon in The Mermaid expressing rancour at the fact that the stone-deaf old lady who kept the local tollgate should have refused to let her Sovereign pass through except after payment of a shilling. What exact treasures of information Mr. James can have extracted as to either the passengers to the golf links or the travelling habits of Edward VII, or what use he expected to make of that information, I do not know. But he had an extraordinary gift of exacting confidences and even confessions so that his collection of human instances must have been one of the vastest that any man ever had. It made him perhaps feel safe—or at least as safe as it was in his nature to feel. He could feel, that is to say, that he knew his own *mileu*—the coterie of titled, distinguished, and "good" people in which he and his books moved and had their beings. And in the special English sense the words "good people" does not mean the virtuous, but all the sufficiently well-born, sufficiently inconspicuous, sufficiently but not too conspicuously opulent, sufficiently but very certainly not too conspicuously intelligent and educated, that supply recruits to the ruling classes of the British Isles. . . .

Of that class he knew the lives and circumstances, at first

perhaps rather superficially and with enthusiasm, and at last profoundly and with disillusionment as profound as his knowledge. . . . And it comforted him to know "things" about the lives of the innumerable not-born that surrounded the manors or the De Vere Street apartments of the people he really knew, in the sense of having them on his calling list—and being on theirs. . . . He saw the "common people" lying like a dark sea round the raft of the privileged. They excited his piqued wonder, his ardent curiosity, he built the most elaborate theories all over and round them, he observed enough of them to be able to give characteristics, phrases, and turns of mind to the retainers of the Privileged, but he never could be brought to think that he knew enough about them to let him project their lives on to paper. He noted admirably the very phraseology of Mrs. Wicks, the faithful attendant of Maisie who lived for ever in fear of being "spoken to," and with equal admirableness the point of view of poor Brooksmith, the gentleman's valet who "never *had* got his spirits up" after the loss of his one wonderful master. But if, as happens to us to-day, he had been confronted by a Radical Left clamouring that he must write about the proletariat or be lost, he would just for ever have dismissed his faithful amanuensis and relapsed into mournful silence.

He had that conscientiousness—or if you will, that precautiousness . . . and that sense of duty to his public. He set himself up—and the claim was no little one—as directing his reader as to the fine shades of the psychology of a decorative and utterly refined world where it was always five o'clock. He makes the claim with the utmost equanimity again and again in his Prefaces, only abandoning it to say that if the world did not in fact contain any creatures of such hypersensibility and sensitiveness as those he rendered in his later work, the world ought, if it was to lay claim to being civilized, to contain nobody else. . . . Yet he actually knew so many details of the lives of the poorer people about him in Rye that, as I have elsewhere related, I once asked him why he did not for once try his hand at something with at least the local peasantry for a *mileu*. The question was prompted more by wonder at the amazing amount he did know than by any idea that he would possibly consider having a try at it. After all, in masterpieces like *The Spoils of Poynton*, which remains for me the technical high-water mark of all James's work—and can't I remember the rapturous and shouting enthusiasm of Conrad over that story when we first read it together so that that must have been the high-water mark of Conrad's enthusiasm for the work of any other writer? In masterpieces, then, like *The Spoils of Poynton*, James, who fifteen years or so before must have been utterly foreign to the *mileu*, had got completely and mercilessly under the skin of the English ruling classes. So that if he could penetrate one foreignness, why not another? And I cited his other great and impeccable masterpiece, *The Real Thing*, which shows members of the ruling classes reduced by financial disaster to complete pennilessness. He replied, pausing for a moment whilst the heights of Iden with its white, thatched farmhouses formed a background to his male and vigorous personality—for it was always on the Winchelsea Road that we conversed . . . he replied then:

"My dear H, you confuse the analogies. You might say that I came to this country *from* comfortable circumstances *into* comfortably circumstanced circles. Though no further uptown than Washington Square, the Washington Square of my youth was almost infinitely divided, by gulfs, chasms, canyons, from the downtownnesses round Trinity Spire where, you understand, they worked—mysteriously and at occupations as to which we of Washington Square hadn't the very ghost of an inkling. . . . And if, as you have heard me say, the comfortably circumstanced of that day were not by any manner of means luxuriously—or even hardly so much as comfortably caparisoned or upholstered or garnished at table or horse-furnitured when they rode in their buggies . . . or, if in the Mecca of good society, internationally of the highest cultivation and nationally of all that the nation had of the illustrious to offer . . . if, then, on descending the steps of the Capitol *on trébuchait sur des vaches* as the Marquis de Sabran-Penthièvre remarked in the seventies . . . if they still, at Washington, D.C., not Square, they still, to the embarrassment of the feet of visiting diplomatists, pastured cows on the lawns outside the White House, nevertheless the frame of mind . . . the frame of mind, and that's the important thing, was equally, for the supporters of the initials as for those of the Square, that of all the most comfortable that the world had to offer. . . . I do not suppose that, with the exception of the just-landed relatives of my parents' Nancies or Biddies or Bridgets in the kitchen visiting their kinsmaids, I ever saw to speak to a single human being who did not, as the phrase is—and Heaven knows, more than the phrase is and desperate and dark and hideously insupportable the condition must be—the verb's coming now . . . didn't know where their next day's meals were coming from . . . who were, that is to say, of that frame of mind, that, as the lamentable song says: 'They lived in a dive and sometimes contrived to pick up a copper or two.' . . . For of course, as you were kind enough to say, in *The Real Thing* I have sufficiently well rendered the perturbations of the English comfortable who by financial disaster were reduced, literally, to complete vagueness as to the provenance of their next day's breakfast, lunch, tea, and dinner. . . . Or, as in the sketch—it isn't sufficiently complete of the more than reduced circumstances of the fathers of Kate Croy in m . . . mmm. . . ." He stopped and surveyed me with a roguish and carefully simulated embarrassment. For it was established sufficiently between us that in the longish, leanish, fairish Englishman who was Morton Densher of *The Wings of the Dove*, he had made an at least external portrait of myself at a time when he had known me only vaguely and hadn't imagined that in the ordinary course of things the acquaintance would deepen. . . . So he began again:

"Consider," he said with a sort of appalled vehemence, "what it must be—how desperate and dark and abhorrent —to live in such tenebrousness that all the light that could fall into your cavern must come in through a tiny orifice which, if it were shuttered by a penny, would give you light, warmth, sustenance, society, even . . . and that, if it were absent, that penny would disclose nothing but unmeasured blackness that penetrated to and pervaded your miserable lair. . . . All light, all hope, all chance in life or of heaven dependent from that tiny disc of metal. . . . Why, how could you enter into a frame of mind similar to that, and still more, if you were a writer, how could you render such circumstances and all their circumambiences and implications? . . . And you ask me, who *am*, for my sins, of the same vocation as the beautiful Russian genius—who am, I permit myself to say, a renderer of human vicissitudes . . . of a certain conscience, of a certain scrupulousness . . . you ask *me* to mislead my devotees by the rendering of caves as to which I know nothing and as to the penetration or the mere imagination of which I truly shudder? . . . Perish the thought . . . I say perish, perish the damnable thought. . . . ." He walked on for some time in a really disturbed silence, muttering every two or three seconds to himself—and then turned on me almost furiously.

"You understand," he said, "the damnable thought is not that I might be poor. If I had to be poor I should hope to support the condition with equanimity. . . ." And he went on to explain that it wasn't even the idea of contemplating, of delving into the poverty of others. What he shrank from was the temptation to treat themes that did not come into his province—the province that he considered the one in which he could work assuredly and with a quiet conscience.

Once he stopped suddenly on the road and said, speaking very fast:

"You've read my last volume? . . . There's a story in it. . . ." He continued gazing intently at me, then as suddenly he began again: "There are subjects one thinks of treating all one's life. . . . And one says they are not for one. And one says one must not treat them . . . all one's life. All one's life. . . . And then suddenly . . . one does . . . *Voilà!*" He had been speaking with almost painful agitation. He added much more calmly: "One has yielded to temptation. One is to that extent dishonoured. One must make the best of it."

That story was *The Great Good Place*, appearing, I think, in the volume called *The Soft Side*. In it he considered that he had overstepped the bounds of what he considered proper to treat—in the way of his sort of mysticism. There were, that is to say, mysticisms that he considered proper to treat and others whose depths he thought should not be probed—at any rate by his pen. For there were whole regions of his character that he never exploited in literature, and it would be the greatest mistake to forget that the strongest note in that character was a mysticism different altogether in character from that of the great Catholic mystics. It resembled rather a perception of a sort of fourth dimensional penetration of the material world by strata of the supernatural, of the world of the living by individuals from among the dead. You will get a good inkling of what I mean if you will read again *The Turn of the Screw* with the constant peepings-in of the ghosts of the groom and the governess with their sense of esoteric evil—their constant peepings-in on the haunted mortals of the story. For him, good and evil were not represented by acts; they were something present in the circumambience of the actual world, something spiritual attendant on actions or words. As such he rendered them and, once convinced that he had got that sense in, he was content—he even took an impish pleasure in leaving out the renderings of the evil actions.

Of that you can read sufficiently in his enormous and affrighting Prefaces. . . . He never specifies in *The Turn of the Screw* what were the evil deeds of the ghostly visitants, nor what the nature of the corruption into which the children fell. And, says he in the Preface to the story:

> "Only make the reader's vision of evil intense enough, I said to myself—and that is already a charming job—and his own experience, his own sympathy (with the children) and horror (of their false friends) will supply him quite sufficiently with all the particulars. Make him *think* the evil, make him think it for himself, and you are released from weak specifications."

It is an admirable artistic maxim. But it did not—and that

is what I am trying to emphasize as the main note of this paper—dispense him, in his own mind, from having all the knowledges, whether of esoteric sin or the mentality of butlers, that were necessary to make him feel that he knew enough about his subject to influence the reader's vision in the right direction. As far as I know—and if diligence in reading the works of James gives one the right to know, I ought to have that right—not a single rendering of esoteric sin, sexual incidents, or shadowing of obscenities exists in all the works of the Master, and his answer to D. H. Lawrence or to Rabelais would, for him, have been sufficiently and triumphantly expressed in the sentences I have just quoted.

But that did not prevent him—when he considered the occasion to serve—from making his conversation heroically Rabelaisian, or, for me, really horrific, on the topics of esoteric sin or sexual indulgence. I have attended at conversations between him and a queer tiny being who lay as if crumpled up on the stately sofa in James's magnificent panelled room in Lamb House—conversations that made the tall wax candles seem to me to waver in their sockets and the skin of my forehead and hands prickle with sweat. I am in these things rather squeamish; I sometimes wish I was not, but it is so and I can't help it. I don't wish to leave the impression that these conversations were carried on for purposes of lewd stimulation or irreverent ribaldry. They occurred as part of the necessary pursuit of that knowledge that permitted James to give his reader the "sense of evil." . . . And I dare say they freed him from the almost universal proneness of Anglo-Saxon writers to indulge in their works in a continually intrusive fumbling in placket-holes as Sterne called it, or in the lugubrious occupation of composing libidinous Limericks. James would utter his racy "Ho-ho-ho's" and roll his fine eyes whilst talking to his curious little friend, but they were not a whit more racy and his eyes did not roll any more than they did when he was asking a housemaid or a parson's wife for advice as to the advisability of employing a Lady's Help, or than when he was recounting urbane anecdotes at tea on his lawn to the Ladies So-and-So and So-and-So. It was all in the day's work.

Exactly what may have been his intimate conviction as to, say, what should be the proper relation of the sexes, I don't profess to know. That he demanded from the more fortunate characters in his books a certain urbanity of behaviour as long as that behaviour took place in the public eye, his books are there to prove. That either Mr. Beale Farange or Mrs. Beale committed in the circumambience of *What Maisie Knew* one or more adulteries must be obvious, since they obtained divorces in England. But the fact never came into the foreground of the book. And that he had a personal horror of letting his more august friends come into contact through him with anyone who might be even remotely suspected of marital irregularities, I know from the odd, seasonal nature of my relations with him. We met during the winters almost every day, but during the summers only by, usually telegraphed, appointment. This was because during the summer Mr. James's garden overflowed with the titled, the distinguished, the eminent in the diplomatic world . . . with all his *milieu*. And, once he had got it well fixed into his head that I was a journalist, he conceived the idea that all my friends must be illegally united with members of the opposite sex. So that it was inconceivable that my summer friends should have any chance to penetrate on to his wonderfully kept lawns. I do not think that I knew any journalists at all in those days, and I am perfectly certain that, with one very eminent exception, I did not know anyone who had been so much as a plaintiff in the shadow of the divorce courts. I was in the mood to be an English country gentleman and, for the time being, I was. . . . It happened, however, that the extraordinarily respectable wives of two eminent editors were one week-end during a certain summer staying in Winchelsea—which was a well-known tourist resort—and they took it into their heads to go and call on James at Rye.

I had hardly so much as a bowing acquaintance with them. But the next day, happening to go into Rye, I met the Old Man down by the harbour. Just at the point where we met was a coal yard whose proprietor had the same name as one of the husbands of one of those ladies. James stopped short and with a face working with fury pointed his stick at the coal man's name above the gate and brought out the exasperated words:

"A couple of jaded . . . WANTONS! . . ." and, realizing that I was fairly quick on the uptake, nothing whatever more. . . . But, as soon as the leaves fell, there he was back on my doorstep, asking innumerable advices—as to his investments, as to what would cure the parasites of a dog, as to brands of cigars, as to where to procure cordwood, as to the effects of the Corn Laws on the landed gentry of England. . . . And I would accompany him, after he had had a cup of tea, back to his Ancient Town; and next day I would go over and drink a cup of tea with him and wait whilst he finished dictating one of his sentences to his amanuensis and then he would walk back with me to

Winchelsea. . . . In that way we each got a four-mile walk a day. . . .

No, I never did get any knowledge as to how he regarded sexual irregularities. . . . I remember he one day nearly made me jump out of my skin during a one-sided discussion as to the relative merits of Flaubert and Turgenev—the beautiful Russian genius of his youth

Turgenev was for him perfection—in person, except that his features were a little broad, in the Slav manner; in his books; in his manners; in his social relations, which were of the highest; in what was aristocratic. But Flaubert, James went on and on hating and grumbling at to the end of his days. Flaubert had, as I have elsewhere related, once been rude to the young James. That James never mentioned. But he had subsequently received James and Turgenev in his dressing-gown. . . . It was not, of course, a dressing-gown, but a working garment—a sort of long, loose coat without revers—called a *chandail*. And if a French man of letters received you in his *chandail*, he considered it a sort of showing honour, as if he had admitted you into his working intimacy. But James never forgave that—more perhaps on account of Turgenev than himself. . . . Flaubert for ever afterwards was for him the man who worked, who thought, who received, who lived—and perhaps went to heaven in his dressing-gown! . . . In consequence he was a failure. All his books except one were failures—technical and material . . . and that one, *Madame Bovary*, if it was a success in both departments . . . well, it was nothing to write home about. And Flaubert's little *salon* in the Faubourg Saint-Honoré was "rather bare and provisional," and Flaubert cared too much for "form," and, because he backed bills for a relation, died in reduced circumstances. . . .

Flaubert was in short the sort of untidy colossus whom I might, if I had the chance, receive at Winchelsea, but who would never, never have been received on the summer lawns of Lamb House at Rye.

And suddenly Mr. James exclaimed, just at the dog-leg bend in the road between the two Ancient Towns:

"But Maupassant!!!! . . ." That man apparently was, for him, the real Prince Fortunatus amongst writers. I don't mean to say that he did not appreciate the literary importance of the author of *La Maison Tellier*—who was also the author of *Ce Cochon de Morin* and, alas, of *Le Horla*, so that whilst in 1888 James was writing of him the words I am about to quote, that poor Prince was already gravitating towards the lunatic asylum. But, writes Mr. James:

"What makes M. de Maupassant salient is two facts: the first of which is that his gifts are remarkably strong and definite and the second that he writes directly *from* them. . . . Nothing can exceed the masculine firmness, the quiet force of his style in which every phrase is a close sequence, every epithet a paying piece. Less than anyone to-day does he beat the air; more than anyone does he hit out from the shoulder. . . ."

sentiments which seem—but only seem—singular in view of the later convolutions of epithet that distinguished our Master. . . .

And those considerations in his conversation Mr. James completely omitted. On the Rye Road, Maupassant was for him the really prodigious, prodigal, magnificent, magnificently rewarded Happy Prince of the Kingdom of Letters. He had yachts, villas on the Mediterranean, "affairs," mistresses, wardrobes of the most gorgeous, grooms, the entrée into the historic salons of Paris, furnishings, overflowing bank balances . . . everything that the heart of man could require even to the perfectly authentic *de* to ally him to the nobility and a public that was commensurate with the ends of the earth. . . . And then, as the top stone of that edifice, Mr. James recounted that once, when Mr. James had been invited to lunch with him, Maupassant had received him, not, be assured, in a dressing-gown, but in the society of a naked lady wearing a mask. . . . And Maupassant assured the author of *The Great Good Place* that the lady was a *femme du monde*. And Mr. James believed him. . . . Fortune could go no further than *that*! . . .

Manners, morals, and the point of view have so changed since even 1906 when Mr. James must have recounted that anecdote that I am not going to dilate upon it. And you have to remember that some years after the 1888 in which he wrote the words I have quoted, Mr. James underwent an experience that completely altered his point of view, his methods, and his entire literary practice. His earlier stages, Mr. James the Second contrived entirely—or almost entirely —to obscure in a sort of cuttlefish cloud of interminable phrases. Until the middle nineties nothing could have exceeded the masculine firmness, the quiet force of his writing, and of no one else than himself could it more justly be written that "less than anyone did he beat the air, more than anyone did he hit out from the shoulder."

That is amazingly the case. I have more than once proclaimed the fact that there were two Jameses. And yet no one could be more overwhelmed than I at re-reading in their earliest forms, after all these years, his early masterpieces as they were written and before he went over and elaborated their phrases. Thus to re-read is to realize with immense force that more than anyone else, in the matter of approach to his subjects, Maupassant rather than Turgenev must have been the young James's master. *Daisy Miller;* that most wonderful *nouvelle* of all, *The Four Meetings; The Pupil; The Lesson of the Master; The Death of the Lion,* and all the clear, crisp, mordant stories that went between, right up to *The Real Thing* and *In The Cage*—all these stories are of a complete directness, an economy, even of phrase, that make James one of the great masters of the *nouvelle*, the long or merely longish short story.

But at a given date, after a misfortune that, for the second time, shattered his life, and convinced him that his illusions as to the delicacies of his "good" people of a certain *milieu* were in fact . . . delusions; after that he became the creature of infinite precautions that he was when I knew him best. I had, that is to say, a sight—two or three sights—of him in the previous stage. Then he resembled one of those bearded elder statesmen—the Marquis of Salisbury, Sir Charles Dilke, or the Prince who was to become Edward VII. He was then slightly magisterial; he cross-questioned rather than questioned you; he was obviously of the *grande monde* and of the daily habit of rubbing, on equal terms, shoulders with the great.

But about the later James, clean-shaven, like an actor, so as to recover what he could of the aspect of youth; nervous: his face for ever mobile; his hands for ever gesturing; there hung continually the feeling of a forced energy, as if of a man conscious of failure and determined to conceal mortification. He had had two great passions—the one for a cousin whom he was to have married and who died of consumption while they were both very young, and the other for a more conspicuous but less satisfactory personage who in the end at about the time when the break occurred, let him down mercilessly after a period of years. And the tenacity of his attachments was singular and unforgetting.

"*The Wings of the Dove* [he writes in his Preface of 1909 to that novel], published in 1902, represents to my memory a very old —if I shouldn't perhaps say a very young—motive. I can scarcely remember the time when the motive on which this long-drawn fiction mainly rests was not vividly present to me. The idea, reduced to its essence, is that of a young person conscious of a great capacity for life, but early stricken and doomed, condemned to die under short respite while also enamoured of the world. . . . She was the last fine flower—blooming alone for the fullest attestation of her freedom—of an old New York stem, the happy congruities thus preserved being matters that I may not now go into, although the fine association . . . shall yet elsewhere await me. . . ."

I do not know anywhere words more touching. . . . And I do not think that, in spite of the later obscuration, the image of the Milly Theale of that book was ever very far away from his thoughts. I remember that when, in 1906, I told him that I was going to America, his immediate reaction was to ask me to visit his cousins, the Misses Mason at Newport, Rhode Island, and to take a certain walk along the undercliff beneath Ocean Avenue and there pay, as it were, vicarious honour to the spot where, for the last time, he had parted from his dead cousin. It was the most romantic—it was the only one that was romantic—of the many small jobs that I did for him. . . . And in one of the fits of apologizing that would occasionally come over him—for having physically drawn myself in the portrait of Morton Densher, who was, to be sure, no hero if he wasn't more than only very subterraneously discreditable—he once said:

"After all you've got to remember that I was to fabricate a person who could decently accompany, if only in the pages of my book, another person to whom I was—and remain, and remain, Heaven knows—let us say, most tenderly attached. . . ." As if to say that, in fabricating such a person, his mind would not let him portray someone who was completely disagreeable.

The other attachment was completely detrimental to him. Its rupture left him the person of infinite precautions that I have here rather disproportionately limned. It was as if, from then on, he was determined that nobody or nothing— no society coterie, no tram-conductor, no housemaid, no *femme du monde*—should ever have the chance, either in life or in his books, to let him down. And it was as if he said the very same thing to the phrases that he wrote. If he was continuously parenthetic, it was in the determination that no word he wrote should ever be misinterpreted, and if he is, in his later work, bewildering, it was because of the almost panicked resolve to be dazzlingly clear. Because of that he could never let his phrases alone. . . . How often when waiting for him to go for a walk haven't I heard him say whilst dictating the finish of a phrase:

"No, no, Miss Dash . . . that is not clear. . . . Insert before 'we all are' . . . Let me see. . . . Yes, insert 'not so much locally, though to be sure we're here; but temperamentally, in a manner of speaking.' " . . . So that the phrase, blindingly clear to him by that time, when completed would run:

"So that here, not so much locally, though to be sure we're here, but at least temperamentally in a manner of speaking, we all are."

No doubt the habit of dictating had something to do with these convolutions, and the truth of the matter is that during these later years he wrote far more for the ear of his amanuensis than for the eye of the eventual reader. So that, if you will try the experiment of reading him aloud and with expression, you will find his even latest pages relatively plain to understand. But, far more than that, the underlying factor in his later work was the endless determination to add more and more detail, so that the exact illusions and the exact facts of life may appear, and so that everything may be blindingly clear even to a little child. . . . For I have heard him explain with the same profusion of detail as he gave to my appalled and bewildered housemaid—I have heard him explain to Conrad's son of five why he wore a particular hat whose unusual shape had attracted the child's attention. He was determined to present to the world the real, right thing!

I will quote, to conclude, the description of myself as it appears in *The Wings of the Dove* so that you may have some idea of what was James's image of the rather silent person who walked so often beside him on the Rye Road.

"He was a longish, leanish [alas, alas!], fairish young Englishman, not unamenable on certain sides to classification—as for instance being a gentleman, by being rather specifically one of the educated, one of the generally sound and generally civil; yet, though to that degree neither extraordinary nor abnormal, he would have failed to play straight into an observer's hands. He was young for the House of Commons; he was loose for the Army. He was refined, as might have been said, for the City and, quite apart from the cut of his cloth, sceptical, it might have been felt, for the Church. On the other hand he was credulous for diplomacy, or perhaps even for science, while he was perhaps at the same time too much in his real senses for poetry and yet too little in them for art. . . . The difficulty with Densher was that he looked vague without looking weak—idle without looking empty. It was the accident possibly of his long legs which were apt to stretch themselves; of his straight hair, and well-shaped head, never, the latter neatly smooth and apt into the bargain . . . to throw itself suddenly back and, supported behind by his uplifted arms and interlocked hands, place him for unconscionable periods in communion with the ceiling, the tree-tops, the sky. . . ."

That, I suppose, was the young man that James rather liked.

# Henry James in Rye

a) A. G. Bradley, 'Henry James As I Knew Him: The Human Side of a Great Novelist', *John O' London's Weekly* (18 December 1936)
b) Ella Hepworth Dixon, *As I Knew Them* (London: Hutchinson & Co., 1930)
c) Matilda Betham-Edwards, *Mid-Victorian Memories* (London: J. Murray, 1919)
d) Anon., 'General Gossip of Authors and Writers', *Current Literature* (January 1900)

In addition to Garland (see section 11), many other friends and acquaintances wrote reminiscences of James during his residence in Lamb House. Arthur Granville Bradley (1850–1943), a historian and travel writer whose works included *Avon and Shakespeare's Country* (1927), was a friend and neighbour of Henry James's in Rye. He wrote several works on colonial America including *The Fight with France for North America* (1908). 'Henry James as I Knew Him' emphasises James's geniality as a neighbour and describes his surprisingly successful integration into Rye society.

Ella Nora Hepworth Dixon (1857–1932) was a novelist and journalist who wrote under the pseudonym Margaret Wynman. Her most significant work was her New Woman novel *The Story of a Modern Woman* (1894). She wrote articles on topics relating to women's position in society and edited the *Englishwoman* between March and August 1895. Her sketch of James reveals the different aspects of his persona; his chilling aloofness when dismissing the hostess who bores him contrasts with his ability to be entirely unaffected and warm in the company of those (whether children or golfers) with whom he apparently had little in common. (A similarly contradictory account of James's blend of consideration and waspishness is sketched by Edward Marsh in *A Number of People* (London: William Heinemann, 1939), pp. 114–15.)

Matilda Betham-Edwards (1836–1919), novelist and travel writer, published her first novel, the very popular *The White House by the Sea*, in 1857. The daughter of a Suffolk farmer, she went on to write several accounts of French rural life and agriculture as well as many more successful novels including *Kitty* (1869). She was socially very active and her close friends included Barbara Leigh Smith Bodichon and George Eliot as well as Henry James. James described her as 'a very gallant little mid-Victorian lady' (*Notebooks*, p. 306). Her sense of the closeness of their relationship seems rather exaggerated. Like Dixon, she reveals a James whose characteristic thoughtful courtesy is leavened by moments of sardonic humour.

The final piece included in this section is an unsigned article which appeared in *Current Literature*, a New York-based journal which ran from 1888 to 1912. The anecdote of James coming to the aid of a fellow writer's children after his death is a reference to the American novelist Stephen Crane, who also lived in Sussex.

# Henry James As I Knew Him.
## THE HUMAN SIDE OF A GREAT NOVELIST.
### By A. G. BRADLEY.

AS an early reader of Henry James's novels (though not, I fear, in full sympathy with their atmosphere) I had vaguely pictured the author as a thin, taciturn, rather stand-offish man. When in 1905 I went to live in Rye and found myself, to my surprise, a neighbour of the famous novelist, it was an even greater surprise to find him a stout, cheerful, humorous and altogether delightful person with a noble head and a twinkling eye which did not, however, detract from an abiding sense of dignity.

This sounds cryptic. But Henry James as a man is indescribable. It is only his lighter and more human side that I am attempting to sketch within the compass of this article.

\* \* \*

HE occupied a charming Georgian house and garden in the heart of Rye, which town in those days (1905-1914) retained the delightful air of repose so befitting its ancient streets and buildings, an atmosphere now destroyed by motor traffic and encircling red brick horrors. What Henry James would now think of the place he lived in and loved for twenty years, I cannot imagine. His leisurely chatty progress down its High Street would be now unthinkable.

Rye society consisted in his day of perhaps a score of households, besides others in the neighbourhood, a few literary or artistic, the majority just "retired" gentle-folk, civil or military, with the local parsons, doctors and lawyers. Henry James was no recluse: he was fond of his fellow creatures—after three p.m., till which hour his privacy was sacrosanct. He attended Rye tea parties freely, had beautiful manners and no aversion to local gossip, which was, of course, in his favour.

\* \* \*

HIS talk over the tea table was generally quite light and human, but always whimsical. He had no trace of American accent. Indeed, his diction was ultra-fastidious, like that of the older University dons. There was more than a touch of his books in his talk, when he would raise his hand and half close his eyes in quest of exactly the right word, which, when found, not seldom brought a twinkle into his eyes as he met yours. For the gesture had a half-conscious touch of humour in it.

He was always very nice to me, partly because I had written a good many books, though they were not the sort he read—when he read anything—and also because I was the only person in the locality who knew America as a former resident, and understood his personal and local allusions. Not that he was partial to his countrymen in general. The tone in which he pronounced the word "Middle West" was worth hearing. Of the South, my particular section, he had no personal knowledge and no great

*Henry James was born in New York in 1843, came to Europe in 1869, became a naturalized British subject in 1915, and died in 1916, shortly after he had been awarded the Order of Merit. From 1875, when he became famous for his novel "Roderick Hudson," he poured out a steady stream of novels and sensitive criticism which ended in 1914 with his masterly "Notes on Novelists." To-day he is read perhaps only by the few—the subtlety and elegance of his style, indeed, always kept the wider public at arm's length—yet his influence on the development of the psychological novel has been profound.*

opinion—"a provincial people" and, in his sense, quite uncultured. Of the practical and physical side of America he neither knew nor cared much. His America was represented by a few cultured centres in the East associated with his personal friends and his own childhood days, which he greatly cherished.

\* \* \*

TILL his years advanced I used often to take country walks with him. He loved the quiet English landscape, but, characteristically, had not the faintest knowledge of the rural industries that went to the making of the picture. He was a subscribing member to our famous Rye golf club. But he would have been the first to make merry at the idea of his swinging a club. Occasionally, however, after a walk on the shore he would look in at the club for tea and be greeted with a shout by any friends present. His fine mobile face would then light up as with characteristic elaboration he delivered some humorous repartee in the Jamesian fashion.

As an old bachelor, though well served, he had, of course, his occasional domestic trials, and could be very funny in talking of them. One of his manservants—a lad about five feet high, and an enthusiastic light-weight boxer—provided him with much amusement as well as faithful service. The adventures of a favourite dog—and of dogs he knew absolutely nothing —also supplied material for whimsical comments.

\* \* \*

TOURING sketching classes sometimes filled the narrow streets and crowded on to his doorstep, all unconscious of the distinguished occupant, because it commanded a popular view. H. J. used to declare that on these occasions he couldn't get out of his house without "taking a flying leap over the heads of art and industry"—the vision of his stout unathletic frame and short legs in the air being his little joke.

He had a hobby for inspecting empty houses, and could hardly pass one in the hands of workmen without dashing in and examining every room. Murder cases, too, intrigued him vastly. Walking down Rye High Street with a friend of mine one day when an interesting case was in the papers, he met our principal solicitor, buttonholed him, and eagerly inquired his opinion of it. The old gentleman leisurely replied that he hadn't given any thought to the subject. H. J. almost flung away, remarking, " The man's a d——d fool."

\* \* \*

I ALWAYS recall one delightful scene during a musical afternoon in a large house near Rye. I was sitting exactly opposite Henry James, who was perched on a cushioned window-seat with a lady beside him. An orchestral piece was in progress. He was not, I think, musical, and was sitting wrapped in thought, his eyes fixed on the floor and a frown of concentration on scenes remote all over his face. His neighbour, obviously a musical enthusiast, was swaying her head to the music, as some ladies do. She had a tall, upright feather in her hat with a drooping tip to it. Each time she swayed in her abstracted neighbour's direction the tip of it touched and tickled his broad bald head.

At every contact, mistaking it for a fly, and without moving a muscle of his solemn abstracted face, he shot his arm up and slapped his crown in impatience at the persistency of the supposed insect. This little scene went on till the conclusion of the piece aroused him from his reverie and the swaying lady had settled down, to ask him, no doubt, what he thought of the performance.

\* \* \*

THE unabashed Philistine who cared for nothing but sport and fancies himself on that account alone, a fairly common type in England, was a real puzzle to Henry James. He sometimes cited a certain prosperous neighbour as a luminous example of this, to him, bewildering type. When taken by his wife to Rome for the first time and asked what he thought of it, he replied, " Nothing at all. It has the worst golf course in Europe." This gave H. J. huge delight. It was not the mere absorption in amusements that puzzled him, but the self-complacency which so often accompanied it.

Americans, with or without introductions, would sometimes break in on his working hours. " My devastating countrymen," he called them, and used to tell us about them

## A. G. Bradley: 'Henry James As I Knew Him'

afterwards. But he was actually most forbearing, much as he might curse them subsequently in his quaint manner.

He read very little in his last few years, but wrote innumerable letters. Even in local notes

**HENRY JAMES.**

regarding a mere social appointment he would often cover with his large handwriting two or three pages with quaint superfluities. I have kept several of these as typical.

\* \* \*

WALKING uphill began to tire Henry James as his years increased, and he acquired the habit of stopping at particular points and carrying on his conversation face to face with his companion. It so happened that on a certain occasion he was in the funeral procession of a deceased local official. They were a large company marching two and two, he and a friend of mine, an occasional companion of his walks, being about the middle of the long column.

On this solemn occasion, when on the road up to the cemetery they reached one of the spots where he was accustomed to halt and hold forth, an absent-minded fit seized him. He

---

### PROVENÇAL CAROL.
(*After Clement Marot, 1495-1544.*)

A SHEPHERD and a shepherdess
   Who danced together in the shade ;
   They played upon their flutes, and this
Is what one to the other said :
   Lithe
   Shepherd lad,
   Blithe
   Shepherd maid,
Now let us leave our flutes, they said,
And sing Noël, Noël, instead.

Remember what the prophet said
In telling of the great things done
In heaven, how the perfect maid
Would bring to birth the perfect son ;
   The thing
   Is done,
   We sing
   The son
Of the perfect maid on heaven's throne ;
Sing Noël, Noël, everyone.
               R. N. CURREY.

---

stopped as usual, and, turning round to his companion, began an oration. Some dozen or more couples behind him, being thus brought to a standstill, were impatiently marking time, while the foremost half of the column were marching on up the hill. His friend, not a little embarrassed, managed to hook the great man by the arm and gently slip out of the procession to take last place in the rear, which did not catch up with the main body till the cemetery was nearly reached.

\* \* \*

MY memories of H. J.'s abounding kindness of heart were revived while I was writing these lines by a lady, hitherto a stranger to me, who once met him under the following circumstances.

Just before the War she was visiting Rye for the day with her son of eighteen and a boy friend of his. The two lads were intelligently discussing the beauties of some old houses when an elderly gentleman, attracted by their comments, joined them and gave the party a long talk on the subject. More than this, when he found that they were staying at Bexhill, having made himself known to them, he invited the two boys to come over and spend a day with him at Lamb House, which they did, to their great enjoyment.

\* \* \*

ON another occasion William Meredith, son of George Meredith, and then senior partner in Constable and Co., my publishers, was spending the week-end with us at Rye. On the Sunday afternoon he went up with me to pay his respects to Henry James. We were sitting in the garden, and before we left our host's long-sustained efforts to send a suitable greeting to Meredith's father gave us immense entertainment.

I don't know what intimacy there may have been between these two celebrities: some feeling, no doubt, as both were considered unintelligible to the common herd. "William," began Henry James—I can see him now on that garden bench, with closed eyes and the frown of concentration on his fine massive face—"William, tell your dear father"—a pause, then a slap on the head. After another pause—"Tell your father, William———" Another slap and a longer pause, a suitably composed message still struggling for birth. But, despite two or three more urgent bangs on the head, it finished in anti-climax, and "William, give your father my love" was all Meredith had to convey to his father. It was not often, however, that the great man failed to express himself to his satisfaction.

\* \* \*

THE last time I met Henry James was early in the War. I found him deep in a letter from his relatives in America, and was greatly surprised at his reading most of it aloud to me. He was much irritated, as it was a defence of President Wilson's reluctance to join the Allies, while his own feeling, as is well known, was so passionately pro-British that he had become a naturalized British citizen.

His death followed soon after, hastened undoubtedly by the tragedy of the War. I have read many autobiographies since of prominent men who more or less knew and met Henry James. But it is fairly obvious that few of them had any notion of how he appeared to his neighbours in Rye, among whom he lived for so many years and was so popular.

———:———

THE lives and ways of the mountain caribou, the black bear, the Canada moose and many other wild inhabitants of the Canadian National Parks are described in *Animals of the Canadian Rockies*. (Lovat Dickson, 12s. 6d.), by Mr. *Dan McGowan*. The book is illustrated from photographs taken by the author, who has had a long experience of animal photography.

———:———

CONTENT lodges oftener in cottages than palaces. —THOMAS FULLER.

# HENRY JAMES

§

WHEN I look back, it seems to me that Henry James was the most profoundly sad-looking man I have ever seen, not even excepting certain members of the house of Rothschild. His eyes were not only age-old and world-weary, as are those of cultured Jews, but they had vision—and one did not like to think of what they saw. It is true that Henry James had plenty of sardonic humour, but he too often used it at the expense of his friends and protégés. It was always a mystery to me how the writer who gave to the world that exquisite story, *An Altar of Friendship*, could be so biting (though always humorous) about the people he dined with, entertained, and " protected " in a literary sense. It was impossible not to like him, but one was continually startled at what he had to say about his contemporaries and juniors. At one time I used to meet him at certain famous " dinners of eight," given by a woman of many graces and achievements, who easily got "all London" round her.

One day I asked him why he no longer dined with Lady X. " I find it more and more difficult, more and more difficult " (Henry James could not say a sentence without repeating himself) " to put up with the second-rate," which was rather hard on our mutual hostess, who had justly made a name by her dinner-parties.

At houses where he was more at home, Henry James could be excellent company. I vividly recollect one Christmas dinner at the house of Sir Claude Phillips, the art critic, when we all sat on the drawing-room floor and blew small feathers across a sheet. The face of Henry James, puffed with heroic effort, rising above the whiteness of the cloth, was irresistibly droll, though perfectly serious. Probably he played these childish games on Christmas night because he had a great liking for Eugénie Phillips, Sir Claude's sister, whose friendship was of the rare and exquisite kind.

Henry James at home at Lamb House, Rye, was a much more genial person than the lion of London drawing-rooms. But he had, there, too, his odd unaccountable moments. He loved his beautifully proportioned Georgian house, with its large, white panelled rooms furnished in the " period," and a butler who always reminded me of Cyrano de Bérgérac. How he could possibly have " missed " the lovely amethyst-and-copper lustre tea service which I picked up one day, for ten shillings, almost within sight of his door I can only attribute to his habit of procrastination. His chagrin when I told him of my bargain was real. " You don't mean to say—to say, my dear young lady—that you've actually bought it ? For six weeks—for six weeks I have been deliberating—deliberating—whether I should acquire that tea-service—and now—in five minutes, yes, in five minutes, it is yours ! "

If I had behaved like a true disciple (I had been " brought up," in a literary sense, on Henry James) I should have offered it, there and then, to the Master. But I am ashamed to say I did not, and it served at tea-time for many other amusing people in our drawing-room in London.

That day he gave signs of the over-strain which he was suffering from when he was writing that *macabre* story, *The Turn of the Screw*. Having invited Mrs. Hodgson Burnett and the whole of her house-party to luncheon at Lamb House, he began the affair handsomely enough, talking to all his guests, playing the perfect host. Suddenly, in the middle, he got up from his place, walked out without any apology, and could be seen, by his amazed guests, pacing the green garden outside the windows in a brown study. Cyrano de Bérgérac continued, meticulously, to hand the dishes, and no one said a word about the strange disappearance of our host. Neither did he make any pother about it when we met again, in the drawing-room, and he showed us, with all the householder's pride, the upstairs and downstairs of his engaging English home.

Henry James chose Rye as a residence because, he declared, he liked golfers in plus-fours. It was characteristic of him that he never wanted to talk " literature," but was profoundly interested in Life. He himself has said that he was half an Englishman because, as a small boy in Boston (or was it New York ?), he was always immersed in a newly arrived number of *Punch*.

The clip-clop of hansom cab horses on a wet and slightly foggy night in London would cause in Henry James the same kind of ecstasy as " autumnal leaves which strew the brooks in Vallombrosa " arouse in cultured English spinsters in quest of emotion on a first visit to Italy.

Another visit which I paid to Lamb House remains in my memory. A guest at Maytham Hall, Mrs. Hodgson Burnett's country home, had acquired a motor-bicycle to which was attched a " trailer," and on this truly infernal conveyance he persuaded me to go and see our mutual friend at Rye. The roads were then guileless of tar ; the summer dust was thick and when we arrived, after much peril, at Lamb House, I was so white from head to foot that only with an effort could Henry James recognize this draggled creature out of a flour mill.

But our afternoon was a success. Our host was fresh from America (one of his rare visits) and he wanted to talk of his experiences. The bane of his visit, he said, had been " the Japanese." Students from that great country, of all shapes and sizes, speaking an incredible version of the English language, had pestered him all day and night. The rest of America, he declared, seemed to be inhabited by Italians, and you heard no English in the streets. As for New York, he said, it had been pulled down and rebuilt at least twice since his last visit ; the city was, to the man who remembered it in the 'seventies and 'eighties, unrecognizable. To find an old friend in the same house was impossible.

Henry James' face was so tragic in repose, that when he smiled it was an event which made the whole room light up. Not long before he died, I was talking to Sir Claude Phillips in a picture gallery when we came across him face to face. The sad features lit up. " And here is Claude," he murmured, " and here is Ella . . ." as if he were counting over carefully the part (and mine was singularly insignificant) which we had, as individuals, played in his life. The little incident was as slight as one in a story of his own, but one could not forget it. If Henry James dwelt on trifles by the strange alchemy of his genius, they suddenly became of profound significance.

All his English friends were profoundly touched, when, impatient at President Wilson's " notes," and prolonged neutrality in the War, Henry James naturalized himself an Englishman, and so proved his sympathy with us in our agony. I wrote him one line : " Quel beau geste ! " But it was almost the last gesture he was to make. Yet like his countryman, the American Ambassador, Walter Page, Henry James was intensely aware of the amazing, the stupendous effort Great Britain was making in the War.

## VI

## HENRY JAMES

### I

Dear Henry James! My heart glows as I recall our long, warm friendship, from first to last not the faintest cloudlet casting a shadow. We valued, I may say we loved, each other, with a brotherly, sisterly affection deeper, more sympathetic perhaps than are often these blood relationships. On neither side was there exaggeration or conventionality. Our respective literary achievements for the most part were not touched upon. Indeed, the only direct criticism he ever passed on a novel of mine was the reverse of flattering.

On June 9, 1913, he had written: "I am very glad to hear of the good fortune of your *Lord of the Harvest*" (just included in the Oxford World's Classics). But alas! the gilt was soon taken off the gingerbread. A little later he paid me a visit, and referring to the story, which he had read, "I should have liked more of a tangle," he said; and, as far as I remember, that was the only direct allusion he made to any work of mine. Indirectly I learned from other sources that he especially valued my studies of French life and literature. And was not his friendship the highest of all compliments?

Our meetings were arranged in this way. I would get a telegram from Rye, answer prepaid, to this effect :

" Can you receive me at five o'clock this afternoon ? " and of course the answer was always Yes. At five precisely his cab would climb the hill, stopping short at a sharp curve of the road, many drivers refusing to attempt an ascent so difficult for their hacks.

Thus it happened now, and well I remember how laborious and painful the footing of that hundred yards or so proved to my great visitor. He had hardly passed his prime, but was ponderously built and moved with the heaviness of age.

Once having regained breath in my little parlour on the ground floor—I never invited him to my study above, although there were many treasures there that would have interested him—he settled himself entirely to his satisfaction. The first thing he did was to study the physiognomy of his hitherto unknown hostess. Indeed, before opening his lips he looked me through and through with those large eyes that seemed to see below the surface of others. Then, that rather staggering attention over, he glanced from the window with its matchless view, wide sweep of sea, red-roofed old town nestled amid verdant heights, high above the walls of the Conqueror's castle crowning the panorama.

Next he looked immediately about him, and I never knew anyone so sensitive to surroundings.

"What a chair is this!" he said. "It has a positive psychology of its own."

The chair in question was a present to me from India, of native cane, high-backed, its proportions exactly suited to the frame and well cushioned; it invited to repose but not inanition.

Then, after a glance at the opposite wall, he added:

"And those fine old engravings."

These were heirlooms, views of my native Ipswich with its twelve churches and fine river and of Bury St. Edmunds with its noble Abbey Gate and ruined tower.

"And yonder magnificent old oak chest?"

"Ah!" I replied, "that is my most cherished heirloom."

A bridal chest, perhaps destined for some noble bride imitating royal example, this curio had long been in the De Betham family, and had indeed served as my mother's linen chest.

It is a most beautiful and highly elaborate specimen of English workmanship, highly polished, its panels showing inlaid canaries and pomegranate, fruit and foliage, under the splendid lock inlaid the figures *1626*.

1626, the year of Charles the First's second Parliament, the year in which, on hearing that Eliot had branded his favourite Buckingham as Sejanus, he had uttered the threat, "If then he is Sejanus, I must be Tiberius"—which he tried to be to his cost!

Henry James next examined the family portraits on the side wall, all three sitters of which have a place in Sir Sidney Lee's *Dictionary of National Biography*—the Rev. W. Betham, Sir William Betham, Ulster king-at-arms, and Matilda Betham. And here I made an unlucky remark.

"Yonder old cleric, my grandfather," I narrated, "a curate for the greater part of his life, lived to be ninety-two and without ever having lost his health or his temper. A few days before his death, as he slowly paced the room leaning on my mother's arm, he made a pun : ' I am walking very slowly, Barbara, but I am going very fast.' "

"A delightful record, but I could have wished without the pun," was my visitor's comment.

I took no notes of those delightful monologues, nor was it necessary ; they imprinted themselves on the memory.

I remember well his description of Sarah Bernhardt's impersonation of Jeanne d'Arc, of the wonderful way with which she baffled her tormentors, keeping them at bay, foiling every trap laid for her tongue.

Of France and French subjects we talked much, and yet have Henry James's novels found favour in the land *par excellence* of crystal clear speech and logical expression?

He would sit down to the tea-table, though rarely taking tea, and of course I could not help talking of his own books. One I mentioned with great appreciation, the inimitable *Three Meetings*. This was on the occasion of his second visit, whereupon he said quickly:

"You shall have my new book."

"No," I said, glancing at my faithful maid in attendance, "pray give her one instead."

"Do you like reading?" he asked; and on her hearty reply in the affirmative, he said:

"I will, I will, I will."

True enough, the promise was kept, and some time after a copy of *The Better Sort* duly arrived, having on the fly-leaf the following inscription:

"*To Emily Morgan, with all good wishes.*
                                HENRY JAMES."
*Jan.* 5, 1912.

And with it this letter to myself:

"I can now tell you the sad story of the book for Emily Morgan, which I am having put up to go to you with this, as well as explain a little my long silence. The very day, or the very second after last seeing you, a change suddenly took place, under great necessity, in my then current plans and arrangements. I departed under that stress for London, practically to spend the winter, and have come back but for a very small number of days, and I return there next week.

"'But,' you will say, 'why didn't you send the promised volume to E. M. from London, then? What matters to us where it came from so long as it came?' To which I reply: 'Well, I had in this house a small row of books available for the purpose and among which I could choose. In London I should have to go and *buy* the thing, my own production, while I leave two or three brand-new volumes, which will be an economy to a man utterly depleted by the inordinate number of copies of *The Outcry* which he has given away and of which he has had to pay for —his sanguinary (admire my restraint!) publisher allowing him half!' 'Why, then, couldn't you write home and have one of the books sent you, or have it sent to Hastings directly from your house?' Because I am the happy possessor of a priceless parlourmaid who loves doing up books and other parcels and does them up beautifully, and if the vol. comes to me here, to be inscribed, I shall then have to do it up myself, an act for which I have absolutely no skill and which I dread and loathe, and tumble it forth clumsily and insecurely. Besides, I was vague as to which of my works I did have on the accessible shelf (and I only know I had some, and would have to look and consider and decide). And the thing will be beautifully wrapped. 'That's all very well:

but why, then, didn't you write and explain why it was that you were keeping us unserved and uninformed?' Oh, because from the moment I go up to town I *plunge*, plunge into the great whirlpool of postal matters, social matters, etc."

I do not give the rest.

Note his redundancy—a couple of pages and dozens of words when two lines would have sufficed.

His last note, dated August 13, 1914, thanked me for my welcoming him "into this ancient fold," *i.e.* his naturalisation as a British subject on the outbreak of the war.

And his last visit—a most delightful one despite an inauspicious beginning—was paid in the autumn of that year.

I have already explained that his cab always stopped just below High Wickham Terrace, drivers refusing to try their hacks' knees with the short, sharp upward hundred yards or so, and still more fearful of their nerves if putting them to the downward ordeal. Hitherto my visitor had footed the corner without apparent difficulty. This time he arrived breathless and almost in a state of collapse. The intervening years and the war had aged him greatly.

Fortunately, a physician was at hand. My good friend and benefactor, Dr. Dodson Hessey, happened to call just before, and at my instance waited to renew an acquaintance that had previously proved highly agreeable to both. "A nice man," had been Henry James's summing-up after their first meeting, and, as I have shown, no one was less addicted to compliments. Vainly did the doctor now advise a cordial. The very mention of brandy made the patient worse. However, he did induce him to take a cup of tea and a slice of bread and butter, these very seldom indulged in when visiting me, and, gradually reviving, Henry James was himself again. A genial, animated, and generous self he became, giving us of his best.

Over an hour's tripartite conversation we enjoyed, turning upon literature and winding up with lady novelists of the day—Miss Braddon, Miss Broughton, and, gallantly added the author of *Daisy Miller*:

"Miss Betham-Edwards, whom I love best of all."

Had he dubbed me a second George Eliot on the spot, I could not have crowed more.

I give one of the last letters I received from him. The others appear in his Life.

LAMB HOUSE, RYE, SUSSEX,<br>*August* 16, 1911.

DEAR MISS BETHAM-EDWARDS,—All thanks for your kind note. I *am* back in England, after a whole year's absence and terrible period of six or seven months of extreme and confining illness, mostly in my bed, for six or seven months before that. I was spoiling for that dire collapse when we last communicated in the autumn of 1909. I was to have gone over to see you then, but was in the event unable either to go or to make you a sign. Then began the very bad time on which I hope my return to England now will have finally and strongly closed the gates. I will make you with pleasure that so long-delayed visit, but I will, by your leave, wait till the "holiday" (God save the mark!) turmoil of communication between this and Hastings shall have somewhat abated. It's a sorry squeeze now—and long drawn out with delays. I rejoice to infer that you remain stalwart and patient and good-humoured—as I try withal to do—even if we neither of us emulate the surprising Hale White.[1] This is disappointing of him— a false note in his fine figure. However! I shall make you a sign by and by and appear; and am all faithfully yours,

HENRY JAMES.

[1] Mark Rutherford, whose novels he admired. I forget to what incident this remark refers. Alas! I never saw him again.

Surrounded by its tiny burial yard, the Rye church lies in the very centre of the city, though hidden from profane eyes by the ivy-covered brick wall that surrounds it. Directly behind the church, with only its front visible from the street, as a wall encloses it also, stands a three-storied house of brick, with white stone trimmings and green window frames, from which swing outward, disclosing the leaded panes, old-fashioned blinds of the same color. To the left of the house as you face it, in the angle made by the street end and the church, you may catch a glimpse of a single story addition, dating back maybe 100 years, but with very modern windows, that look out upon a lovely garden behind the wall.

"This is Lamb House," said my friend, "and for many, many years it was the official home of the Mayor of Rye. The last Mayor, however, had a new modern little place of his own, so this lovely spot fell upon the market. Henry James discovered it one day during a roam through the town, and immediately leased it. He has been living here for two or three years now, alone, save for his butler and his housekeeper."

We ascended the four stone steps at the massive black oak door and sounded the lizard knocker. Instantly the door was swung open by a man whose every feature spoke the butler.

Yes, Mr. James was in.

We were ushered into a dainty little drawing-room, on the left of the door, carpeted with rugs of deep red, where we sat upon Louis Quinze chairs until, from some inner recess, emerged a man. He was dressed comfortably in striped trousers that touched the floor at his heels and a loose negligee shirt. Of a height a shade below medium, he looked a most ordinary person. His hair was streaked with gray, but not so thickly as his ragged, square-cut beard. Seeing us, his eyes assumed a light that spoke of gladness, and at once he took us by the arms and led us out of the neat, exact little drawing-room into the one-storied addition to the house that we had seen from the street as we mounted the steps to the doorway.

Henry James' brown eyes glanced with pride about the room, then turning to us he said, "Isn't this grand?" and stooping he flipped back a corner of the rug that my heel had scuffed up. "Now make yourselves comfortable, light a cigarette and let's talk. I have worked all day, and was about to go out for a little wheel ride when my man announced you. I am so glad you came; I was beginning to bore myself."

The cigarettes were offered. I noticed that Mr. James, when the ash had collected at the end of his would walk the length of the study and snip it out the open window. That act struck me as one cue to Henry James' manner, both as a man and as a literary artist.

There is no writer of the English language to-day who takes such infinite pains as Henry James. His sentences may be two pages long, but you will notice, despite this confusing fact, that his verbs are always of the same number as his nouns. His study looked as though he must have spent at least three hours, standing the books up vertically on the shelves and arranging his letters in little piles of the same size upon the three desks that stand before the windows. Each bit of rug fringe upon the floor of Henry James' study is in place. If you were to change the position of one book, the author would, while continuing to talk to you, nonchalantly step over to the case and put the book back where, to his mind, it belonged.

No, it isn't old-maidishness, it is simply an abnormally developed neatness, a neatness that appalled me, and struck me dumb. When I got to know James better, I told him so. He only laughed and said, "Well, a man gets into ways, you know; a man gets into ways."

The window at which Henry James does the greater part of his literary labor looks out upon the garden hidden from the street by the high brick wall of which I have spoken. There is a long expanse of turf as green as emerald, and in the centre a bed of brilliant scarlet flowers. Just outside the window an apple tree of years that go beyond three score and ten spreads forth its branches. Upon the writing desk, the day I called, there lay some fifteen sheets of manuscript written in the sprawling, scrawling hand that is the vexation of printers when any of Henry James' copy comes to them. That is the one incongruous characteristic of Henry James. With all his other neatnesses, he writes a hand that nigh appalls the reader. I have a letter from him before me now. The signature I know to be "Henry James." You might take it for Henrik Sienkiewicz.

There has been out, in England, not many weeks, a book by Mr. James entitled The Two Magics, and he is at work now upon a volume of short stories in the tenor of the two that comprise the former book.

"And when will it be ready?" I asked him.

"Oh, I never know," he said. "I work by easy stages."

Which is true. Now and again a book that bears his name appears. Once off the press, the author of it rushes for Italy to spend a month with Frank Marion Crawford, where he forgets that he writes for a living. Alone as he is, loving only his work and the people who take off their hats to him in the streets of Rye, Henry James is one of the gentlest spirits in the literary world to-day. You will be astonished possibly to know that his income from his writing is a scant three hundred pounds a year, though in spite of this, there has never come a man in need to Henry James to whom he has not offered a part of what he calls his own. Not so long ago a novelist in England died. He left two little children, absolutely alone in the world. One of that man's friends put by a little sum for them, and out of the kindness of his heart wrote to other literary men soliciting their help. He sought a maker of books, whom he knew to have an income of over twenty thousand pounds from his literary work. "Won't you aid these little folk?" he asked. Not one cent was forthcoming Henry James was written in the matter. By return mail came a check for fifty pounds, one-tenth of his whole year's income.

His wonderful neatness is one, the above recorded incident offers another, cue to the character of the man.

# Henry James and his Photographers

a) Alice Boughton, 'A Note by his Photographer', *Hound and Horn* (1934)

b) Alvin Coburn, *Men of Mark* (London: Duckworth & Co., 1913)

During Henry James's visit to the Unites States (1905–6) he sat for two well-known photographers, both of whom recorded their memories of these encounters. Alice Boughton (1865–1943) studied painting in Paris and Rome, and became a Fellow of the Photo-Secession, a society established by Alfred Stieglitz in order to promote innovative and experimental photography. For a while she worked in the studio of another successful female photographer, Gertrude Kasebier. She is typical of the group in her interest in techniques which compromise photographic realism. Boughton went on to photograph Henry James's brother William James in 1907. Her book, *Photographing the Famous*, was published in 1928.

Alvin Coburn (1882–1966) was another member of the Photo-Secession group, and became a successful photographer of celebrities including George Bernard Shaw and Thomas Hardy. Shaw described him as 'one of the most accomplished and sensitive artist-photographers now living' (Edel, v, p. 341). He explored the possibilities of nonrepresentational photography and in 1916 invented a device which Ezra Pound called a 'vortoscope', an arrangement of mirrors allowing him to take multiple-image photographs or 'vortographs' of objects such as lumps of wood.

Coburn photographed James in New York for *Century* magazine in 1905. In a letter to the literary agent James Brand Pinker, Henry James writes enthusiastically about the young photographer:

> Also, I am happy to say, I have a very good & right (& beautifully done) photographic portrait, at last, which I will bring you when I come. The gifted youth comes down next week again to do the House. (Horne, p. 436)

James commissioned Coburn to take a series of photographs to be used as frontispieces for the Collected Edition. In December 1906

James, clearly enthused by the project, wrote to Coburn congratulating him on the fine photographs he had taken in the Wallace Collection – the 2/6 was a tip for the attendant – and anticipating eagerly Coburn's trip to Venice in order to take photographs for *The Wings of the Dove*:

> My Dear A. L.!
> I rejoice in your good news & yearn over your visible results. Hooray for your fine day, your nine exposures, & the effect of your 2/6 (a postal order for which I by the way enclose). Make your Mother dress you warmly for the journey to Venice – which I think (I am in fact sure) you will, with the elasticity of youth, really enjoy. (Horne, pp. 443–4)

James's jaunty optimism was misplaced, for Coburn later wrote of the Venice trip in his autobiography: 'Never before or since have I felt so miserably cold and damp' (Horne, p. 443).

# A Note by His Photographer

Alice Boughton

HENRY JAMES was, I may truthfully say, the only sitter who ever terrified me. I was to do him for publication, and though the time was set for early afternoon, he did not come until nearly four o'clock. It was April, and a warm day, ending in a thunder shower, the sky getting blacker by the minute and the light going. Finally he came, dignified and impressive, with manners almost courtly, and wearing a top hat several sizes too big. I saw that he took in everything in the room, and his keen, keen eye followed me about as I moved around, trying for the best spot, and to squeeze out as much light as possible from the leaden sky. When I could no longer endure the eye, I went to the book-shelves and took down *The Amazing Marriage* and asked him to read while I got ready. He took the book but continued to watch me over the top, then I said, "Please pay no attention to me but read —really read, and I will tell you when I am ready." And so he did, and became so absorbed, that when I wanted him to look into the camera I failed to get his attention. For the third time I said, very loudly, "Mr. James, look into the camera!" He came to quickly, turned his head and uttered a sharp "Eh?" And there you are! At the time, my latest acquisition was a small painting of a mother and child by Arthur Davies. This was hanging near the door, and on his way out Mr. James stopped before it and looked at it a long time, bending forward, in his top hat, his stick behind him. "Just one more, please—I must do this, for you look like a Daumier!" He seemed really amused, but remained in the same position until I photographed him again. Then we shook hands and he departed. My assistant, who had none too much reverence in her makeup, looking out of the window after he had gone, said "He's trying to find the subway and he does look like the Mad Hatter." Not more than five or ten minutes after he had gone, Mr. Davies came in, and I told him about Mr. James standing in his top hat, hands behind him, examining the painting, and how he looked so like a Daumier picture. To which Mr. Davies replied, "Very tactful of you to tell him that!" "Why tactful?" "Because Mr. James has always been a great admirer of Daumier and years ago wrote an article about him for Harper's." It was luck, not tact, on my part.

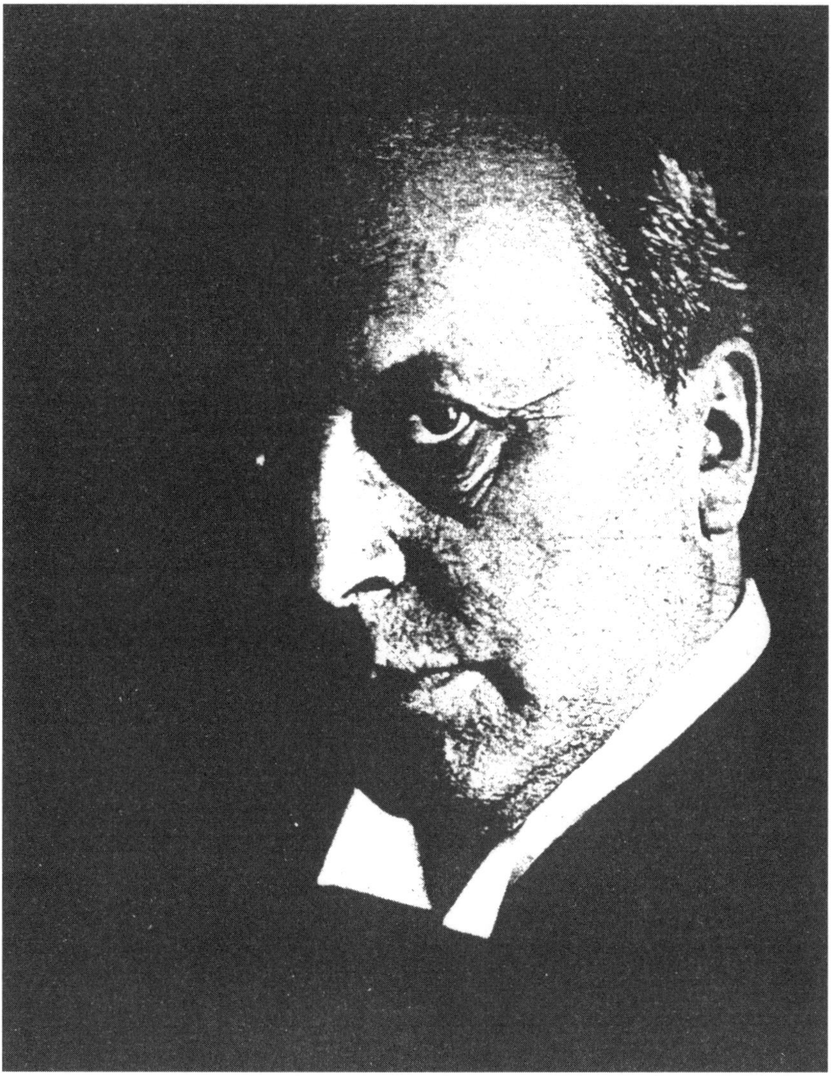

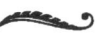

I made my first portrait of Henry James in New York on the twenty-sixth of April 1905, but the one reproduced in this volume was made at his home in Rye, over a year later. The late Richard Watson Gilder, at that time the Editor of the Century Magazine, gave me a letter of introduction to Mr. James, which I sent to him just on the eve of his departure for California. I received a pleasant letter asking me to write to him to an address in New York which he gave me, towards the end of April, and one day I received by way of reply a telegram asking me to come the next morning with my camera. Mr. James was stopping with friends in one of those dignified old " brown stone fronts " that are gradually being replaced by office buildings in that part of New York between Washington Square and the Plaza. Each year makes a change, and streets which one has known are often, after a comparatively short absence, altered beyond recognition. I made the acquaintance of Mr. James and took a number of photographs of him, and on my mentioning that I expected to return to England before very long, he very kindly invited me to come and see him in Rye. It was over a year, however, before the opportunity came for me to accept: part of the time he was away, and I made a journey to Italy and Sicily, and had a serious illness which nearly ended this volume when only a third of the portraits had been made. In June 1906, I went to the little town in Sussex where the grass grows up between the old-fashioned rounded paving-stones of the streets. It seems to have been passed by and forgotten by the modern rush and bustle, and it was here in the beautiful garden of the old-world house that I made the portrait of Mr. James in this volume, and also the one that is the frontispiece of the first volume of the collected edition of his works.

Having made the photograph for the first volume, it occurred to Mr. James that I might do some of the other illustrations for the edition, and so I did first one and then another, until we discovered that the better part of a year had passed and that I had made the entire series of frontispieces for the twenty-four volumes! This had necessitated journeys to Paris and Italy, and innumerable delightful rambles about London in the company of the author to Hampstead Heath, to Kensington, and also to St. John's Wood, where, getting hungry in our search for just the right picture for the second volume of "The Tragic Muse," we stopped at a baker's shop, the same shop I was told by my companion that he had known as a youth, and went on down the street munching Bath buns from a paper bag! Mr. James has immortalised our search for frontispieces in the Preface of the first volume of "The Golden Bowl" in the definitive edition in such a delightful way that there is really nothing further to be said about the matter. I cannot refrain from quoting one paragraph which sums up in crystallised form not only the essence of our pursuit of these pictures for his books, but also the production of any pictures whatsoever made by photography. He writes: "Both our limit and the very extent of our occasion, however, lay in the fact that, unlike wanton designers, we had not to 'create,' but simply to recognize—recognize, that is, with the last fineness." Mr. James, although he is not literally a photographer, must have, I believe, sensitive plates in his brain with which to record his impressions. He always knew exactly what he wanted, and what we did was to browse diligently until we found such a subject. It was a great pleasure to collaborate in this way, and I number the days thus spent among my choicest recollections.

It was at this time that I first met and photographed Arthur Symons. He was living at St. John's Wood, and his "Studies in Seven Arts" had just appeared. I have an inscribed copy which he gave me on the day I took him his portraits. I also showed him some of my photographs of London, and we came to talk of a volume to be called "London, a Book of Aspects," which he was to write and to which I was to contribute the pictures. This was eventually accomplished, but they did not appear together, and I very much fear they never will. The Symons' text was privately printed by my friend Mr. Edmund D. Brooks of Minneapolis, and as I read again the exquisite description of the Thames from Hungerford Bridge, I think of the night I took Mr. Symons there and rejoice that I was partly responsible for this gem of prose. We walked all the way from St. John's Wood through a thin mist which lessened as we got to the river, but which still made the distances mysterious. We leaned over the parapet of the bridge for I should say about half an hour. "The Surrey side is dark, with tall, vague buildings rising out of the mud on which a little water crawls : is it the water that moves or the shadows ? " is a passage that Whistler would have revelled in. " From one of the tallest chimneys a reddish smoke floats and twists like a flag" is a line that has a haunting beauty.

John S. Sargent I photographed in his studio in Chelsea. It was at the time that I was making the frontispieces for Mr. James, and knowing that they knew each other, I asked the latter for a letter of introduction. It was a very charming epistle and told that I had been labouring for him ceaselessly for months and as a recompense asked only for this letter. Needless to say it brought a favourable response, and an invitation to come with my camera on a certain morning, for who could refuse an invitation so charmingly worded as that which my good friend Mr. James wrote for me ? I found Mr. Sargent most friendly and willing to help me in every way to get my result. A portrait by photography needs more elaboration between the sitter and the artist than a painted portrait, and Mr. Sargent having had some experience in portraits himself realized this. To make satisfactory photographs of persons it is necessary for me to like them, to admire them, or at least to be interested in them. It is rather curious and difficult to exactly explain, but if I dislike my subject it is sure to come out in the resulting portrait. The camera is all recording and very sensitive to the slightest gradation of expression of the personality before it ; also the impression that I make on my sitter is as important as the effect he has on me. I make friends quickly and am interested in the mental alertness of the people I meet. You can know an artist or an author, to a certain extent, from his pictures or books before you meet him in the flesh, and I always try to acquire as much of this previous information as possible before venturing in the quest of great ones.

# Hugh Walpole, 'Henry James; A Reminiscence', *Horizon* (February 1940)

Sir Hugh Seymour Walpole (1884–1941) was one of several young men to whom James was romantically attached in his later years. Particularly important to him were the sculptor Hendrik Andersen and a young Irishman, Jocelyn Persse. His friendships with Persse and Walpole endured until his death and James left both men (as well as Lucy Clifford) £100 in his will. Walpole's affection and admiration for James are very apparent in this essay, as is his determination to paint a true picture of his friend. He feels that the real James has been obscured by the legend – 'he seems a mythical figure, like one of the Blake presences in *The Book of Job*' (p. 261).

Walpole was born in New Zealand but lived in England for most of his life. He published his first novel, *The Wooden Horse*, in 1909. His output was both prolific and varied – it included his series of semi-autobiographical novels about a boy named Jeremy, historical romances, most notably *Rogue Herries* (1930), as well as works of fantasy and horror. He was knighted in 1937.

He first became acquainted with Henry James after writing to introduce himself in 1908 – the two already had a number of mutual friends including A. C. Benson and the novelist Lucy Clifford. They met over dinner at the Reform Club, and Walpole recorded his first impressions of James in his diary:

> Dined with Henry James alone at the Reform Club. He was perfectly wonderful. By far the greatest man I have ever met – and yet amazingly humble and affectionate – absolutely delightful. (Edel, v, p. 407)

James was equally delighted with his new acquaintance and wrote to their mutual friend, A. C. Benson, thanking him for helping bring Walpole to his attention:

> It isn't only that I owe you a letter, but that I have exceedingly wanted to write it – ever since I began (too many weeks ago) to feel the value of the gift that you lately made me in the form of the acquaintance of delightful and interesting young Hugh Walpole ... I feel him at any rate an admirable young friend, of the openest mind and most attach-

ing nature, and anything I can ever do to help or enlighten, to guard or guide or comfort him, I shall do so with particular satisfaction, and with a lively sense of being indebted to you for the interesting occasion of it. (*Letters*, iv, pp. 522–3)

The ambitious and charming young writer soon became a close friend of James, and, according to Somerset Maugham, Walpole claimed that he once sexually propositioned James, but was refused. However James was clearly deeply attached to the younger novelist and this passionate fondness is reflected in his letters. James was less enthusiastic about Walpole's novels and in a letter written in 1910 takes him to task for the shortcomings of *Maradick at Forty* (1910):

> Your book has a great sense and love of life – but seems to me very nearly as irreflectively juvenile as the Trojans, and to have the prime defect of your having gone into a subject – i.e. the marital, sexual, bedroom relations of M and his wife – the literary man and his wife – since these *are* the key to the whole situation – which have to be tackled and faced to mean anything. You don't tackle and face them – you *can't* ... And you have never made out, recognized, nor stuck to, *the centre of your subject*. But can you forgive all this to your fondest old reaching-out-his-arms-to-you [H. J.?] (*Letters*, iv, p. 552)

According to Compton Mackenzie, when quizzed about his real opinion of Walpole's works Henry James confided that 'so far he had written absolutely nothing at all' (Andro Linklater, *Compton Mackenzie: A Life* (London: Chatto & Windus, 1987), p. 138).

'Henry James: A Reminiscence' is a warmly affectionate tribute which includes lively sketches of many of James's other close friends, including Gosse, Sturgis and Persse. Like Gosse, Walpole includes a version of James's mysterious 'figure at the window' anecdote which he associates more explicitly than Gosse with sexual frustration. (compare section 3). Walpole's friendship for James appears to have been tinged by competitiveness and jealousy, and he is alert to the perceived intellectual shortcomings of rivals (including Persse and even Wharton) and presents his own character and behaviour with a mixture of self-deprecation and vanity.

SIR HUGH WALPOLE
# HENRY JAMES
## A Reminiscence

I remember some years ago mentioning Henry James to a friend and hearing St. John Ervine's voice growling behind me: "Talking about that old bore again." Possibly at one time I did speak of James too often and, in any case, he would be altogether beyond Ervine's ken. But he—James, not Ervine—was so very much the greatest man I have ever known. That was my excuse: that I gave myself pleasure by thinking of him.

Nevertheless what wars can do to extend horizons! James died in the middle of the 1914-1918 War and now in the 1939-? War he seems a mythical figure, like one of the Blake presences in *The Book of Job*. It is in fact because of a legend that has grown up around him that I write these few words now. He wasn't, in reality, at all like the stuttering word-spinning priest of Nothingness that modern literary criticism pictures him.

The legend comes, I think, a good deal from Ford Madox Ford whose books of reminiscence were often fairy-tales—lively, entertaining, provocative and always romantic. It was, of course, perfectly true that James would stand at the windiest corner of the street and sustain one of his necromantic séances until a bad cold was inevitably caught by all. He was not aware that his long, slow, careful speech-windings were anything unusual or out of the way. I remember once, when staying with him at Rye, that, walking on a golf-course, we encountered two small children. James gave them some money with which to buy sweets but, when he had given it, began an oration to them as to what they should do with their money, the *kind* of sweets they should buy, the best time of the day for the consumption of sweets and so on. They listened for a long time, staring up into his smooth Abbé-like face, then cast the coins on the ground and ran, screaming.

He was greatly distressed by this. What had frightened them? What had they seen or heard?

Here I must explain my own status in regard to those high vague figures, so dim now and tenebrous, before 1914.

I see at this distance James, Gosse, Colvin, Hewlitt, Arthur Benson as beneficent witches from *Macbeth*.

Beneficent they certainly were, but for the rest the parallel is very close. As they stood screaming over the literary cauldron, the wind blowing up over the heath ' very nasty indeed ', each had, with several and individual pride, his own future Thane of Cawdor, and even, with a little necromancy, a possible King. It was a time when Literary reputations were of very much more importance than they are today. When James wrote his articles in *The Times* on " The Younger Novelists " there were battles of the most ferocious kind. Those named by him would have been triumphant indeed had they only been certain as to whether they were praised or blamed by him.

Gosse and Colvin were two rival witches, one thin, pink, precise and Puritan, the other piratical, feline, generous and wonderful company. Nature, who sees to everything, saw to it that Gosse should wear a black patch over one eye for several years before his death—just like John Silver!

Hewlitt was black, foreign-looking, sardonic, courageous, a grand man whose proper estimate has yet to be made.

They were all grand men and of a kindliness of heart that I do not find among many literary men today. But that is because literary men today are not expected to be anything but sensible—and as little in evidence as possible!

When I came to London in 1908 I was quite determined to get on and waste no time about it, but so soon as I met, through Robbie Ross, Wells and Max and Clutton Brock, I lost a great deal of my personal aggressiveness. I was so happy to be in the company of these great men that I truly did not think of myself at all. I went to Wells on Sunday in Hampstead and to Gosse on Sunday in Regent's Park. I had worshipped Arthur Benson at Cambridge and had watched with awe the wonderful mental processes of Percy Lubbock, Gazelee and Howard Sturgis. Sturgis was a stout old-maidish person with a very sharp tongue who worked at embroidering in his fine house in the country. He wrote *Belchamber*. I was terrified of him.

All these persons were kind to me because of my vitality. They all hoped that in time I might mature and learn some taste, discretion, wisdom. What they most of them lacked was this same physical vitality. If only I might combine it with a few brains! they murmured. I well remember eagerly breaking into a conversation between Benson and Lubbock as to the *real* meaning of the end of *The Wings of the Dove*. I highly, eloquently explained it. I can still see Benson's stare as the most sophisticated of cows might incredibly survey a gambolling, presumptuous calf.

There I met Henry James. Immature though I was I perceived instantly his inevitable loneliness. He was lonely in the first place because, an American, he was never really at home in Europe. Nor was he at home in America for when he was there he longed for the age, the quiet, the sophistications of Europe.

He was lonely in the second place because he was a spectator of life. He was a spectator because his American ancestry planted a reticent Puritanism in his temperament and this was for ever at war with his intellectual curiosity.

Sexually also he had suffered some frustration. What that frustration was I never knew but I remember his telling me how he had once in his youth in a foreign town watched a whole night in pouring rain for the appearance of a figure at a window. " That was the end . . ." he said, and broke off.

His passion for his friends—Lucy Clifford, Edith Wharton, Jocelyn Persse, Mrs. Prothero, among others—was the intense longing of a lonely man. It was most unselfish and noble. His love for his own relations, his brother William, his nephew, had a real pathos for although they beautifully returned it they could never be so deeply absorbed in him as he was in them. I went once to Brown's Hotel to say goodbye to him before his departure for America with William James who was very ill. While I was with him a message came and he hurried away. I waited and waited but no one came, so at last I started downstairs. I passed an open bedroom door and saw William lying on the floor and Henry standing over him. As I hurried down I caught an expression of misery and despair on Henry's face that I shall never forget.

It has become, in these fierce and bitter days, suspicious to speak of nobility of character but it must be risked when one speaks of Henry James. He had in relation with his friends so many things to put up with! First of all our intellects. Edith Wharton alone seemed to satisfy him intellectually and that I always thought odd for, with the exception of *Ethan Frome* I always considered her, and consider her still, a flashy, superficial novelist. But James was never a good critic of contemporary writers. "Poor, poor Conrad!" he would say. And he wrote of D. H. Lawrence "trailing in the dusty rear" in those famous *Times* articles. He could see little in the novels of E. M. Forster. Wells and Bennett were to him intolerably diffuse.

He did, quite naturally, wonder why novelists in general paid so little attention to form, did not consider more seriously their 'subjects', and so on. All this is, of course, generally known. What is *not* so generally known is that the failure of his own *Collected Edition* struck him a blow from which he never properly recovered.

The night when the gallery booed him at the first performance of *Guy Domville* and the days when he realized that the Collected Edition over which he had worked for years, re-writing the earlier novels, composing the marvellous Prefaces, was not only not selling but was also not reviewed—these were catastrophes for him. He was as little vain and conceited as any man, but his art was something that had a value and importance altogether outside himself and his own popularity.

Just as Wells hoped that, if he kept on long enough, human beings would learn some wisdom before it was too late, so James hoped, that if *he* kept on long enough, writers would learn something of the sacrifice and service and discipline that Art demanded. But of course no one learned anything: it has needed something very much more terrible than Wells' Encyclopædia and James' cadences to bring about a realization. . . .

So James fell back on his friends. I soon began to wonder at the contrast between the simplicity of his heart and the complexity of his brain. I knew him only after he had shaved his beard and Sargent's portrait in the National Portrait Gallery presents him exactly as he was except when in the company of his close friends. At parties and places where people gathered together he was as ceremonial as an Oriental and many people found it very tiresome to stand at attention and wait for the long unrolling of the sentences and think of something to say in reply that was not completely idiotic. But alone with the people he loved, his humour was over all and his tenderness beneficent.

He could not do too much for his friends, could not be too close to them, could not hear too many details of their daily lives. It mattered nothing to him if their tastes were not his if he loved them. Jocelyn Persse, for example, liked horses rather than the Arts and pretended none other, but Henry was never happier than when he was in Jocelyn's company.

My enthusiasms often exasperated him and once he was really angry, with a ferocity, over some would-be critical article of mine but he accepted me for better or worse and protected me often enough against the ill humours and scorns of others.

I look back to one especial case of protection that for me illuminates the whole distant scene with a nostalgic light. Some ten years ago I described it in a small privately-printed book and now, writing in a second war, the figures are yet more distantly removed, more ghostly but, for myself, more real.

It began with Henry James' Seventieth Birthday. His friends agreed to give him a replica of the Golden Bowl and his portrait painted by Sargent. A letter must be sent out asking for subscriptions. Edmund Gosse, as James' oldest literary friend, I as his youngest, were deputed to write and despatch this letter.

So soon as I heard of this I implored to be spared. I loved Gosse and was terrified of him. I was sure, in my heart, that I would make a mistake and then that cold, bitter anger would slay me—and I passionately did not want to be slain!

Henry James calmed my fears. He assured me that all would be well. He himself would see to it. So, after a beautiful letter had been composed by Gosse and a list of grand and memorable names compiled, I went down to the printers in the City to arrange for the printing and despatch. Henry James accompanied me " so that nothing might be wrong ".

Two days later I dined alone with Maurice Hewlitt. For one reason or another he did not at that time care for Gosse. He met me in the hall. His sardonic eye flashing, his little " goatee " pirouetting with pleasure on his elegant chin, he said, as he took my hand: " Dear Hugh, I knew that you were fond of me. But I did *not* know until this morning that Gosse was. In fact I thought the contrary. I have, however, received so affectionate a letter from Gosse and yourself that I am flattered and proud." My heart sank. Something dreadful had occurred. " For God's sake tell me," I murmured.

With delight he showed me the letter. James and I had forgotten altogether to fill in the names of those to whom the letter was sent. The letter, therefore began: " Dear " and ended: " We are, Dear, yours sincerely, Edmund Gosse, Hugh Walpole." And this to people as dignified, as unassailably great as John Morley and Mrs. Humphrey Ward!

Oh yes, Gosse was angry! I have his letter still.

But the real point of it is that Henry James took the

blame entirely upon himself and chose the reception day for the subscribers at Sargent's studio to explain the facts.

He stood beside the Portrait and, as each person approached, explained that it had been *his* fault and neither Gosse's nor mine that the names had been omitted. And his explanations took a very long time. And the queue grew ever longer and longer. And I stood for hours blushing and confused. It was an amazing scene but a beautiful one.

Time we are told is no longer Time. And so, at this moment, as I write, Henry, in his brown buff waistcoat, his dark elegant clothes, is standing beside his Portrait, courteous, anxious, explanatory, helping a young friend, apologizing for a breach in good manners that he had not himself committed.

[*Henry James*, 1898: *Lithograph drawing by Sir William Rothenstein.*

W. R.

# Muriel Draper, *Music at Midnight* (London: Heinemann, 1929)

The portrait of James included in *Music at Midnight* contrasts with Walpole's portrait through its elaboration of (and perhaps evasion of) reality (see the Introduction, p. xv). Muriel Draper, neé Sanders (1886–1952) was born in Massachusetts, but travelled widely in Europe before settling in London with her husband Paul Draper, a singer. Paul Draper's sister was the successful monologuist Ruth Draper, herself a friend of James. Muriel Draper was a prominent society hostess and her guests included Osbert Sitwell and Arthur Rubenstein as well as Henry James. Muriel later divorced her husband and returned to New York where she worked as an interior decorator and journalist. Here too she was a noted figure on the social scene, associated with artists and writers such as Carl Van Vechten. Her memoir, *Music at Midnight*, was published in 1929. Subsequently Draper developed a career as a lecturer, with a particular interest in women's rights and in 1942 helped established the National Council of American-Soviet Friendship. Her account of the older James is typical of portraits of the 'Master' in its focus on his impressive physical presence and extraordinary conversation. Her descriptions of the latter are especially baroque. Like Desmond MacCarthy (see section 7) she identifies a marked detachment in James which sets him apart from others while allowing him to observe and analyse them with exceptional acuity:

> He seemed to be possessed of an inner secret delight. It was as if he were playing a powerful game of the intellect, a game the rules of which he had himself invented, the honours of which were inalienably his. It appeared to absorb, amuse, and frighten him a little as well. Fright could have been lessened only at the cost of diminished absorption and amusement, a price he would not pay. (p. 278)

Many years passed and I saw him. Though by that time perfectly aware that still other geniuses were alive, I could never quite dissociate him in my mind from the reverent amazement I had felt upon first hearing that a genius lived in the same world with myself. He stood, a solid squared ashlar of wisdom, with a magnificently domed head atop, in Mrs. Napier's drawing-room. I walked up to him as bravely as I could, and we met. I told him how it had come about that he had entered my childhood as a uniquely living genius. He listened, with a burdened smile on his full lips, he who had to hear so much, and then it began. With a labouring that began stirring in the soles of his feet and worked up with Gargantuan travail through his knees and weighty abdomen to his heaving breast and strangled column of a throat, hoisted up by eyebrows raised high over the most steadily watching eyes I have ever looked into, he spoke. Having imaginatively participated in every effort his body had made, I was exhausted by the time the words were finally born, but had awaited them too long not to rally my attention when I heard them. They were about like this:

" My dear,—if I may call you so, my dear,—my even now—if I may yet further without permission so invade your, to be sure, passing years—child, my dear child. How right and yet how perfectly—if perfection can so enter, how perfectly wrong they both were, *you* were, all of you were."

I sat down. He sat beside me, and in a kind of mutual agony, we continued. I was later to discover that there was a way of communication with him that avoided all this amazing difficulty, which allowed the rich vein of his knowledge of human beings and events to flow unchecked, and which made listening to him and talking with him one of the rare values of my life, but this first time was agony. Again and again, in that memorable conversation, he would raise those cornices of eyebrows in an effort to build under them the astounding structure of words that so decorate his written page, and again and again would fail to find them. He seemed to listen for them with his own ear as eagerly as I with mine and even kept his eye alert for the possible shape of one that might appear by happy accident. Rejecting any less felicitous expression of his thought than one that would perfectly convey it, he would throw one phrase after the other away on its tremendous journey up from the soles of his feet. A patient " er—er—er " was the only sign that another had fallen by the wayside. Once, with temerity, I offered him one, almost beseeching him to take it as agreed counterfeit until such time as real gold would be passed over the counter and this soul-racking barter cease. But no, with the dear heavy smile leaving his lips to rest for a moment somewhere under his eyes, he cast it aside. So it went. The weight of his thought, the penetrating justice of his wit, and the impact of his whole being were such that I would gladly have suffered the pain of its articulation through years of silence, had they not seemed to me also " to be sure, passing years."

We spoke of America a little tentatively, a little anxiously and very tenderly. We spoke of families. He heard there was a son. He wanted to know him. He spoke of Ruth Draper and her talent. He spoke of music and asked to come one night to Edith Grove and listen. And then, as I pulled myself up and away from his side, fascinated, exhausted and adoring, his eyes travelled up from under the corniced eyebrows and saw my hat. It was a small white satin affair, with a cluster of tiny white love birds perched at the front. He gasped with horror, pointed his finger, and said with utter kindness, " My child " (it came easier this time), " my very dear child—the cruelty—ah! the cruelty of your hat! That once living—indeed yes, loving,—creatures should have been so cruelly separated by death to become so unhappily and yet, ah! how becomingly united on your hat."

I had met Henry James!

Soon after he came to lunch. Crossing the threshold of Edith Grove, he questioned me as to the tenure of the house. How long a lease did we have? How long would we be there? I told him it was a twenty-one year lease and he sighed ponderously, saying, " long enough to see me out, my child, long enough to see me out. Stay me out, I beg—stay me out." He had asked to be quite alone, so Paul and I sat one on either side of him and listened. After lunch he and I went down to the studio through the staircase where the lady harpist had remained so long imprisoned. He asked to see my son, so that young person was sent for. The Irish angel brought him. He was only a little over three years old, and a few days before had been found asleep with a copy of Henry James' book, *Letters of a Son and Brother*, under his pillow, his hand slipped in at a page upon which a photograph of Henry and his brother William standing close to their father's knee was reproduced. The tale of this incident had moved Henry James and when my son came into the room he fastened his accurately wise eye upon him. The Irish angel had brushed his hair until it shone, and dressed him in his best afternoon raiment, which consisted of long linen trousers and suspenders cut out of one piece, fastened to a frilled white shirt at the shoulders by a huge pearl button. The devouring James focused his gaze on that button and held it there as the child crossed the vast room. Spontaneously glad to see this grown-up who in his youth had leaned so trustingly at his father's knee, my son had entered the room on the run, but faced with the arresting force of his gaze, his footsteps faltered and his pace slackened, so that by the time he came to within three feet of Henry James, he stopped short and remained motionless as that great man began to address him:

"Ah! my boy. So here you come, faithfully—as it were, into view—with buttons, yes, *buttons*. . . ." Here he paused while the yeast that would eventually give rise to the ultimate word began to ferment in the soles of his feet: as it reached his knees he repeated, " Buttons, that are, er—that are—er er . . ." By this time the poor child was intimidated by the intensity of tone and started to back away, but Henry James began a circular movement in air with the fore-finger of his right hand and continued—" buttons that have been— er,"—and then in a shout of triumph—" *jettés-D*, as it were, yes, *jettés-d*,"—his voice quieting down as the word emerged—" *jettés-d* so rightly, so needfully, just there, my child," pointing in the direction of his small shoulder. But my child heard him not. At the first burst of " *jettés-D* " he had fled terrified from the room, the discovery of which brought forth from Henry James the mournful reflection, " Would I had remained a photograph! "

To be called to the telephone by Henry James was an experience in itself. The first time it happened I, all unaware, took up the receiver eagerly, and said, " Yes—this is Muriel."

A voice that began to twist and turn on the other end of the wire, finally spoke.

" Would you be—er—or rather, my dear,—er—my very dear, if I may call you so, child, would you,—not by—er—er *arrangement*, but would you—more—er— truthfully speaking—be—er—er— NATURALLY at home—this afternoon? "

By that time I was not naturally anything at all, and could only gasp, " Yes, always, any time—yes, yes, this afternoon at five, I will, unnaturally or not, be here— yes," and hung up.

It was during this visit that I learned to talk with him and listen to him, by withdrawing the weight of my attention from his actual words and the anguished facial contortions that accompanied them, and fastening it on the stream of thought itself. I even diverted my eyes from that part of his face from which the phrases finally emerged, namely, his mouth, and directed them to a more peaceful spot between his eyes, which I imagined to be the source of thought. It proved helpful. Evidently released from some bondage which the eye and ear of a listener imposed upon him, he seemed to feel more free. My effort to ignore the words and extract the meaning by a sense of weight, inflection and rhythm which emanated from him, removed the burden he must have felt at keeping me—anyone—waiting so long, and gradually the full current of his thought was flowing steadily, pauses and hesitations becoming accents rather than impediments. It proved an excellent *modus operandi* from then on, and only at those times when he had an audience of more than one person did the old difficulties return.

A few nights after this lunch, Thibaud, Casals, Rubinstein, Kochanski and Sczymanowski were to be the nucleus of an evening at Edith Grove; so I sent a line to Henry James informing him of this and begging him to join us. He arrived early and sledged down the stairs into the room with that extraordinary density of movement that was characteristic of him. He did not give the impression of putting one foot before the other in order to carry his torso and its appendages into the room. He came in all at once. Head, shoulders, arms, body, legs, arrived at the same time, inexorably displacing space and leaving an almost visible vacancy in his wake. Solid purposeful wholeness impelled him. All of him was there, nothing left behind. He sat quietly on the sofa beside me and awaited silently the first notes of the Brahms B Major piano trio which was to begin the evening's programme. As the music progressed and the incomparable tone of Casals' cello was heard in the short solo passage of the first movement, his solemnly searching eyes fastened on Casals' face, and he seemed to listen by seeing. When Thibaud began the brilliant passage for violin in the second movement, his eyes left Casals, as if he had drunk him all in through his organs of sight—music, hands, bowing and all—and centred on Thibaud, whom he watched with meticulous care during the whole second movement. During the last, when Arthur Rubinstein was burning the music out of the piano with an accumulating speed that left even those great artists somewhat breathless as he rushed them up to the high climax of the trio, H. J. turned the attention of his listening eyes toward him and kept it there until the performance came to a close. Only then did he begin to question me and greet one or two of the artists as they came up. His need for exhaustive analysis of each one separately made it difficult for him to take them in collectively, and I left him talking tortuous French to Thibaud. Casals was clamouring for the Schubert octet which was his favourite, as the Mendelssohn was Thibaud's. He said " one drank fresh milk" in listening to it, and could he please hear it through instead of playing it. As soon as enough artists had arrived to make up the necessary parts, it began—Thibaud, playing first violin, Bauer and Mr. Edith playing second violins, (yes, Bauer, whose great pleasure it occasionally was when circumstance allowed, to play the violin in a familiar work), one of the Goossens boys playing the horn, Harold Bauer's sister Gertrude playing viola, Rubio playing the cello, the faithful Watson double-bass, a friend of his snatched from back-stage by the method outlined earlier in this narrative, playing the clarinet. Casals sat on one side of me smoking a huge cigar, which was one of his few indulgences, and Henry James on the other, watching, absorbing, recording every gesture and expression of each man or woman in the room, and each object or article of furniture in relation to them. His appreciation was for and in terms of images. No sounds passed unsifted through that battery of image attention he so skilfully employed.

He seemed to be possessed of an inner secret delight. It was as if he were playing a powerful game of the intellect, a game the rules of which he had himself invented, the honours of which were unalienably his. It appeared to absorb, amuse, and frighten him a little as well. Fright could have been lessened only at the cost of diminished absorption and amusement, a price he would not pay.

He took in the fragile, minute and blonde delicacy of Mme. Thibaud as she sat in timorous sprightliness in an enveloping arm-chair of exaggerated dimensions, under a vase of heavily blossoming, formally petalled pink and white camellias, gleamily bending through glossy dark green leaves. He did not neglect Mme. Suggia, the gifted cello-playing friend of Casals before he married Susan Metcalf, who sat in swarthy gold, white, and black of dress and skin and hair on a small upright Chinese Chippendale chair in the spectral shadow of paling almond flowers. He saw the sensitive aloof protection which Karol Sczymanowski threw about himself and the life-defying speed with which Arthur Rubinstein managed to stand still. To all this he gave the steady orderliness of his observation. Toward the end of the octet, Montague Vert Chester, in a new pair of white gloves, came into the room. As was the unvarying custom at Edith Grove he crept into the nearest seat he could find without even a whisper of greeting, and listened with the rest. It happened to be a seat on the other side of James, and when the music was over, I presented him. " Chester, this is Mr. James." Chester, with a scant nod, for he had no social grace, said, " Good evening, Mr. James," and began to talk across him to me. Knowing that Chester admired his works with an enthusiasm that he rarely accorded anything other than music, my son and pink food, I added, " Mr. Henry James, Chester." He bounded up from his seat and shouted with excitement:

" What, not *the* Mr. James? Not the great Henry James?" offering his white-gloved hand in clumsy respect, eyes popping from his head.

From under benevolent eyebrows *the* Mr. James looked up and said soothingly, "Take it gently, my good man, take it gently."

Chester sat down.

In a corner formed by three folds of the Kien Lung screen, lighted by a Burmese chandelier of carved golden flowers and leaves that trailed downward over her head, I had placed a Chinese stone statue of the Goddess of Charity. Her right arm held in calm closeness to her side under gracious folds of modest raiment, her left hand outstretched to offer a basket filled with fruits of human kindness, eyes drooping to veil from sight the need of those who took, she stood forever in impassioned serenity. It was to Henry James a source of unending wonder. Standing before it the first time, he turned to me and chanted:

"Ah! My child, what a lesson to the artists of to-day on where to begin and to the women of to-day on where to leave off!"

So I could go on for pages, but as it has been decided that this is not to be a book on Henry James, I offer this mere handful of impressions caught at random from the air he so invaded. I will add that when fate determined that I should leave London during 1915, I saw him one long last time. Invalided, sickened with a grief and distress that need no retelling, he heard my news. After an unforgettable silence, he said:

"So my child, my very dear child, you are not staying me out. You are returning to that America we..."

Here his pause was not for lack of words, but the more

clearly to convey the unspoken. And then—" Ah! Well —perhaps one day I may do some faint far justice to all this,"—with a wave of the arm that encircled the room and everything that had ever been seen, spoken or heard in it—" to all this you have given me—to all this," and he patted my hand. He did not say goodbye, but sledged slowly, sadly, wisely out, the domed head disappearing like a silvered sun at the top of the stairs. I never saw him again.

# Interviews

a) Witter Bynner, 'A Word or Two with Henry James', *Critic* (February 1905)
b) Preston Lockwood, 'Henry James's First Interview', *New York Times* (21 March 1915)

Henry James expressed his exasperation with the media in a notebook entry made in 1887:

> One sketches one's age but imperfectly if one doesn't touch on that particular matter: the invasion, the impudence and shamelessness, of the newspaper and the interviewer, the devouring *publicity* of life, the extinction of all sense between public and private. (*Notebooks*, p. 40)

It is hardly surprising, given these views, that James granted very few interviews, and these only with the greatest reluctance. One of James's American publishers, George Harvey, persuaded him to give the first – this was 'Henry James in the Serene Sixties' by Florence Brooks which was published in the *New York Herald* in 1904.

The second was with Witter Bynner (1881–68), a poet and man of letters whose 'interview' with James was a record of previous conversations which James reluctantly allowed him to publish in this form. In fact James's supposed parting remarks are lifted almost verbatim from a letter written by James to Bynner.

> I have a constituted and systematic indisposition to 'having anything to do,' myself, personally, with anything in the nature of an interview, report, reverberation; that is to adopting, endorsing, or in any way otherwise taking to myself, anything that anyone may be presumed to have contrived to gouge, as it were, out of me. It has, for me, nothing to do with *me – my* me at all; but only with the other person's equivalent for that mystery, whatever it may be; and thereby *his* little affair exclusively. (Letter to Witter Bynner (24 December 1904). Houghton Library, Harvard University, bMS Am 1891.19:14)

James agreed to be interviewed by Preston Lockwood in order to publicise his work with the American Volunteer Motor Ambulance Corps. Henry James disapproved of the first draft and dictated a revised version to Lockwood. Realising this perhaps reinflects our impression of the interview, making us aware of how carefully and subtly James controlled his publicity, contriving a kind of struggle between the interviewer and interviewee (with James wanting to talk only about the War opposed by Lockwood who wants to draw him out about literary matters). Although James seems to lapse involuntarily into discussion of literature and language in fact he was fully in control of the interview's final form. As Olga Antsyferova observes, 'in this publication Henry James accepts his public image as a recluse and enemy of the press. But at the same time he masterfully and self-consciously plays with that image' ('Three Interviews of Henry James: Mastering the Language of Publicity', *The Henry James Review*, 22:1 (2001), p. 87).

# A Word or Two with Henry James

### By WITTER BYNNER

MR. JAMES was in New York for practically the first time in almost twenty years. As we walked he told me of his first flying visit a month or two ago, and thence the talk led to various topics:

"My renewal of acquaintance with New York was not to begin with altogether happy. This second visit is more satisfactory than that first pause of a day or two. I arrived in the sultry last part of August and was absolutely overwhelmed with the heat of the city and its other terrors. It was not at all the place I had known as a boy.

"My friends elected luckily to bring me straightway to the Players' Club, which I then thought and think still an oasis of quietness and atmosphere. It suggested to me, as I looked about, the Garrick Club in London and its fine collection of paintings. Amid the abundance of portraits and photographs in the Players', I came upon a case of daguerreotypes full of faces so many of which were familiar to me, that I realized I must have been fortunate enough as a boy to be in the hands of parents who were fond of the theatre. They must have taken my brother and me to the playhouse rather prematurely, I judge, else I should not have known all those faces and recovered so many half-lost sensations. Leaning stiffly on pillars for instance there were two girls with long hair, the Bateman sisters, whom I used to see on the stage. I remembered them, of course, the better, in having known them, since those times, as two very charming women in England. But there were others, such as the Florences, who once impressed me with their singing; Maggie Mitchell, over whom I went fantastically mad, though she was undoubtedly a barbarian and would nowadays be taken for such; and there was one woman with the face and curls of a school-mistress, draped in some ghastly pseudo-classic hangings short at her shapeless knees, whom I indubitably once took with admiring seriousness. Those were emphatic events in my boyhood, those visits to the theatre. I remember wondering how I could possibly live the time through from a Tuesday to a Friday, and then, when once I was seated in the theatre with my eyes on the old green curtain, feeling quite convinced that in the few minutes before that curtain should rise, I was doomed to be removed by accident or death or some unforeseen punishment. Those were palpitations that are immemorable; I seem hardly to have been done with them yesterday.

"Equally as recent seem the old sensations produced on me by my previous life in New York. Gramercy Park and such other places as I found unchanged stand about me this time and give me the same sense of existence as though it were last week instead of twenty years ago that I was calling on a relative or on the way to my own home. I was born in Washington Place and lived afterwards in Fourteenth Street near Sixth Avenue. Those parts of the town are, of course, all gone,—that is, as I knew them. I cannot give you an inkling of what a queer, ghostly, melancholy experience it is to go about a town and find here and there a piece of it, a fragment of it, so to speak, with great stretches between, where it has crumbled away and been replaced by size and strangeness. Suddenly while walking along, as we are walking now, I will come upon a house, or a block of houses or even a section, unchanged, and will discover and snugly recognize, be aware of the old town again, only to lose it all the next minute and to seem almost not on *terra firma*.

"Naturally I cannot know in a day what there is to be known about New York; even to know again what I used to know about it would take many days. Although I have an exemplary memory for rubbish, more important facts do not seem to stay by me. Not that I must complain of my memory; I suppose it has served me well, accurately, ardently for the writing of picturesque trash. During that day or two in New York before I left for Boston, I had, for instance, in the Players' I believe, a dish that I have not tasted in over sixteen years and remember, not only as an American food but, if I mistake not, as an idiosyncrasy of New York — brandied peaches!

"In the Players' Club, as in other New York clubs (and there are so many!) I was impressed with the sociability of club life here in America. The clubs in London, as I at least have observed them, serve purposes rather of utility and political coagulation than of consociation. Men take meals at their clubs in London, it strikes me, much as they would eat at a small and absolutely nice hotel, whereas here I notice that you eat in groups and have altogether amiable, chatty times together. That's the point,—you are more gregarious, more sociable at your clubs, more *en famille*.

"After the shock of New York in those one or two hot days, I was glad to be back again in Boston, the city with the charm exclusively its own. Its distinction is, of course, its oneness, its completeness, its homogeneity, qualities it has retained almost precisely as it had them when I was a boy, and it was a rural, or rather a rustic city, the conservative, collective and representative capital of New England. One feels, to be sure, the disadvantages of such advantage. Boston's standard of comparison is bounded entirely by its own precincts. It is given to bidding you to swan and setting you goose. But this very stiffness, stuffiness, this very inaccessibility to a breath of outer air, produces, in however close an atmosphere, a demeanor of self-respect and of patrician dignity.

"How many men, by the bye, New England contributes to New York, and how few New York to New England! It would seem to me that, when I was a boy, not so many would leave us for New York. I remember feeling the proximity in Boston of its imposing figures, with most if not all of whom I came, through my father, in some touch, except, I believe, with poor Hawthorne. My father used to take me now and again to luncheons of the Saturday Club, active, at that time, with its gifted founders.

"Writing seems nowadays so different a matter from what it then was. I judge it may have come to much the same pass with you in America as with us in England, where training in journalism and, before that, training in public schools, has given, to a multitude, a sort of pseudo-form, a largeness, looseness, and elasticity of talk which has flooded the country with an enormous sea of chatter. As soon as any man has anything at all to say to anybody, it is puffed about the country in distended and distorted shape. To blame for this, of course, there is the accessibility of print on the one hand, and the dissemination of it on the other. All this chatter must have its uses. There must be a public for it. Indeed I have a reason or two to believe there persists a public for it.

"But I must make no statements! Sometimes I think I shall never speak again; particularly, that is, when some remark or other which I have made in all obviousness, is fostered, to my detriment, annoyance, and ill-temper by persons who have mistakenly interpreted it as a clever saying. I had that trial, for instance, with a chance and simple remark about my friend, Henry Harland. I make mention of it since the ghost of its murdered sense has pursued me even to America. With somebody of presumable intelligence, I was speaking of Harland's last three books and, in common with all the world, was admiring his ability to make one situation serve him thrice. I stated the mere fact that in his first book a nobly-descended young Englishman hires a castle of an Italian or Austrian princess and that the two fall in love, that in his second book, the princess hires the house of the nobly-descended young Englishman and that the two fall in love, and that in the third book, the princess and the nobly descended young Englishman are together hiring the same house and that the two fall in love. It is as though there were a red glass, a blue glass, and a green glass, rearranged in various order. And to the artist who can rearrange the combination with, each of three times, an equally charming effect, there is deference. Nothing in what I said is to be translated beyond appreciation of Harland's handling of his material, which, after all, is the material he knows and loves and can write best about. One may be entertained with his skill of trickery, but the man who laughs aloud at my little word of observation is a silly donkey.

"There is something wonderfully engaging in Harland's fresh boyishness. Never so young as with pen in hand, he is, after all, the eternal boy! It is a disappointment to me that now when I have come to America he has returned again to England. He desired me to visit him in his beloved Norwich and I should so much have liked to see him there.' Probably no one ever bore towards Norwich so strong an affection as Harland's for the town. Probably Norwich feels that in his love for her there is untoward excess — something not wholly proper, not wholly licit.

"The poor man has not of late been well. It was suggested to me that he should seclude himself for a period in one or another of the dry Western States, but it is altogether likely that the mental emigration, segregation, deprivation therein would be too much; he could not be without his grand duchesses and his princesses and his nobly-descended young men.

"Partly it's a great compliment to his books that I remember them so clearly; for, on the whole, I seldom can recollect as stories even the books that I most enjoy. On the other hand, for my comfort on this score, I am convinced that many of the best effects derived from reading or, it may be, from experience, come to us by a process quite distinct from that of remembrance. Germs of evil influence we remember all too clearly, but salutary effects softly enter into us without our realizing just how or when. One does not much remember the plot of a book by Meredith, for instance, but looks back on it, finds retrospect, retains vision, in something deeper than memory.

"I believe this is the afternoon when I am to be taken to hear 'Parsifal,' to which I have agreed to go on the condition that I be not expected to return for the second instalment."

He relieved me with the dexterity of a pickpocket, while we shook hands, of my scruples as a highwayman:

"May I add, since you spoke of having been asked to write something about me, that I have a constituted and systematic indisposition to having anything to do myself personally with anything in the nature of an interview, report, reverberation, that is, to adopting, endorsing, or in any other wise taking to myself anything that any one may have presumed to contrive to gouge, as it were, out of me? It has, for me, nothing to do with *me—my* me, at all; but only with the other person's equivalent for that mystery, whatever it may be. Thereby if you find anything to say about our apparently blameless time together,—it is your little affair exclusively."

## HENRY JAMES'S FIRST INTERVIEW

Noted Critic and Novelist Breaks His Rule of Years to Tell of the Good Work of the American Ambulance Corps.

By Preston Lockwood.

ONE of the compensations of the war, which we ought to take advantage of, is the chance given the general public to approach on the personal side some of the distinguished men who have not hitherto lived much in the glare of the footlights. Henry James has probably done this as little as any one; he has enjoyed for upward of forty years a reputation not confined to his own country, has published a long succession of novels, tales, and critical papers, and yet has apparently so delighted in reticence as well as in expression that he has passed his seventieth year without having responsibly "talked" for publication or figured for it otherwise than pen in hand.

Shortly after the outbreak of the war Mr. James found himself, to his professed great surprise, Chairman of the American Volunteer Motor Ambulance Corps, now at work in France, and to-day, at the end of three months of bringing himself to the point, has granted me, as a representative of THE NEW YORK TIMES, an interview. What this departure from the habit of a lifetime means to him he expressed at the outset:

"I can't put," Mr. James said, speaking with much consideration and asking that his punctuation as well as his words should be noted, "my devotion and sympathy for the cause of our corps more strongly than in permitting it thus to overcome my dread of the assault of the interviewer, whom I have deprecated, all these years, with all the force of my preference for saying myself and without superfluous aid, without interference in the guise of encouragement and cheer, anything I may think worth my saying. Nothing is worth my saying that I cannot help myself out with better, I hold, than even the most suggestive young gentleman with a notebook can help me. It may be fatuous of me, but, believing myself possessed of some means of expression, I feel as if I were sadly giving it away when, with the use of it urgent, I don't greatefully employ it, but appeal instead to the art of somebody else."

It was impossible to be that "somebody else," or, in other words, the person privileged to talk with Mr. James, to sit in presence of his fine courtesy and earnestness, without understanding the sacrifice he was making, and making only because he had finally consented to believe that it would help the noble work of relief which a group of young Americans, mostly graduates of Harvard, Yale, and Princeton, are carrying on along their stretch of the fighting line in Northern France.

Mr. James frankly desired his remarks to bear only on the merits of the American Volunteer Motor Ambulance Corps. It enjoys today the fullest measure of his appreciation and attention; it appeals deeply to his benevolent instincts, and he gives it sympathy and support as one who has long believed, and believes more than ever, in spite of everything, at this international crisis, in the possible development of "closer communities and finer intimacies" between America and Great Britain, between the country of his birth and the country, as he puts it, of his "shameless frequentation."

There are many people who are eloquent about the war, who are authorities on the part played in it by the motor ambulance and who take an interest in the good relations of Great Britain and the United States; but there is nobody who can tell us, as Mr. James can, about style and the structure of sentences, and all that appertains to the aspect and value of words. Now and then in what here follows he speaks familiarly of these things for the first time in his life, not by any means because he jumped at the chance, but because his native kindness, whether consciously or unconsciously, seemed so ready to humor the insisting inquirer.

"It is very difficult," he said, seeking to diminish the tension so often felt by a journalist, even at the moment of a highly appreciated occasion, "to break into graceful license after so long a life of decorum; therefore you must excuse me if my egotism doesn't run very free or my complacency find quite the right turns."

He had received me in the offices of the corps, businesslike rooms, modern for London, low-ceiled and sparely furnished. It was not by any means the sort of setting in which as a reader of Henry James I had expected to run to earth the author of "The Golden Bowl," but the place is, nevertheless, today, in the tension of war time, one of the few approaches to a social resort outside his Chelsea home where he can be counted on. Even that delightful Old World retreat, Lamb House, Rye, now claims little of his time.

The interviewer spoke of the waterside Chelsea and Mr. James's long knowledge of it, but, sitting not overmuch at his ease and laying a friendly hand on the shoulder of his tormentor, he spoke, instead, of motor ambulances, making the point, in the interest of clearness, that the American Ambulance Corps of Neuilly, though an organization with which Richard Norton's corps is in the fullest sympathy, does not come within the scope of his remarks.

"I find myself Chairman of our Corps Committee for no great reason that I can discover save my being the oldest American resident here interested in its work; at the same time that if I render a scrap of help by putting on record my joy even in the rather ineffectual connection so far as 'doing' anything is concerned, I needn't say how welcome you are to my testimony. What I mainly seem to grasp, I should say, is that in regard to testifying at all unlimitedly by the aid of the newspapers, I have to reckon with a certain awkwardness in our position. Here comes up, you see, the question of our reconciling a rather indispensable degree of reserve as to the detail of our activity with the general American demand for publicity at any price. There are ways in which the close presence of war challenges the whole claim for publicity; and I need hardly say that this general claim has been challenged, practically, by the present horrific complexity of things at the front, as neither the Allies themselves nor watching neutrals have ever seen it challenged before. The American public is, of course, little used to not being able to hear, and hear as an absolute right, about anything that the press may suggest that it ought to hear about; so that nothing may be said ever to happen anywhere that it doesn't count on having reported to it, hot and hot, as the phrase is, several times a day. We were the first American ambulance corps in the field, and we have a record of more than four months' continuous service with one of the French armies, but the rigor of the objection to our taking the world into our intimate confidence is not only shown by our still unbroken inability to report in lively installments, but receives also a sidelight from the fact that numerous like private corps maintained by donations on this side of the sea are working at the front without the least commemoration of their deeds—that is, without a word of journalistic notice.

"I hope that by the time these possibly too futile remarks of mine come to such light as may await them Mr. Norton's report of our general case may have been published, and nothing would give the committee greater pleasure than that some such controlled statement on our behalf, best proceeding from the scene of action itself, should occasionally appear. The ideal would, of course, be that exactly the right man, at exactly the right moment, should report exactly the right facts, in exactly the right manner, and when that happy consummation becomes possible we shall doubtless revel in funds.''

Mr. James had expressed himself with such deliberation and hesitation that I was reminded of what I had heard of all the verbal alterations made by him in novels and tales long since published; to the point, we are perhaps incorrectly told of replacing a "she answered" by a "she indefinitely responded."

I should, indeed, mention that on my venturing to put to Mr. James a question or two about his theory of such changes he replied that no theory could be stated, at any rate in the off-hand manner that I seemed to invite, without childish injustice to the various considerations by which a writer is moved. These determinant reasons differ with the context and the relations of parts to parts and to the total sense in a way of which no a priori account can be given.

"I dare say I strike you," he went on, "as rather bewilderedly weighing my words; but I may perhaps explain my so doing very much as I the other day heard a more interesting fact explained. A distinguished English naval expert happened to say to me that the comparative non-production of airships in this country indicated, in addition to other causes, a possible limitation of the British genius in that direction, and then on my asking him why that class of craft shouldn't be within the compass of the greatest makers of sea-ships, replied, after brief reflection: 'Because the airship is essentially a bad ship, and we English can't make a bad ship well enough.' Can you pardon," Mr. James asked, " my making an application of this to the question of one's amenability or plasticity to the interview? The airship of the interview is for me a bad ship, and I can't make a bad ship well enough."

Catching Mr. James's words as they came was not very difficult; but there was that in the manner of his speech that cannot be put on paper, the delicate difference between the word recalled and the word allowed to stand, the earnestness of the massive face and alert eye, tempered by the genial " comment of the body," as R. L. Stevenson has it.

Henry James does not look his seventy years. He has a finely shaped head, and a face, at once strong and serene, which the painter and the sculptor may well have liked to interpret. Indeed, in fine appreciation they have so wrought. Derwent Wood's admirable bust, purchased from last year's Royal Academy, shown by the Chantrey Fund, will be permanently placed in the Tate Gallery, and those who fortunately know Sargent's fine portrait, to be exhibited in the Sargent Room at the San Francisco Exhibition, will recall its having been slashed into last year by the militant suffragettes, though now happily restored to such effect that no trace of the outrage remains.

Mr. James has a mobile mouth, a straight nose, a forehead which has thrust back the hair from the top of his commanding head, although it is thick at the sides over the ears, and repeats in its soft gray the color of his kindly eyes. Before taking in these physical facts one receives an impression of benignity and amenity not often conveyed, even by the most distinguished. And, taking advantage of this amiability, I asked if certain words just used should be followed by a dash, and even boldly added: " Are you not famous, Mr. James, for the use of dashes? "

" Dash my fame! " he impatiently replied. " And remember, please, that dogmatizing about punctuation is exactly as foolish as dogmatizing about any other form of communication with the reader. All such forms depend on the kind of thing one is doing and the kind of effect one intends to produce. Dashes, it seems almost platitudinous to say, have their particular representative virtue, their quickening force, and, to put it roughly, strike both the familiar and the emphatic note, when those are the notes required, with a felicity beyond either the comma or the semicolon; though indeed a fine sense for the semicolon, like any sort of sense at all for the pluperfect tense and the subjunctive mood, on which the whole perspective in a sentence may depend, seems anything but common. Does nobody ever notice the calculated use by French writers of a short series of suggestive points in the current of their prose? I confess to a certain shame for my not employing frankly that shade of indication, a finer shade still than the dash. * * * But what on earth are we talking about? " And the Chairman of the Corps Committee pulled himself up in deprecation of our frivolity, which I recognized by acknowledging that we might indeed hear more about the work done and doing at the front by Richard Norton and his energetic and devoted co-workers. Then I plunged recklessly to draw my victim.

"May not a large part of the spirit which animates these young men be a healthy love of adventure?" I asked.

The question seemed to open up such depths that Mr. James considered a moment and began:

" I, of course, don't personally know

many of our active associates, who naturally waste very little time in London. But, since you ask me, I prefer to think of them as moved, first and foremost, not by the idea of the fun or the sport they may·have, or of the good thing they may make of the job for themselves, but by that of the altogether exceptional chance opened to them of acting blessedly and savingly for others, though indeed if we come to that there is no such sport in the world as so acting when anything in the nature of risk or exposure is attached. The horrors, the miseries, the monstrosities they are in presence of are so great surely as not to leave much of any other attitude over when intelligent sympathy has done its best.

" Personally I feel so strongly on everything that the war has brought into question for the Anglo-Saxon peoples that humorous detachment or any other thinness or tepidity of mind on the subject affects me as vulgar impiety, not to say as rank plasphemy; our whole race tension became for me a sublimely conscious thing from the moment Germany flung at us all her explanation of her pounce upon Belgium for massacre and ravage in the form of the most insolent, 'Because I choose to, damn you all!' recorded in history.

" The pretension to smashing world rule by a single people, in virtue of a monopoly of every title, every gift and every right, ought perhaps to confound us more by its grotesqueness than to alarm us by its energy; but never do cherished possessions, whether of the hand or of the spirit, become so dear to us as when overshadowed by vociferous aggression. How can one help seeing that such aggression, if hideously successful in Europe, would, with as little loss of time as possible, proceed to apply itself to the American side of the world, and how can one, therefore, not feel that the Allies are fighting to the death for the soul and the purpose and the future that are in *us*, for the defense of every ideal that has most guided our growth and that most assures our unity?

" Of course, since you ask me, my many years of exhibited attachment to the conditions of French and of English life, with whatever fond play of reflection and reaction may have been involved in it, make it inevitable that these countries should peculiarly appeal to me at the hour of their peril, their need and their heroism, and I am glad to declare that, though I had supposed I knew what that attachment was, I find I have any number of things more to learn about it. English life, wound up to the heroic pitch, is at present most immediately before me, and I can scarcely tell you what a privilege I feel it to share the inspiration and see further revealed the character of this decent and dauntless people.

" However, I am indeed as far as you may suppose from assuming that what you speak to me of as the 'political' bias is the only ground on which the work of our corps for the Allies should appeal to the American public. Political, I confess, has become for me in all this a loôse and question-begging term, but if we must resign ourselves to it as explaining some people's indifference, let us use a much better one for inviting their confidence. It will do beautifully well if givers and workers and helpers are moved by intelligent human pity, and they are with us abundantly enough if they feel themselves simply roused by, and respond to, the most awful exhibition of physical and moral anguish the world has ever faced, and which it is the strange fate of our actual generations to see unrolled before them. We welcome any lapse of logic that may connect inward vagueness with outward zeal, if it be the zeal of subscribers, presenters or drivers of cars, or both at once, stretcher-bearers, lifters, healers, consolers, handy Anglo-French interpreters, (these extremely precious,) smoothers of the way; in short, after whatever fashion. We ask of nobody any waste of moral or of theoretic energy, nor any conviction of any sort, but that the job is inspiring and the honest, educated man a match for it.

"If I seem to cast doubt on any very driving intelligence of the great issue as a source of sympathy with us, I think this is because I have been struck, whenever I have returned to my native land, by the indifference of Americans at large to the concerns and preoccupations of Europe. This indifference has again and again seemed to me quite beyond measure or description, though it may be in a degree suggested by the absence throughout the many-paged American newspaper of the least mention of a European circumstance unless some not-to-be-blinked war or revolution, or earthquake or other cataclysm has happened to apply the lash to curiosity. The most comprehensive journalistic formula that I have found myself, under that observation, reading into the general case is the principle that the first duty of the truly appealing sheet in a given community is to teach every individual reached by it—every man, woman and child—to count on appearing there, in their habit as they live, if they will only wait for their turn.

"However," he continued, "my point is simply my plea for patience with our enterprise even at the times when we can't send home sensational figures. 'They also serve who only stand and wait,' and the essence of our utility, as of that of any ambulance corps, is just to be there, on any and every contingency, including the blessed contingency of a temporary drop in the supply of the wounded turned out and taken on—since such comparative intermissions occur. Ask our friends, I beg you, to rid themselves of the image of our working on schedule time or on guarantee of a maximum delivery; we are dependent on the humors of battle, on incalculable rushes and lapses, on violent outbreaks of energy which rage and pass and are expressly designed to bewilder. It is not for the poor wounded to oblige us by making us showy, but for us to let them count on our open arms and open lap as troubled children count on those of their mother. It is now to be said, moreover, that our opportunity of service threatens inordinately to grow; such things may any day begin to occur at the front as will make what we have up to now been able to do mere child's play, though some of our help has been rendered when casualties were occurring at the rate, say, of 5,000 in twenty minutes, which ought, on the whole, to satisfy us. In face of such enormous facts of destruction—"

Here Mr. James broke off as if these facts were, in their horror, too many and too much for him. But after another moment he explained his pause.

"One finds it in the midst of all this as hard to apply one's words as to endure one's thoughts. The war has used up words; they have weakened, they have deteriorated like motor car tires; they have, like millions of other things, been more overstrained. and knocked about and voided of the happy semblance during the last six months than in all the long ages before, and we are now confronted with a depreciation of all our terms, or, otherwise speaking, with a loss of expression through increase of limpness, that may well make us wonder what ghosts will be left to walk."

This sounded rather desperate, yet the incorrigible interviewer, conscious of the wane of his only chance, ventured to glance at the possibility of a word or two on the subject of Mr. James's present literary intentions. But the kindly hand here again was raised, and the mild voice became impatient.

"Pardon my not touching on any such irrelevance. All I want is to invite the public, as unblushingly as possible, to take all the interest in us it can; which may be helped by knowing that our bankers are Messrs. Brown Brothers & Co., 59 Wall Street, New York City, and that checks should be made payable to the American Volunteer Motor Ambulance Corps."

# Obituaries

a) *Daily Telegraph* (29 February 1916)
b) *The Times* (29 February 1916)
c) *Daily Mail* (29 February 1916)

As so many of the pieces included in this volume reveal, the last days of Henry James were clouded by his great sorrow over the War, and his frustration at the American government's supine attitude towards the struggle, a frustration which eventually led him to renounce his American citizenship. His great friend Edith Wharton gives a moving account of James's final illness in her memoir *A Backward Glance*:

> His dying was slow and harrowing. The final stroke had been preceded by one or two premonitory ones, each causing a diminution just marked enough for the still conscious intelligence to register it, and the sense of disintegration must have been tragically intensified to a man like James, who had so often and deeply pondered on it, so intently watched for its first symptoms. He is said to have told his old friend Lady Prothero, when she saw him after the first stroke, that in the very act of falling (he was dressing at the time) he heard in the room a voice which was distinctly, it seemed, not his own, saying: 'So here it its at last, the distinguished thing!' The phrase is too beautifully characteristic not to be recorded. He saw the distinguished thing coming, faced it, and received it with words worthy of all his dealings with life.
>
> But what really gave him his death-blow was the war. He struggled through two years of it, then veiled his eyes from the endless perspective of destruction. It was the gesture of Agamemnon, covering his face with his cloak before the unbearable. (Wharton, pp. 366–7)

The three obituaries reprinted here form an interesting contrast. All three writers acknowledge the difficulties of James's writings but whereas the obituaries in *The Times* and the *Telegraph* are respectfully appreciative of his works, the *Daily Mail* piece is rather more caustic in tone, observing that: 'Like caviare, Mr. James is loved by people who have acquired the taste and by people who think such a taste the right thing to acquire' (p. 301).

# DEATH OF MR. HENRY JAMES

## FAMOUS NOVELIST.

We deeply regret to announce the death of Mr. Henry James, O.M., the well-known novelist, which occurred last night at his residence, 21, Carlyle-mansions, Chelsea. In the latter part of last year Mr. James, who was 72, suffered a stroke, and had since been in a very precarious condition of health. Following upon his naturalisation as a British subject last July, and his avowed sympathies with the British cause in the war, Mr. James received in the New Year honours list the Order of Merit, an opportune tribute to his distinguished place in literature.

Although born and brought up in the United States, Mr. Henry James was more English than American, and, perhaps, more cosmopolitan than either. He wrote novels both of English and American life, but in essentials he belonged to the Old World rather than the New. He was content to receive his "impressions" in any gracefully ordered community, but most congenial to him was that refinement and mellowness of the social arts which is to be found more richly in old civilisations. France lent him artistic inspiration. England was his home. In Italy he was a frequent sojourner. His art, like that of J. M. Whistler, another American, who lived and worked in England, was far from expressing the characteristic ideals of the country that gave him birth. In their subtlety, delicacy of technique, their aloofness from obvious and traditional forms of art, the writer and the painter had much besides nationality in common.

Henry James was born in New York on April 15, 1843. His father, the Rev. Henry James, was a man of great charm of disposition, and a picturesque and original writer on theology. He has been described as a Swedenborgian, but his beliefs were not easily classified. Mr. Henry James, senior, conducted the early education of his two sons, and his influence was clearly shown in their respective careers and work. William James became a famous psychologist and metaphysician, with a predominating taste for exploration of the religious consciousness. Henry, also, proved himself an enthusiast in psychology, but he did not share his brother's taste for systematic philosophy. From the novelist's reminiscences, published in April, 1913, it is to be inferred that in their upbringing the boys had their minds directed rather towards inner and spiritual than towards outward and visible things. In his amazing English the autobiographer wrote: "We came more or less to see that our young contemporaries of another world, the trained and admonished, the disciplined and governessed, or in a word the formed, relatively speaking, had been made aware of many things of which those at home had not been." It is inconceivable that the young Jameses ever really appreciated the importance of the "get rich quick" spirit, and Henry, at least, was incapable of "hustle." He recalled as the most delightful experiences of boyhood "long summer afternoons" and "days of ample leisure" spent at his grandmother's home at Albany. He admired rather than desired to imitate William's moral energies and austerities. While greatly loving his wise, kindly father and his industrious, lofty-souled brother, Henry, according to his own modest admission, was content with "wondering and dawdling and gaping." He enjoyed a certain vagueness in life—"just to be somewhere—almost anywhere would do—and somehow receive an impression or an accession, feel a relation or a vibration." In all this the child—strange product of the 19th century and Anglo-Saxon culture—was most truly father to the man.

## DEVOTION TO DICKENS.

Henry's European instincts were early developed. In the days of his youth the proportion of English literature to American circulating in the United States was very large. Most of the books that came into young Henry's hands were English, and from them, he records, he derived his first comprehension of, and inclination towards, the land of his forefathers.

He absorbed all the works of Dickens, and ever after clung to them with an affection which remained independent of a purely literary judgment. Both William and Henry were given a training in art. It was William who was "always drawing, drawing," but Henry's literary style discloses more evidence of the earlier pursuit. Both boys travelled extensively with their father in Europe. They visited London, and Henry was charmed with the quality of the scene. He found in dress, manners, physiognomies, and material background the veracity, not merely of Dickens, but of Hogarth. The education of Henry James, under the continued direction of his father, was varied and informal. He was a student in New York, Geneva, Paris, and Boulogne. He took great delight in French history, and made himself so proficient in the French language that his anonymous essays in that medium were long afterwards commended by the schools as models worthy of imitation by native-born writers.

In 1860 he returned to America, and joined the Harvard Law School; but it was most unlikely that he would become a lawyer or follow any profession of defined scope and limitations. He began to write for the magazines, and soon convinced himself that literature, not law, was his vocation. His first short tale, "The Story of a Year," was published in the "Atlantic Monthly," in 1865. Four years later he severed his domiciliary ties with the United States and made his headquarters in England. London, a city for which he always had a partiality, the Isle of Wight, and Rye, in Sussex, were the chief of his English haunts. His visits to America were rare and brief, but he remained a great Continental traveller, spending much of his time in Paris, where he met those wandering Americans whom he delighted to picture in his novels, and frequenting Italy, a most congenial background.

A fertile, albeit a leisurely writer, Henry James produced works both of fiction and criticism in abundance. Himself divided in his interests between the old and new worlds, and writing for an appreciative circle of readers in both, he practically originated the international novel. It was his custom to bring out his stories at first serially in a magazine, and then to have them published simultaneously in book form in Boston and London, an innovation subsequent writers have not been slow to appreciate as a means of immensely extending their public. Seeing so much of the American abroad, and recognising the contrast between life and manners in such different spheres, the author's novels dwell largely on these differences, his principal characters being as often as not New Yorkers or Bostonians entering European society for the first time, or, conversely, foreigners travelling in the New World.

"DAISIE MILLER."

One of the first of his books, "Poor Richard," was issued serially in 1867, and two years later came "Gabrielle de Bergerac." "Watch and Ward" and "Roderick Hudson," published in 1871 and 1875 respectively, found him in full swing as a writer of growing popularity. "The American," regarded by many competent critics as the author's best work—at all events up to that date—saw the light in 1877, while twelve months later this prolific writer gave to the world "Daisy Miller," a work dealing not very lightly with the extravagances of an American girl plunged into the gaieties of a foreign capital, and compromising herself by ignorance of and disregard for stricter rules of etiquette than she had been accustomed to. Mr. James suffered at the hands of American reviewers for this volume, sensitive critics seeing in it an attempt to deride and belittle their country men and women.

Keen and delicate verbal portraits of women became a feature of Henry James's fiction. Such are to be found in the stories entitled "The Pension Beaurepas"; while the American girl is studied again in "A Bundle of Letters" (1879). American life is the theme of most of the earlier novels. "Washington Square" (1880), a story of a New York family, in which father and daughter are at war over the girl's love affair, exhibited the author in his more incisive and tireless analysis of motives and emotions.

Other longer or shorter stories included "The Portrait of a Lady," in 1881; "The Siege of London" in 1883; "Portraits of Places" written the following year; "A Little Tour in France," being a charming account of travel in the land of vine and olives, published in book form not long afterwards; "Tales of Three Cities," "The Bostonians," and "Princess Casamassima." "Partial Portraits" appeared in 1888, a year that saw no less than twelve or fifteen articles and romances from the writer's busy pen, the following seasons adding to the list " The Tragic Muse," " Terminations," " What Maisie Knew," " In the Page," " The Awkward Age," " The Soft Side," " The Sacred Fount," " The Wings of the Dove," " The Ambassador," " The Golden Bowl," " The American Scene," " The Outcry," " A Small Boy and Others " (1913), and other narratives. Mr. Henry James wrote innumerable articles on books and essays which attracted his attention. whilst amongst his volumes of critical essays will be remembered " French Poets and Novelists," treating of Alfred de Musset, Gautier, Baudelaire, Georges Sand, and other French writers. He was the author of " Hawthorne " in the " English Men of Letters " series, and many scholarly criticisms of literary work on both sides of the Atlantic. In 1914 he published " Notes on Novelists," a study which showed how closely he followed the work of young, contemporary English writers.

Chief exponent of the analytical and metaphysical school of novelists, to which belong Bailey Aldrich and William Howells, Henry James yet stands practically alone in English fiction. His influence is to be found in other younger writers, but it has not been an influence for good. The conventions of his technique, often a stumbling-block in the original, became an intolerable pose and affectation in the imitator. His style was the expression of inherited temperament and tastes, early environment and education, and an immense reading of French authors. Possibly if he had written in French he would not have failed, as he frequently does fail, in lucidity. He contrived to turn the English language to uses for which it was never intended. Not caring much about strict rules of grammar, nor for distinctions between colloquial and formal ways of utterance, but pursuing with never ruffled calm a chosen pattern, he achieved sentences which were marvels of verbal ingenuity. Like all masters of artistic expression, he compelled his medium, however intractable, to obey him. But some degree of initiation is required before an understanding is established between reader and the author. Henry James is a byeway in literature, and not, like Dickens, a high road for the multitude.

*Photo.*] [HOPPÉ.

### LITERATURE OF FINE SHADES.

When everything has been said about Henry James's abstraction and allusiveness, his elliptical dialogue and seemingly undisguised preoccupation with manner, his style will be found to justify itself in total effect. It is suggestive of the fine shades of character which the artist is representing. Its artificiality reflects the artificiality of the civilisation that is being studied. The entirely modern creatures of Mr. James's shadowy romances are infinitely removed in the importances of their existence from primitive humanity. Elemental passions and instincts are exhibited only in the extreme of their teleological reach. The necessities of earning bread and butter, the cruder aspect of sex relations, the dull grind of common rounds and daily tasks, these are not the realities on which Mr. James's attention is focussed. His people usually belong to the class which is materially defended from ugliness of circumstance, which has the leisure for turning human relations and occupations into a covert game.

That game in which the rules are prompted by breeding and intelligence, provides experiences as infinite as life itself. It has its comedies and tragedies, and Mr. James is their reporter.

It is not difficult to understand how very differently such a writer will impress different individuals. To some he will seem painfully prolix, strangely unreal; to be telling at inordinate length and with wilful obscurity a story as elusive and insubstantial as an ill-remembered dream. To others he appears as revealing with astonishing clarity and incomparable sureness of touch processes of the human mind which for most of us are wrapped about in the darkness of our sub-conscious selves. When his work is seen from this point of view it appears as essentially human. For many years past the author has been a cult with an increasing host of readers. The very fact that the atmosphere of his fiction was so far removed from that of the commonplace increased its charm for those who were capable of enjoying it. To care for Henry James's novels is to care with enthusiasm. Such an attitude on the part of his admirers may have its bearing on the fact that America always claimed this devotee of Europe as one of her leading men of letters.

On Mr. James's 70th birthday, April 15, 1913, a large group of his friends on this side of the Atlantic, including the best-known authors of the day, presented him with a reproduction in silver-gilt of a golden bowl of the time of Charles II., on a golden porringer, inscribed, "To Henry James, from some of his friends." The form and substance of this tribute implied graceful reference to a favourite among his novels. A letter accompanying the gift expressed the honour and affection in which the novelist was held by the donors. At the same time one of their number, Mr. J. S. Sargent, was commissioned to paint Mr. James's portrait for his acceptance.

Although, as this testimonial indicated, Mr. James owned popularity in a very wide circle, yet he was a man who enjoyed retirement more than society. He sought above all things peace, and his companions were most often books.

## SYMPATHY WITH ENGLAND.

Quite apart from his literary claims English people have every reason to remember Henry James with affection. During the trial of this war he gave to England his full allegiance and sympathy. In July last he expressed this solidarity with the English cause in the strongest way possible by becoming a naturalised Englishman. In his petition for naturalisation he gave these reasons for his step:

Because of his having lived and worked in England for the best part of forty years; because of his attachment to the country and his sympathy with it and its people; because of the long friendships and associations and interests he has formed here—these last including the acquisition of some property; all of which things have brought to a head his desire to throw his moral weight and personal allegiance, for whatever they may be worth, into the scale of the contending nation's present and future fortune.

Mr. James shared with Mr. Hardy among literary men the honour of having been awarded the O.M. He was unable to attend in person to receive the award from his Majesty, and it was brought to him by Viscount Bryce. Despite his state of illness, Mr. James, it is understood, showed a simple and genuine delight in the possession of this honour. Probably the last literary work to which the stricken writer gave his hand was an introduction to a volume, which is shortly to be published, of letters written from America by Rupert Brooke. In this preface, which is of considerable length, Mr. James has given a delicate appreciation of the young poet who lost his life in Gallipoli.

By the novelist's death a charming personality and a rare talent of challenging interest are lost to the literary world.

# HENRY JAMES O.M
## THE MAN AND THE ARTIST.

Henry James, whose death is announced elsewhere in this issue, was born in New York on April 15 1843. His father, Henry James, senior, was a well known writer and lecturer on theological subjects, an exponent in particular of Swedenberg, and of 'Sandemanianism,' as the doctrine of the Scotch sect founded by John Glas in 1730 was named in America.

The distinguished philosopher William James was the novelist's elder brother. Of their early years a picture, in beautiful and characteristic elaboration, was drawn by the younger brother in 'A Small Boy and Others' (1913) and 'Notes of A Son and Brother' (1914), in which their father's vivid personality stands out against a background of intimate homeliness, leisurely freedom, inquisitive culture, still untouched by the more strident associations of a newer New York. The whole family spent a long period in Europe in the fifties, where the small boy and his brothers received a somewhat spasmodic education, chiefly in Paris and London. At nineteen Henry the younger entered the Harvard Law School, but in the following years literature irresistibly asserted itself against law, and by 1869 had become definitely his profession. It was in that year that he came to Europe for the visit which with few and comparatively brief intervals was to prove lifelong. The first years were largely spent in Italy and France. From about 1880 onwards his home was in England, at first in London, later at Rye, in Sussex. He was never married.

Such was the simple if embracing outline of Henry James's life – in a sense uneventful enough, except for the wide range of its points of social contact, yet in fact charged and brimmed as few lives are with ceaseless adventure of spirit and intelligence. The story is to be read in his long and varied list of writings, which gave year by year the reflection of a mind quietly watchful and critical from the first, and growing, as its store of impressions was enlarged, in power and depth. It is possible to see him, in those of his earlier stories and essays which were finally allowed to survive, as a sharp-sighted and demure young observer of manners – manners American or English, Parisian or Roman – somewhat prematurely sedate, somewhat unpromisingly free, as might have been augured, from the natural crudities and headlong judgements of youth; but obviously endowed not merely with admirable fineness of perception, but with a sense of clear form and proportion altogether new in English fiction.

### An Early Work.

The very maturity, in its lucid self – composure of 'Roderick Hudson' (1875) – not actually his first novel, but the earliest which he afterwards thought worth preservation, so individual in spite of the evident influence of Hawthorne and Turgenev, might suggest that much progress on such lines was hardly to be looked for. Moreover, this finished young citizen of the world was pouring out work at a rate which would soon exhaust a slender vein, and with all its qualities of shrewdness and charm there was not much in those years to indicate that it had any great depth of resource. His critical work, among which may be mentioned the study of Hawthorne contributed to the 'English Men of Letters' series, and the volume of essays called ' Partial Portraits,' showed the same delicacy of discrimination, with a knowledge of French models and an insight into French methods that had perhaps never been matched outside France itself.

Meanwhile novel followed novel in quick succession, among them ' The American' (1878) and 'The Portrait of a Lady' (1881), freely interspersed with short stories and sketches of all kinds, and still it was hardly possible to foresee the profoundly original developments to come. 'The Tragic Muse' (1890), not in itself a very successful book, was really the first to show definite signs of the transition to the art which realised itself finally in the strange and intricate beauty of ' What Maisie Knew' (1897) and the books that followed. Among these was 'The Ambassadors' (1903), which the author himself considered the most happily conceived and fashioned of all his works.

This is not the place, however, for an examination of his work in detail; we only note that the evolution of his art continued to the end to keep pace with the ever-growing complexity of his interest in life. That interest had from the beginning little enough to do with what he described as 'the gross rattle of the foreground'; indeed, it was precisely his predilection for the civilised over the uncivilised, for the finely polished and discreetly veiled over the stripped and the crude, which, while it gave his earlier work a certain thinness and paleness, lead him into such wealth of intricacies. His very cosmopolitanism and detachment gave him a heightened sense of human drama, and enabled him to survey an exceptionally wide variety of types, native and foreign, – though it must be added that his range had very definite limits.

### The American Girl.

He dealt chiefly with two classes – the artistic and the ' leisured' – and of the latter he made one section in particular his own. This was that America of the sixties and seventies and especially that

American girl, who were harvesting in a relish in which there was still some of the excitement of novelty, the fruits of their discovery of Europe. There was a moment when the juxtaposition was at its most telling, full of illumination for Europe as well as for America, and by favour of time and circumstance Henry James was exactly so placed as to be able to record it. He returned to it again and again for different varieties of effect, and with one of them, the story of 'Daisy Miller' (1878), obtained, for perhaps the only time in his life, something of the nature of a 'popular' success. Success in that sense was for his later work out of the question, but he has long had his own intensely – even, as might seem to the uninitiato, fanatically – attached circle of readers. He was deeply interested in the theatre and wrote many plays, a few of which have made brief appearances; but, while his method in fiction had in one sense grown more and more dramatic, he never succeeded, in spite of constant experiment, in so adjusting it as to fit the stage.

In spite of his immense industry and though after some years of London he preferred to work in the serenity of Rye, he enjoyed and valued society, with the enjoyment of one in whom the critical and observant habits so strong that it demanded the pleasure of exercise. Such a book as 'The American Scene' (1907), in which he pictured one of his latest visits to America, after long years of absense, gives the measure of his extraordinary capacity for seizing and disentangling a network of associations. Through all his long residence in Europe, his relations with America were closer and more constant than may perhaps have been generally understood; and the whole America question, in whatever aspect, was one in which he was always eager to keep himself instructured. Indeed, to see him and hear him talk in later years was to feel that his mind contained material enough for another lifetime of creative work. His mellow, expansive humour and humanity were lavished, in a congenial atmosphere, with a generosity in which he himself seemed to share the listener's enjoyment; and if his scorn for what was stale and obvious or second rate sometimes involved him in complicated struggles with his inexhaustible benevolence and courtesy, it was for the listener an added delight to watch his triumphant and always richly tortuous emergence from them. When, at the right time and place, he would give the rein to his power of evoking and peopling a remembered scene, brushing in one vividly-marked figure after another with broad strokes of a vocabulary unmatched for splendour and grace, the finished picture was a work of art unforgettably enhanced by the careful deliberation of speech, the expressive gesture, the mobility of the finely-modelled face. At such times it was possible to realize a little how the passion for 'form', in the critical and brooding mind of a consummate artist, could never rest, never be set aside, never be satisfied with anything short of the full imaginative possession and poetic re-creation of all experience.

### The Order of Merit.

In 1913, on the occasion of his 70th birthday, some 250 of his friends, new and old, on this side of the Atlantic, united in inviting him to sit to Mr Sargent for his portrait, the painter himself being among the number. It is agreeable to remember that he was pleased and touched by this spontaneous expression, not merely (or chiefly) of admiration for his genius, but of the affection and honour of all who knew him. The portrait is destined in due course to be offered to the nation. It will remain as a two-fold monument to Henry James – to the creator of the some of the furthest and rarest refinements of art to be found in any literature – and to the friend whose friendship has meant so much and to so many. None of them will ever forget the noble and passionate vehemence with which, from the outbreak of the war, he flung himself into the cause of the Allies. One felt, in listening to the expression of his love for this country and for France, both of which he knew and loved so well, that the issue was met by a heart, a brain, and a temper worth its gravity and its honour. He eagerly helped the magnificent work of certain Americans for the alleviation of suffering in Belgium and France; and at last (July 1915) he took a step which was warmly welcomed by his friends in England and not misunderstood by his friends in America – he became naturalised as an English subject. Giving as his reasons for naturalization Mr Henry James said: –

Because of his having lived and worked in England for the best part of 40 years; because of his attachment to the country and his sympathy with it and its people; because of the long friendships and associations and interests he had formed here – these last including the acquisition of some property; all of which things have brought to a head his desire to throw his moral weight and personal allegiance, for whatever they may be worth, into the scale of the contending nation's present and future fortune.

Not one of us who knew him but must feel proud that he wished to claim citizenship with us. The one and most fitting distinction that could be offered him as an Englishman was the Order of Merit, and it was announced on New Year's Day, 1916, that this had been accorded him. He was already lying in his last illness; but that he was able to appreciate the gift and to take pleasure in the thought of all that it meant, we know and shall gratefully remember.

## DEATH OF MR. HENRY JAMES.

### NOVELIST FOR THE FEW.

We regret to announce the death last night at 21, Carlyle-mansions, Chelsea, London, of Mr. Henry James, the novelist, at the age of seventy-two. He received the Order of Merit at the New Year.

Many regarded Mr. James as an American novelist, but he was not, though he was born in New York. His work is English and, as announced in his own words last July, he was granted British nationality "because of his having lived and worked in England for the best part of forty years; because of his attachment to the country, and his sympathy in it, and its peoples; because of the long friendships and associations and interests he has formed here—these last including the acquisition of some property; all of which things have brought to a head his desire to throw his moral weight and personal allegiance, for whatever they may be worth, into the scale of the contending nation's present and future fortune."

MR. HENRY JAMES.

Mr. James has inspired many people to make witty epigrams. One is that his brother, Mr. William James, late professor of psychology at Harvard, wrote psychology like a novelist while Mr. Henry James wrote novels like a psychologist. Someone else said that when Mr. James wrote fiction you scented the critic; and when he wrote criticism you felt the novelist.

He was all these—a novelist, a psychologist, and a critic. His father was a clever man who taught a kind of Ishmaelitish Swedenborgianism which no one is said to have grasped except, of course, his two sons. Mr. Henry James allowed himself to be influenced by the French school of writing, which, to some extent, may account for his "obscurity." It has been said that if he had moulded himself on Fielding he would have become our greatest novelist.

### UNNAMED HEROINE.

Like caviare, Mr. James is loved by people who have acquired the taste and by people who think such a taste the right thing to acquire. But the average novel reader innocently consuming his works in large quantities would be very like Mr. Wells's Kipps if confronted with caviare. It is, frankly, a surprise. Mr. James frequently had no plot, and in one story, "In the Cage," the heroine's name is never once mentioned. He was a novelist who did not write about the actions of people but of their thoughts; he was like an analyst observing in enthusiastic detachment from the subjects of his analysis. His style was a study in exactitude, the shade of meaning being reached often by involved parenthesis and regularly by delicately applied adverbs.

Among some of his best-known writings are "The American" (1877), "Poor Richard" (1887), "The Bostonians" (1886), "The Tragic Muse" (1890), "The Golden Bowl" (1905), "A Small Boy and Others" (1913).

For many years Mr. James lived in England. He was a bachelor and took great pride in the old Lamb House at Rye, a house George II. used to visit.

Perhaps the critic was uppermost in the character of this many-sided man that day in Bayswater when, so the story goes, Mr. James confessed to Du Maurier, the author of "Trilby," that he had great difficulty in finding plots for his stories. The story continues that Du Maurier made a present of the "Trilby" plot to Mr. James, but it was declined as too valuable a present. What a pity! "Trilby," by Henry James, would have been a most interesting book.

# NOTES

**W. D. Howells**

The wood engraving of HJ at the beginning of Howells's article is by Timothy Cole.

p. 5, col. 1, l. 38: 'Mr Fields's': James T. Fields (1817–81) succeeded James Russell Lowell as editor of the *Atlantic Monthly*.

p. 5, col. 2, ll. 32–4: '"The Atlantic" … "The Century"': American periodicals which combined fiction with features on social and cultural topics.

p. 5, col. 2, l. 45: 'Daisy Miller': This tale was published by *Cornhill Magazine* in 1878 and proved an immediate success.

p. 6, col. 1, l. 14: 'Henrietta Stackpole': a newspaper correspondent, the assertive and independent friend of Isabel Archer in *The Portrait of a Lady* (1881).

p. 6, col. 1, l. 47: 'Mr Tristram': a friend of Christopher Newman in *The American* (1877), a fellow American.

p. 6, col. 1, l. 50: 'Madame de Belgarde': Madame de Bellegarde (Howells misspells this name) is Claire de Cintré's scheming and ambitious mother in *The American*.

p. 6, col. 1, l. 51: 'Newman': Christopher Newman, protagonist of *The American*.

p. 6, col. 2, l. 55: 'Dorothea': Dorothea Brooke is the heroine of George Eliot's *Middlemarch* (1871).

p. 7, col. 1, l. 17: 'Searle': protagonist of 'The Passionate Pilgrim' (1875), an American who covets his English ancestral home.

p. 7, col. 1, l. 46: 'Claire Belgarde': the heroine of *The American* is Claire de Cintré; Claire de Bellegarde was her maiden name.

p. 7, col. 1, l. 47: 'Bessy Alden': Bessie Alden, the heroine of 'An International Episode' (1878), is a spirited young American woman who turns down an offer of marriage from Lord Lambeth.

p. 7, col. 1, l. 54: 'Lord Warburton': a suitor of Isabel Archer.

p. 7, col. 1, l. 55: 'The Touchetts': Mr and Mrs Touchett and their son Ralph are friends and benefactors of Isabel Archer.

p. 7, col. 2, l. 22: 'Osmond's daughter': Pansy Osmond from *The Portrait of a Lady*.

p. 7, col. 2, l . 23: 'Mr Rosier': Pansy's suitor.

p. 7, col. 2, l. 28: 'Valentin Belgarde': the brother of Claire de Cintré, and a friend of Newman.

p. 7, col. 2, l. 49: 'infamous crime': Mme de Bellegarde and her elder son caused the death of the old Marquis, Claire's father, because he opposed his daughter's first marriage.

p. 8, col. 1, l. 16: 'Madame Merle and Gilbert Osmond': Madame Merle encourages Isabel to marry Gilbert Osmond, her own former lover.

p. 8, col. 1, l. 17: 'Miss Light and her mother': Christina Light is the beautiful and ambiguous heroine of *Roderick Hudson* (1876) who reappears as the eponymous Princess Casamassima.

p. 8, col. 1, l. 40: 'Dickens': Charles Dickens (1812–70), the immensely successful novelist.

p. 8, col. 1, l. 40: 'Thackeray': William Makepeace Thackeray (1811–63), novelist whose best known work is *Vanity Fair* (1847–8).

p. 8, col. 1, l. 47: 'Richardson': Samuel Richardson (1689–1761), author of long epistolary novels including *Pamela* (1740) and *Clarissa* (1748).

p. 8, col. 1, l. 48: 'Fielding': Henry Fielding (1707–54), author of robust and satirical novels such as *Tom Jones* (1749).

p. 8, col. 1, l. 50: 'Trollope and Reade': Anthony Trollope (1815–82), a prolific novelist whose *Barsetshire Chronicles* (1855–67) were particularly successful. Charles Reade (1814–84) is perhaps best known now for his historical romance *The Cloister and the Hearth* (1861) although most of his novels in fact focused on the pressing social issues of his own day.

p. 8, col. 1, l. 52: 'Hawthorne and George Eliot': Nathaniel Hawthorne (1804–64), American writer whose novel, *The Marble Faun* (1860), had a strong influence on HJ's works. HJ published a study of Hawthorne's works in 1879. Mary Ann Evans (1819–80), one of the most important novelists of the nineteenth century, wrote under the pen name of George Eliot. HJ admired her works (though not without reservation) and the influence of *Middlemarch* can be traced in *Portrait of a Lady*.

p. 28, col. 1, l. 61: 'Daudet ... Zola': Alphonse Daudet (1840–97), French short story writer and novelist, whose best known work is *Lettres de mon Moulin* (1866). HJ wrote warmly about Daudet in an essay for the *Atlantic Monthly* in 1882. Emile Zola (1840–1902), the most significant exponent of French naturalism. His novels depicting the gritty, violent realities of working class life were considered shocking by many. HJ viewed his works with both admiration and distaste.

p. 8, col. 2, l. 42: 'book of European sketches': *Transatlantic Sketches* (1875).

p. 8, col. 2, l. 46: 'essays on modern French writers': HJ had written numerous such essays for the *Nation* on writers including Sainte-Beuve, Gautier and Sand.

## E. S. Nadal

p. 15, col. 1, l. 14: 'Mrs Pierrepont': wife of Edwards Pierrepont (1817–92), the US Ambassador to Great Britain.

p. 15, col. 1, l. 26: 'Eugene Schuyler': (1840–90), an American diplomat who held posts in Romania, Turkey and Greece.

p. 15, col. 2, l. 4: 'Holland House': a Jacobean mansion in Kensington. Lady Holland presided over a famous salon here early in the nineteenth century. The house was almost completely destroyed during the Blitz.

p. 15, col. 2, l. 30: 'Café Royal': an elegant restaurant in London's Piccadilly, much frequented by Oscar Wilde and his friends.

p. 16, col. 2, l. 56: 'The Reform Club': a Liberal club, located on Pall Mall.

p. 17, col. 1, l. 6: 'Athenaeum': a club associated with the promotion of literary, artistic and scientific excellence.

p. 17, col. 2, l. 41: 'Secretary of Legation in Madrid': probably John Hay (1838–1905), biographer of Lincoln, who held this position from 1868–70.

p. 18, col. 1, l. 20: 'choice of Hercules': The tale of Hercules choosing between the easy path of vice and the rocky path of virtue can be found in Xenophon's *Memoirs of Socrates*.

p. 18, col. 2, l. 12: '*The Nation*': a weekly periodical founded in 1865 by Abolitionists (campaigners for the emancipation of slaves).

p. 18, col. 2, l. 15: 'Grant and Greeley campaign': a reference to the 1872 US Presidential contest between Ulysses S. Grant and Horace Greeley.

p. 18, col. 2, l. 22: 'Dennett': John R. Dennett (1837–74), literary critic at the *Nation*.

p. 18, col. 2, l. 35: 'Garrison': Wendell Phillips Garrison was in charge of book reviews at the *Nation*.

p. 18, col. 2, l. 41: 'Arthur Sedgwick': (1844–1915), lawyer and editor of the *Nation*.

p. 18, col. 2, l. 54: 'two Adamses': One of these two is almost certainly Henry Brooks Adams (1838–1918), the American journalist, historian and novelist whose grandfather and great grandfather were US presidents. Adams and his wife Clover were good friends of HJ. The other Adams may be one of his brothers, several of whom were prominent in public life.

p. 19, col. 1, l. 16: 'Doctor Holmes': The physician and writer Oliver Wendell Holmes (1809–94) coined the phrase 'Boston Brahmin' to describe the city's Anglo-Saxon Protestant elite.

p. 19, col. 1, l. 40: 'Hayes-Tilden affair': In the controversial US Presidential election of 1876 Rutherford Hayes defeated Samuel Tilden.

p. 19, col. 1, l .43: 'Virginia Dare in "Democracy"': *Democracy* was published anonymously by Henry Adams in 1880. Its heroine's name is in fact Victoria Dare – Virginia Dare (b. 1587) was the first child to be born in America to English parents in Roanoke island. The entire settlement had disappeared mysteriously by 1590, and it has been conjectured that some of the colonists might have joined the Croatan tribe.

p. 20, col. 2, l. 32: 'Lowell': James Russell Lowell (1819–91) was one of the 'Fireside' poets, a group which also included Oliver Wendell Holmes and Henry Wadsworth Longfellow. He edited the *Atlantic Monthly* from 1857–61.

p. 20, col. 2, l. 56: 'Baedekers': the well-known series of travel books.

p. 21, col. 1, ll. 22–3: 'just brought out a play': As Nadal dates this visit to 1891 the play must be *The American* although his account tallies better with the reception of *Guy Domville* which was first produced in London in 1895.

p. 21, col. 1, l. 24: 'Grant Duff': Sir Mountstuart Elphinstone Grant Duff (1829–1906) was the Liberal MP for Elgin and a Victorian polymath.

p. 21, col. 1, l. 35: 'Haymarket': The Theatre Royal, Haymarket was particularly associated with successful comedies during this period. The London production of *The American* was in fact performed at the Opera Comique Theatre.

p. 21, col. 1, l. 39: 'Charles Lamb': Also known as 'Elia' (1775–1834), Lamb was an English essayist and poet who produced *Tales from Shakespeare* (1807) with his sister Mary Lamb. The play Nadal refers to is *Mr H—*, a farce which was produced (once only) at Drury Lane in 1807.

p. 21, col. 1, l. 50: 'Bulwer': Edward Bulwer-Lytton (1803–73) was a novelist and playwright whose influential and varied output included the 'silver fork' novel *Pelham* (1828) and the 'Newgate' novel *Paul Clifford* (1830).

p. 22, col. 1, l. 35: 'Burdett Coutts': William Burdett-Coutts (1851–1921) was an American born philanthropist and politician, the husband of the immensely wealthy Angela Burdett-Coutts whose name he adopted.

p. 22, col. 1, l. 42: 'crush-hat': a soft hat which can be crushed flat.

p. 22, col. 1, l. 50: 'Saturday Club in Boston': a literary group whose members included Oliver Wendell Holmes and James Russell Lowell. The club met weekly at Boston's Parker House Hotel.

p. 22, col. 1, ll. 53–5: 'Johnson's Club … Mermaid Tavern': Johnson's Club was formed by the eighteenth-century man of letters, Samuel Johnson. It attracted literary, artistic and political figures. Will's Coffee-House was established in the seventeenth century and was frequented by Pepys and Dryden. The Mermaid Tavern, associated with Shakespeare and Raleigh, was burned down during the Great Fire of London.

p. 22, l. 11, l. 43: 'Bismarck': Otto von Bismarck (1815–98) was Chancellor of Germany between 1871 and 1890.

p. 23, col. 1, l. 45: 'O. Henry's': O. Henry (1862–1910) was the pseudonym of William Sydney Porter, a popular American short story writer, noted for his clever plot twists.

## Justin McCarthy

p. 74, ll. 20–1: 'Robert Louis Stevenson or Thomas Hardy': Stevenson (1850–94), the novelist, poet and short story writer, was a good friend of HJ who admired his works greatly and was deeply saddened by Stevenson's early death. HJ found the works of Thomas Hardy (1840–1928), the famous novelist and poet, far less congenial. He described his last novel, *Jude the Obscure* (1895), as 'ineffably dreary and stupid' (Kaplan, p. 465).

## Edmund Gosse

p. 27, l. 13: '*Life of W. W. Story*': HJ's study of the American sculptor, William Wetmore Story and his friends, was published in 1903.

p. 28, l. 27: 'chimaera bombinating in a vacuum': the chimaera is a monster from Greek myth with a lion's head, goat's body and serpent's tail. To bombinate is to buzz or drone. The image of a chimera bombinating in a vacuum is derived from a satirical attack made by Rabelais in *Pantagruel* on the subtlety of the Schoolmen.

p. 29, l. 28: 'Mr. Percy Lubbock': (1879–1965), literary critic and biographer. Lubbock was an ardent disciple of HJ as a young man and later became an important figure in Jamesian scholarship, and the first editor of his letters.

p. 30, l. 6: 'Veronese': Paolo Veronese (1528–88), the Italian Mannerist painter.

p. 31, l. 34: 'Marivaux': Pierre de Marivaux (1688–1763), an influential French playwright and novelist.

p. 31, ll. 34–5: 'de ne vivre que … pour entendre': to live only to see and understand (French).

p. 32, l. 17: 'Great Malvern': a well-known Victorian spa town in Worcestershire.

p. 33, l. 14: 'Ruskin … Vere': John Ruskin (1819–1900) was an immensely influential Victorian thinker who wrote on numerous topics but is perhaps best known as an art critic. William Morris (1834–96) founded the Arts and Crafts Movement and was well known as an artist, designer and writer of poetry and fiction, as well as being a prominent figure in the socialist movement. Aubrey de Vere (1814–1902) was an Irish poet and critic.

p. 33, l. 33: 'Flaubert and Edmond de Goncourt': Gustave Flaubert (1821–80), the innovative and influential French novelist of the Realist school, best known for *Madame Bovary* (1857); Edmond de Goncourt (1822–96) and his brother Jules de Goncourt (1830–70) were writers of art criticism as well as successful novelists.

308    *Lives of Victorian Literary Figures IV: Henry James*

p. 34, l. 21: 'Turgenev': Ivan Sergeyevich Turgenev (1818–83), Russian writer whose best known work is the novel *Fathers and Sons* (1862). HJ was acquainted with Turgenev and was influenced by his works which he greatly admired.

p. 34, l. 22: 'Guy de Maupassant': (1850–93), French short story writer and novelist, noted for his frank realism and elegantly crafted plots.

p. 24, l. 30: 'François Coppée': (1842–1908), a French poet and dramatist.

p. 36, l. 14: 'Greville or Crabb Robinson': Charles Cavendish Fulke Greville (1794–1865) was a social and political diarist. Henry Crabb Robinson (1775–1867) was a diarist who included many notable figures among his friends.

p. 37, l. 1: 'Mr. (now Lord) Morley': John Morley, Viscount Morley of Blackburn (1838–1923) was a politician and writer who succeeded G. H. Lewes as editor of the *Fortnightly Review*.

p. 37, l. 6: 'George Du Maurier': (1834–1896), born in France but spent his working life in England where he gained success both as a cartoonist and a writer and became a good friend of HJ. Du Maurier's most successful novel was *Trilby* (1894), notable for its creation of the sinister Svengali.

p. 38, l. 20: 'Colonel Higginson': The writer Thomas Wentworth Higginson (1823–1911) was a champion of Emily Dickinson's poetry and a prominent Abolitionist.

p. 39, l. 7: 'his sister Alice': Alice James (1848–92), HJ's gifted younger sister, suffered from ill health for much of her life. Her diaries were published in 1934.

p. 40, l. 12: 'an eminent author': This is a reference to John Addington Symonds (1840–93), the poet and critic. Although (like the author of 'Beltraffio') Symonds married, he was homosexual and wrote frankly and eloquently on behalf of homosexual rights.

p. 40, l. 34: 'the theatre': Many other writers have described HJ's unsuccessful career as a dramatist (see sections 9 and 10).

p. 41, l. 34: 'the Daniel Curtises': Daniel Curtis was a wealthy and cultured Bostonian. HJ stayed with him and his wife Ariana in Venice on several occasions.

p. 41, l. 36: 'Edward Compton': Compton (1854–1918) was an actor and theatre manager. His dealings with HJ are discussed by his son Compton Mackenzie (see section 9).

p. 42, l. 37: '*Tenants ... Disengaged*': *Tenants* (1894), a melodrama originally called *Mrs Vibert*. *Disengaged*, originally called *Mrs Jasper*, was designed and cast in 1893 but never performed. HJ withdrew the play, feeling that its producer, Augustin Daly, was sabotaging its chances of success.

p. 43, l. 6: '*The Album* and *The Reprobate*': two further unproduced plays, published in 1894.

# Notes

p. 43, l. 12: 'George Alexander': Sir George Alexander (1858–1918), the actor and theatre manager, produced and starred in *Guy Domville*.

p. 43, l. 18: 'Domvile': Gosse misspells Domville throughout this piece.

p. 43, ll. 26–7: 'it left all those threads loose as they would be in life': Compare Howells's similar description of HJ as a novelist (section 1, p. 6).

p. 44, l. 11: 'a cabal': Alexander had been sent an unsigned telegram on the opening night 'with hearty wishes for a complete failure'.

p. 44, l. 13: 'Early next morning': Edel suggests that it is unlikely that Gosse called on HJ early in the morning following the opening night of *Guy Domville* or that HJ recovered quite so fully and quickly from the humiliation (Edel, iv, p. 78).

p. 46, l. 4: '*buisson d'épines*': a thornbush – a 'prickly' person (French).

p. 47, l. 19: 'Vivian': Sometimes known as Nimue, in Arthurian legend Vivian was a beautiful enchantress who imprisoned the wizard Merlin in a cave.

p. 48, l. 38: 'Paul Bourget': (1852–1935), French novelist and critic. HJ liked Bourget but did not care for his work.

p. 48, l. 10: 'Maurice Barrès': (1862–1923), French writer and politician.

p. 48, ll. 24–5: 'Archbishop Benson': Edward White Benson (1829–96) was Archbishop of Canterbury between 1883 and 1896. He was also the father of A. C. Benson whose own account of the genesis of *The Turn of the Screw* can be found in section 6.

p. 51, l. 34: '*jeune premier*': juvenile lead (French).

p. 51, l. 38: 'Lacordaire': Jean Baptise Henri Lacordaire (1802–61), a celebrated preacher associated with political reform.

p. 51, l. 39: 'Sainte-Beuve': Charles Augustin Sainte-Beuve (1804–69) was a French literary historian and critic. HJ admired his writings and reviewed his works for the *Nation*.

p. 53, l. 23: 'Edward Burne-Jones': (1833–98), a British painter and member of the Pre-Raphaelite Brotherhood. HJ was a friend of Burne-Jones and admired his works.

p. 53, l .28: 'Vicomte Melchior de Vogüé': (1848–1910), a minor French novelist and critic.

p. 53, l. 31: 'Marion Crawford': Francis Marion Crawford (1854–1909), a prolific American novelist. HJ rather envied his commercial success.

p. 53, l. 14: 'Mr H. G. Wells': Herbert George Wells (1866–1946), novelist and social commentator. Now best known for his science fiction, he was also a noted writer of everyday tales such as *Kipps* (1905). His novel, *Boon* (1915), parodied HJ, offending him greatly.

p. 54, l. 14: 'Mr Rudyard Kipling': (1865–1936), the novelist and short story writer best known for his children's books. HJ was acquainted with Kipling – he had mixed feelings about his works and rather envied his great success.

p. 54, l. 14: 'Mr W. E. Norris': William Edward Norris (1847–1925), a minor novelist.

p. 54, l. 22: 'Mrs Wharton': Edith Wharton (1862–1937) was a highly successful American writer, best known for novels such as *The House of Mirth* (1905) and *The Age of Innocence* (1920). She and HJ were close friends as well as admirers of each other's works.

p. 58, l. 28: 'Hugh Walpole': (1884–1941) was born in New Zealand but lived in England for most of his life. He was a successful and prolific novelist and was knighted in 1937. He and HJ were close friends, and his own account of their relationship can be found in section 15.

p. 58, l. 28: 'Rupert Brooke': (1887–1915) was a 'Georgian' poet, now best known for his patriotic sonnet 'The Soldier'. HJ was very attached to Brooke and deeply shocked by his early death.

p. 59, l. 2: 'Robertson James': (1846–1910), HJ's youngest brother.

p. 59, l. 13: 'Mr. Sargent': John Singer Sargent (1856–1925) was a celebrated American painter who worked largely in Europe and is best known for his society portraits, including a portrait of HJ painted to celebrate his seventieth birthday.

p. 60, l. 25: 'Roland': In the anonymous Old French epic *The Song of Roland*, Roland blows his 'oliphant' horn to summon the forces of Charlemagne.

p. 60, l. 29: 'Entente': The 'Entente Cordiale' or friendly understanding between France and England was signed in 1904.

p. 62, ll. 10–11: 'American Volunteer Motor Ambulance Corps': This was established in 1914 by Richard Norton, a son of Charles Eliot Norton, the Harvard Professor who had been a friend of HJ since 1864.

p. 62, l. 39: 'Mr. Wilson': Dr Thomas Woodrow Wilson (1856–1924) was the US President during World War I.

p. 63, l. 32: 'Lord Bryce': James Bryce, 1st Viscount Bryce (1838–1922) was a British jurist, historian and politician.

## J.-E. Blanche

p. 67, l. 3: 'Miss Norton': probably Grace Norton, sister of HJ's old friend Charles Eliot Norton.

p. 67, l. 7: 'Moore's: George Augustus Moore (1852–1933), Irish novelist, best known for his novel *Esther Waters* (1894), an unsentimental study of an unmarried mother. Moore later became associated with the Celtic revival.

p. 67, ll. 13–14: 'From Europe … William': This letter was written on 29 October.

p. 68, l. 18: 'Jusserand': Jean Jules Jusserand (1855–1932), French literary historian and diplomat.

p. 69, l. 9: 'Bernhard Berenson': more usually known as Bernard Berenson (1865–1959), the Lithuanian born American art critic.

p. 69, l. 15: 'Carl Van Vechten': Van Vechten (1880–64), American writer associated with the Harlem Renaissance. His best known book is *Nigger Heaven* (1926).

p. 69, l. 17: '*Peter Whaffle*': The title is in fact *Peter Whiffle* (1922).

p. 70, l. 22: 'Proust's': Marcel Proust (1871–1922), novelist best known for *À La Recherche du Temps Perdu*, a long and complex autobiographical novel published between 1913 and 1927.

p. 71, l. 9: 'Mrs. S. N.': identified as Mrs Saxon Noble by Simon Nowell-Smith (Nowell-Smith, p. 37).

p. 72, l. 8: 'Joseph Conrad': (1857–1924), born in Poland but became a British citizen in 1886. With their complex narratives and experimental techniques, Conrad's novels can be seen as forerunners of Modernism. Although not a close friend of Conrad, HJ had great respect for him as a writer.

p. 72, l. 14: 'André Gide': (1869–1951), French novelist whose works include *The Immoralist* (1902) and *The Counterfeiters* (1925). He was condemned for his public defence of homosexuality but was awarded the Nobel Prize for literature in 1947. He met HJ just once, in 1912.

p. 72, l. 17: 'Walter Berry': (1859–1927), a close friend of Edith Wharton and through her became acquainted with HJ.

p. 73, l. 6: 'Vermeer': Johannes Vermeer (1632–75), Dutch painter.

p. 73, l. 6: 'Cubism': early twentieth-century art movement associated with artists such as Picasso. Its exponents aimed to view subjects from many angles simultaneously.

p. 73, ll. 16–17: 'a Racine ... Stendahl': Jean Racine (1639–99), French tragedian whose subjects were taken from classical literature; Michel de Montaigne (1533–92), French writer best known for his influential essays; Honoré de Balzac (1799–1850), major French novelist whose many works include *Eugénie Grandet* (1833) and *Le Père Goriot* (1835); Stendhal was the pseudonym of Marie-Henri Beyle (1783–1842), French novelist best known for *Le Rouge et le Noir* (1830).

p. 73, l. 17: 'Freud': Sigmund Freud (1856–1939), founder of psychoanalysis.

**Violet Hunt, 'The Last Days of Henry James'**

p. 79, col. 1, l. 5: 'Peggy': Mary Margaret James, William James's daughter.

p. 79, col. 1, ll. 15–16: 'Mr Bryan': William Jennings Bryan (1860–1925), US Secretary of State during World War I, a passionate pacifist who eventually supported the US entry into the war.

p. 79, col. 1, l. 19: 'Purple Patch': Violet Hunt was fond of purple, a fashionable colour at this time. In the American edition of *The Flurried Years* she describes how her purple coat and veil were remarked on by the ladies of Rye.

p. 79, col. 1, ll. 38–40: 'he allowed ... cause': This interview, by Preston Lockwood, can be found in section 17.

p. 79, col. 1, l. 10: 'Book of France': *The Book of France in Aid of the French Parliamentary Committee's Fund for the Relief of the Invaded Departments*, edited by Winifred Stephens (London: Macmillan, 1915).

p. 79, col. 1, l. 61: '*narquois*': mocking, sardonic (French).

p. 80, col. 1, l. 69: 'a little story in the *Cornhill*': *Daisy Miller* (1878).

p. 80, col. 1, l. 91: 'La Maison de Pêché': house of sin (French).

**Violet Hunt, *The Flurried Years***

p. 81, l. 21: 'the editor': Ford Madox Ford, the editor of the *English Review*.

p. 82, l. 19: '*Morituri te Salutant*': 'Those who are about to die salute you' (Latin). Popularly attributed to gladiators, this declaration is more firmly linked with participants in Roman mock naval battles.

p. 82, l. 24: '*Modeste Mignon*': Balzac's novel of 1844.

p. 82, l. 32: 'montée': well set up, well equipped (French).

p. 82, l. 34: 'New Reform Club': a club in Adelphi Terrace.

p. 83, l. 3: 'Mr. Bernard Shaw': George Bernard Shaw (1856–1950), playwright and critic. He was a member of the Fabian Society, and was associated with various progressive causes including spelling reform, rational dress and vegetarianism.

p. 83, l. 8: 'Mona Maltravers': The tale, published in 1909, is in fact called 'Mora Montravers'.

p. 86, ll. 14–15: '*es wäre so schön gewesen*': it would have been so nice (German).

p. 88, ll. 25–7: '*sans peur ... sans reproche*': The French military hero Bayard (1474–1524) was known as 'le chevalier sans peur et sans reproche', the knight without fear or reproach (French).

p. 88, l. 4: 'Smeeth': a village in Kent.

p. 89, l. 2: '*laches*': cowardly actions (French).

p. 89, l. 15: '*rixe*': scuffle (French).

p. 89, l. 17: 'Cranford': Elizabeth Gaskell's best loved novel, *Cranford* (1851) is a study of a provincial town and its (predominantly female) inhabitants.

p. 89, l. 26: 'Mrs. P.': This may be either Frances Prothero or Brigit Patmore.

p. 89, l. 29: 'Mrs. Frank Hill': Jane Dalzell Finlay married newspaper editor Frank Harrison Hill (1830–1910) in 1862.

- p. 90, l. 1: 'Mary Martindale': Ford Madox Ford's sister-in-law, with whom he had earlier had an affair.
- p. 90, ll. 29–30: '*Götterdämmerung*': the last opera of Wagner's *Ring* cycle, first performed in 1876.
- p. 90, l. 30: 'Mrs Clifford': Lucy Clifford (1846–1929), who wrote under the pseudonym John Inglis, was a successful writer whose novels focused on the sometimes painful realities of women's lives. She was a great friend of HJ.
- p. 90, l. 31: 'just published – something very strange': perhaps *The Wife of Altamont* (1910).
- p. 91, l. 3: 'the Beauty's': Violet Hunt's favourite niece, Rosamond Fogg Elliot.
- p. 92, l. 15: 'little Miles': Miles dies suddenly at the end of *The Turn of the Screw*.
- p. 93, ll. 14–16: 'there was … had repented': an allusion to Luke's Gospel, 15:7.
- p. 93, l. 32: 'Joseph Leopold': When Ford Madox Ford was baptised as a Catholic in 1892 he took the names 'Joseph Leopold Ford Hermann Hueffer'.
- p. 93, l. 34: 'Adrienne Dayrolles': a French actress who took the part of Noémie Nioche in *The American*. She did not act in *Guy Domville*.
- p. 94, l. 26: 'Mary Robinson': Agnes Mary Frances Robinson (1857–1944), a writer, scholar and poet.
- p. 95, l. 14: 'Le don de l'amoureuse merci': the gift of loving mercy (French).
- p. 95, l. 27: 'Mondaine': society woman (French).
- p. 96, l. 17: '*herzen's gut*': literally 'heart's good', good hearted (German).
- p. 96, l. 18: 'Elizabeth Schultz': a protégée of Ford Madox Ford.

## Vincent O' Sullivan

- p. 98, l. 3: 'the Exhibition at Earl's Court': In the late nineteenth century, exhibitions were regularly held at Earl's Court.
- p. 98, ll. 8–9: 'she may be perfectly respectable': It was somewhat unusual for women to eat alone in restaurants at this time, but HJ is right to insist that perfectly respectable women sometimes did so.

## A. C. Benson

- p. 103, l. 9: 'Fred Myers': Frederic William Henry Myers (1843–1901) was a classicist, psychical researcher and essayist.
- p. 103, ll. 19–20: 'Miss Laura Tennant … Alfred Lyttelton': Alfred Lyttelton (1857–1913) was a sportsman and politician. His wife Laura died after giving birth to their first child less than a year after their marriage.

314     *Lives of Victorian Literary Figures IV: Henry James*

p. 104, l. 12: 'King's': the famous chapel of King's College, Cambridge was completed in 1547.

p. 105, l. 2: 'collapse': a reference to *Guy Domville*.

p. 105, l. 16: '*Two Magics*': Two tales, *The Turn of the Screw* and *Covering End*, were published as *The Two Magics* in 1898.

p. 109, l. 6: 'Nardi parvus onyx eliciet cadum': 'a tiny shell of spikenard will coax out a jar'(Latin), Horace, *Odes* IV.12.

p. 109, l. 11: 'Fitzgerald': Edward Fitzgerald (1809–1883). Writer, best known for his translation of Omar Khayyam's *Rubaiyat* (1859). Benson wrote the volume on Fitzgerald in the 'English Men of Letters series' in 1905.

p. 112, ll. 23–4: 'He does not take a side': Compare Howells (section 1, pp. 5–6).

p. 113, l. 4: 'Robert Browning': (1812–89) gave voice to fictional villains in several dramatic monologues. A striking example is 'Porphyria's Lover' (1834) whose disturbed narrator describes how he strangled his mistress with her own hair.

p. 114, ll. 30–2: 'So ... the distinguished thing': This anecdote is also reported by Edith Wharton (Wharton, pp. 366–7). The lady in whom he confided was Frances Prothero.

**Desmond MacCarthy**

p. 122, l. 3: 'Gyp': Sibylle Martel de Janville, a popular French novelist with strong anti-Dreyfus views.

p. 122, l. 21: 'Froude': James Anthony Froude (1818–94), an English historian, and Carlyle's biographer.

p. 122, l. 23: 'Carlyle': Thomas Carlyle (1795–1881) was an extremely influential Scottish historian whose best known work is his history of *The French Revolution* (1837). His marriage to Jane Welsh Carlyle (1801–66), an important letter writer in her own right, has been much discussed.

p. 124, l. 5: '*gemütlich*': pleasant and welcoming (German).

p. 126, l. 10: 'Pecksniff': an unpleasant hypocrite in Dickens's *Martin Chuzzlewit* (1843–4).

p. 126, l. 12: 'the Dove': Milly Theale, heroine of *The Wings of the Dove* (1902).

p. 127, l. 4: 'Ibsen': Henrik Ibsen (1828–1906), the controversial and highly influential Norwegian dramatist. Although HJ had reservations about his works Ibsen's influence can be traced in his own later novels.

p. 127, l. 25: 'Meredith': George Meredith (1828–1909), poet and novelist whose works were often experimental in form and controversial in subject. He and HJ met in 1878 and remained friends.

p. 129, l. 6: 'Dostoevsky': Fyodor Dostoevsky (1821–81), Russian novelist whose works reflect his concern with moral, philosophical and spiritual questions.

p. 129, l. 19: 'Mr. Chesterton': Gilbert Keith Chesterton (1874–1936) is now best known for his detective stories about Father Brown. In his autobiography Chesterton describes HJ as a very formal and courtly man, who never quite understood the English.

p. 130, l. 1: ' the pattern in the carpet': in 'The Figure in the Carpet' (1896), HJ describes a novelist who tells an admirer that discerning readers will be able to spot a single unifying pattern in all his works.

p. 132, l. 29: 'Maggie Verver': heroine of *The Golden Bowl* (1904).

p. 132, l. 31: 'Kate Croy and Charlotte Stant': equivocal characters from *The Wings of the Dove* and *The Golden Bowl* respectively.

p. 133, ll. 29–32: ' Wilkie Collins … She': Wilkie Collins (1824–89), successful novelist of 'sensation' novels, most famously *The Woman in White* (1860); Marie Corelli (1855–1924) was the pseudonym of Mary Mackay, a writer of popular supernatural thrillers; Stanley Weyman (1855–1928), writer of historical adventures and romances; Sir Walter Scott (1771–1832), Scottish poet and novelist best known for historical romances such as *Waverley* (1814) and *Ivanhoe* (1820). Mary Braddon (1835–1915), another 'sensation' novelist, author of the best selling *Lady Audley's Secret* (1862); *The Deemster*, Thomas Hall Caine's romantic novel of 1887, set on the Isle of Man; *She* (1887) is H. Rider Haggard's still popular novel of African adventure.

p. 133, l. 37: 'Dean Farrar's school stories': Frederic William Farrar (1831–1903) was a theological writer, now remembered for the school story *Eric, or Little by Little* (1858).

p. 134, ll. 7–8: 'Sir William Harcourt's public speeches': Harcourt (1827–1904) was a prominent liberal politician.

p. 137, l. 30: 'Muffs': a muff is a foolish, clumsy person.

p. 138, l. 8: 'City of destruction': starting point of Bunyan's Christian in *The Pilgrim's Progress* (1678).

p. 138, l. 30: 'Cowley and Donne': Abraham Cowley (1618–67) and John Donne (1572–1631) were English metaphysical poets.

**Frank Moore Colby**

p. 140, col. 1, l. 2: 'an essay on women': 'George Sand: The New Life' (1902).

p. 140, col. 1, l. 23: 'George Sand': pen name of Amandine Aurore Lucile Dupin (1804–76), successful French novelist whose lifestyle was considered scandalous.

p. 140, col. 1, l. 28: 'Augustus the Strong': King of Poland and Elector of Saxony (1670–1733). He was said to have sired 365 children.

p. 140, col. 2, l. 38: 'Mme. Karénine': Anna Karenina, adulterous heroine of Tolstoy's famous novel (1877).

**Mrs Humphrey Ward**

p. 145, ll. 2–3: 'the love-story of Chateaubriand … Beaumont': François-René, Vicomte de Chateaubriand (1768–1848) was a French Romantic writer and diplomat who had a love affair with Pauline de Beaumont.

p. 145, l. 4: 'Eleanor': *Eleanor* was published in 1900.

p. 146, l. 1: '*villegiatura*': country residence during the summer holidays (Italian).

p. 146, l. 28: 'Knossos': famous Bronze age site on Crete.

p. 146, l. 29: 'Barberini bees': The Barberini were a powerful Italian family whose crest consisted of three bees.

p. 146, l. 32: 'Domitian': Roman Emperor (AD 51–96).

p. 147, l. 30 'Risorgimento': term used to describe the gradual unification of Italy in the nineteenth century.

p. 147, l. 30: '*connaissances*': learning, attainments (French).

p. 148, l. 17: 'F. T. Palgrave': Francis Turner Palgrave (1824–97), best known as editor of the *Golden Treasury* (1861), a hugely popular anthology of English poems.

p. 148, l. 18: 'Pindar': Greek fifth-century lyric poet, famous for his Odes.

p. 149, l. 23: 'daughter D---': Dorothy.

p. 150, ll. 5–6: 'un dolce come si deve': a pudding as it should be (Italian).

p. 150, l. 18: 'Diana Nemorensis': 'Diana of the Nemi' or 'Diana of the Grove' (Latin). The site was excavated in 1885.

p. 150, l. 19: '*fattoria*': site office (Italian).

p. 150, l. 28: 'ex-votos': votive offerings made to a deity.

p. 150, l. 29: '*fragole*': strawberries (Italian).

p. 150, l. 32: 'Lord Savile': the English Ambassador at Rome who undertook these excavations.

p. 151, l. 21: '*flânerie*': sauntering aimlessly, idling (French).

p. 151, l. 33: 'crypto-porticus': a concealed or enclosed portico.

p. 152, l. 8: 'Stocks': Mrs Humphrey Ward's large country house near Aldbury in Hertfordshire.

p. 152, l. 23: '*beau geste*': a gracious gesture (French).

p. 154, ll. 11–24: 'A mortal … and were glad': the quotations are from Matthew Arnold's 'The Youth of Nature', a poem on the death of Wordsworth.

p. 154, l. 28: 'old Laertes': Laertes is described working in rags on his farm, sure that his son Odysseus is dead, in Book 24 of Homer's *Odyssey*.

p. 154, l. 30: 'Olive Chancellor': a central character from *The Bostonians* (1886).

p. 154, l. 31: 'Madame Mauve': 'Madame de Mauves', a short story published in 1874.

p. 155, l. 2: 'St. George': Henry St George is a character in 'The Lesson of the Master' (1888).

p. 155, l. 4: 'Brooksmith': a tale written in 1891.

p. 155, ll. 11–12: '"Ann Veronica" and the "New Machiavelli"': *Ann Veronica* (1909), a novel by H. G. Wells which features an unusually feminist heroine; *The New Machiavelli* (1911) is a semi-autobiographical novel by Wells whose central character flouts society when he leaves his wife for another woman.

p. 155, l. 30: 'Tolstoy': Leo Tolstoy (1828–1910), great Russian novelist, author of *Anna Karenina* and *War and Peace* (1865–9).

p. 156, l. 21: 'The Ambassador': *The Ambassadors* (1903).

p. 156, l. 34: '*rive gauche*': the 'Left Bank', region of Paris on the southern bank of the Seine, an area associated with artists (French).

p. 157, l. 3: 'Daubigny': Charles-François Daubigny (1817–78), French painter, a precursor of impressionism.

p. 157, ll. 19–20: 'Cartmel Chapel … Levens': Cartmel and Levens are both small villages in Cumbria.

**Compton Mackenzie**

p. 163, ll. 9–10: 'Saraste … Thomas Hughes': Pablo de Saraste (1844–1908), a Spanish violinist and composer; Sir Charles Hallé (1819–95), the German-English conductor and pianist; Wilson Barrett, (1846–1904), English actor and playwright; William Gorman Wills (1828–91), a playwright; Thomas Hughes (1822–96), writer best known for *Tom Brown's Schooldays* (1857).

p. 165, ll. 17–18: 'Tennyson … *Queen Mary*': Alfred, Lord Tennyson (1809–92), Poet Laureate from 1850 and best known for *In Memoriam* (1850). His poetic drama, *Queen Mary*, was published in 1875.

p. 165, l. 24: '*The School for Scandal*': highly popular comedy by Richard Brinsley Sheridan (1751–1816).

p. 166, l. 11: 'Melpomene and Thalia': the Muses of Tragedy and Comedy.

p. 166, l. 20: 'Oscar': Oscar Wilde (1854–1900). His great success with *The Importance of Being Earnest* was cut short when he was arrested and charged with 'acts of gross indecency with other male persons'.

p. 166, l. 24: '*An Ideal Husband*': another successful comedy by Wilde, first performed in 1895.

p. 167, l. 5: 'William Heinemann': publisher (1863–1920).

p. 167, l. 7: '*The Passionate Elopement*': This novel was eventually published in 1911 by Martin Secker.

p. 167, l. 21: 'J. B. Pinker': James Brand Pinker (1863–1922) was a literary agent whose clients included Ford Madox Ford and Violet Hunt.

p. 167, l. 23: 'Mackenzie's "*Sinister Street*"': highly successful and well-regarded semi-autobiographical novel (1914).

p. 168, l. 29: 'Arnold Bennett's': Bennett (1867–1931), writer best known for his novels set in the Staffordshire 'Potteries' such as *The Old Wives' Tale* (1908) and *Clayhanger* (1910).

p. 170, l. 3: '*obiter dicta*': incidental remarks (Latin).

p. 170, l. 9: '*Carnival*': a novel (1912) based on Compton Mackenzie's experiences of the theatre world.

p. 171, ll. 9–10: '*Notes on Novelists*': volume of essays (1914) which includes assessments of Balzac, Flaubert and Sand as well as of young British novelists such as Mackenzie.

p. 171, l. 13: 'Y.Z.': Hugh Walpole.

## W. Graham Robertson

p. 175, l. 30: 'Marion Terry': actress (1852–1930), sister of Ellen Terry.

p. 175, l. 31: 'Miss Millard': Evelyn Millard (1869–1941) played the part of Mary Brasier.

## H. M. Walbrook

p. 181, l. 5: '*Pall Mall Gazette*': an evening newspaper founded in 1865.

p. 181, l. 21: 'lately plotted fireside': untraced.

p. 182, l. 25: 'Vedrenne-Barker': Harley Granville-Barker and John E. Vedrenne took over the Royal Court Theatre in Chelsea in 1904. They produced experimental and innovative works by playwrights such as Ibsen and Shaw.

p. 182, l. 39: 'Miss Horniman': Annie Horniman (1860–1937) was a theatre patron and manager.

p. 183, l. 5: '*Impressions and Opinions*': a collection of essays on art and literature published in 1891.

p. 183, l. 22: 'Sarcey': Francisque Sarcey (1827–99), French drama critic and journalist.

p. 183, l. 38: 'Coquelin': Benoît Constant Coquelin (1841–1909), a celebrated French comic actor.

p. 183, l. 39: 'Tartuffe and Cyrano de Bergerac': Tartuffe, a religious hypocrite, is the eponymous hero of one of Molière's most famous comedies (1664); Cyrano de Bergerac was a seventeenth-century French writer and the subject of a well-known play by Edmond Rostand (1897).

p. 183, l. 40: '*diseur*': reciter (French).

p. 183, l. 2: 'Henry Irving's': Sir Henry Irving (1838–1905), acclaimed actor and manager of the Lyceum.

p. 184, ll. 17–18: 'Miss Githa Sowerby's ... *and Son*': the play was first produced in 1912 and is the story of the tensions between a successful industrialist and his rebellious children.

**Hamlin Garland**

p. 189, l. 7: 'The Minister's Charge': novel by Howells published in 1887.

p. 190, l. 7: 'Rose of Dutcher's Coulée': normally 'Coolly', Garland's 1895 novel about a Midwestern farm girl who goes to college and becomes a writer.

p. 190, l. 22: 'cryptograms, or palimpsests': a cryptogram is a document written in cipher; a palimpsest is a manuscript which has been reused and overwritten by another text.

p. 193, l. 29: 'Wynchelsea': the correct spelling is Winchelsea.

p. 195, l. 12: 'Owen Wister's work': (1860–38), American writer of Western novels.

p. 195, l. 13: 'Valley of Decision': a two volume historical novel set in eighteenth-century Italy published in 1902.

p. 198, l. 18: 'Clemens': Samuel Langhorne Clemens (1835–1910), better known as Mark Twain, the popular and influential American writer whose works include *The Adventures of Huckleberry Finn* (1884).

p. 199, l. 8: 'young woman stenographer': As Garland visited HJ in 1906 this must have been a temporary secretary as Mary Weld had by then left her post and she was not replaced by Theodora Bosanquet until 1907.

**Ford Madox Ford**

p. 203, l. 14: 'Mr. H. M. Tomlinson': Henry Major Tomlinson (1873–1958) was a British writer and journalist.

p. 204, l. 30: 'Lady Help': This story seems to be a fantasy, although HJ certainly had problems with his servants. The sister of his housekeeper, Mrs Smith, worked for Alfred Austin, and the story related here also recollects the hiring of both Burgess Noakes and Mary Weld.

p. 208, l. 10: 'Southey': Robert Southey (1774–1843).

p. 208, l. 10: 'Bridges': Robert Bridges (1844–1930).

p. 208, l. 15: 'Swinburne': Algernon Charles Swinburne (1837–1909). Recurring themes in his poetry are sadomasochism and lesbianism so he might have been considered a curious choice for the Laureateship.

p. 208, l. 16: 'Mr. Alfred Austin': (1835–1913), appointed Poet Laureate in 1896.

p. 209, ll. 7–9: 'Sir Ponsonby ... Tintagel and Camelot': These are made up names.

p. 209, ll. 11–12: 'Methusaleh ... Mariner': Methusaleh is mentioned in Genesis – his name has become synonymous with great age; 'Mariner' is a reference to Samuel Taylor Coleridge's poem 'Rime of the Ancient Mariner' (1797).

p. 209, l. 13: 'the author of *Kubla Kahn*': poem by Coleridge published in 1816.

p. 211, l. 15: 'Mrs Wicks': in fact Mrs Wix, the governess of Maisie in *What Maisie Knew* (1897).

p. 212, l. 22: '*The Real Thing*': famous 1893 tale of genteel but impoverished artist's models who represent the aristocracy much less successfully than professional working class models.

p. 213, l. 12: '*on trébuchait sur des vaches*': one stumbled over cows (French).

p. 213, l. 29: 'that lamentable song': untraced.

p. 214, l. 29: 'the beautiful Russian genius': Turgenev (see note to Gosse, p. 34, l. 21).

p. 215, l. 27: '*The Great Good Place*': a fantasy with homoerotic overtones about a mysterious retreat (1900).

p. 217, l. 10: 'D. H. Lawrence': David Herbert Lawrence (1885–1930), novelist and poet famous for the sexual frankness of novels such as *Lady Chatterley's Lover* (1928). HJ did not admire his works.

p. 217, l. 11: 'Rabelais': François Rabelais (1493–1553), French writer best known for *Gargantua* and *Pantagruel*, and noted for his bawdy and scatological humour.

p. 217, l. 18: 'queer tiny being': Jonathan Sturges, an American journalist and great friend of HJ who had been crippled by polio as a child.

p. 27, ll. 31–2: 'fumbling in placket-holes as Sterne calls it': A placket-hole is an opening in an outer skirt which gives access to an inner pocket. There are several bawdy references to placket-holes in *Tristram Shandy*, the best known work of Lawrence Sterne (1713–68).

p. 218, ll. 15–16: 'Mr. Beale Farange or Mrs. Beale': the parents of Maisie.

p. 221, l. 8: 'Prince Fortunatus': in Straparola's story collection *Nights* (1550–3), a fairy tale prince who possessed an inexhaustible purse.

p. 221, ll. 10–11: '*La Maison Tellier* ... *Le Horla*': *La Maison Tellier* was a collection of tales published in 1881; *Ce Cochon de Morin*, a tale published in 1882; *Le Horla* (1887) is a striking horror story.

p. 221, l. 14: 'the lunatic asylum': Maupassant was declared insane in 1891. His mental instability may have been caused by syphilis.

p. 222, l. 1: '*de*': 'of' in French. Like the German 'von', 'de' before a French surname denotes noble birth.

p. 222, l. 8: '*a femme du monde*': a society lady (French).

p. 223, l. 17: 'the Marquis of Salisbury': the 3rd Marquis (1830–1903), Prime Minister from 1885–6, 1886–92 and 1895–1902.

p. 223, l. 17: 'Sir Charles Dilke': writer and politician (1843–1911).

p. 223, l. 20: '*grande monde*': high society.

p. 223, l. 28: 'two great passions': the cousin Ford refers to here is Minnie Temple who died in 1870 aged twenty-four. Ford overstates HJ's relationship with Minnie – there was no engagement although she was undeniably an important influence in his life and on his work. Simon Nowell-Smith suggests that the second passion Ford mentions is in fact for the Tragic Muse rather than a real individual (Nowell-Smith, pp. xxxii–iii).

## A. G. Bradley

p. 232, col. 1, ll. 12–13: 'a lad about five feet high': Burgess Noakes, who entered HJ's service as a houseboy soon after he moved to Rye and stayed in his employment until HJ's death.

## Ella Hepworth Dixon

p. 235, l. 4: 'the house of Rothschild': a reference to the famous German banking family.

p. 235, l. 10: '*An Altar of Friendship*': she is probably referring to 'The Altar of the Dead' (1895).

p. 235, l. 27: 'Sir Claude Phillips': (1846–1924), an art critic and museum curator.

p. 236, l. 27: 'Mrs Hodgson Burnett': Frances Hodgson Burnett (1849–1924), writer now best known for her children's novel, *The Secret Garden* (1911).

p. 237, l. 6: 'Boston (or was it New York?)': It was New York.

p. 237, ll. 10–11: 'autumnal leaves … Vallombrosa': a quotation from Milton's *Paradise Lost*, I.302–3.

## Matilda Betham-Edwards

p. 239, l. 13: '*Lord of the Harvest*': This novel, set in Suffolk, was first published in 1899.

p. 241, l. 3: 'the Conqueror's castle': Hastings Castle, built around 1067.

p. 242, l. 4: 'Eliot': John Eliot (1592–1632), English statesman.

p. 242, l. 5: 'Buckingham': George Villiers, 1st Duke of Buckingham (1592–1628) was the favourite of both James I and Charles I. He was assassinated.

p. 242, l. 5: 'Sejanus': Sejanus (20 BC–AD 31), an ambitious soldier who was executed after he tried to seize power from the Emperor Tiberius.

p. 242, l. 11: 'Sir Sidney Lee's … *Biography*': Lee (1859–1926) was the second editor of the *Dictionary of National Biography*.

p. 242, ll. 27–8: 'Sarah Bernhardt's ... Jeanne d'Arc': Bernhardt (1844–1923), the famous actress, acted in Barbier's *Jeanne d'Arc* in 1898.

p. 243, l. 10: *'Three Meetings'*: The title is in fact 'Four Meetings', an 1877 tale of an American spinster's thwarted longing to visit Europe.

p. 243, l. 20: *'The Better Sort'*: a collection of tales published in 1903.

p. 246, l. 14: 'Miss Broughton': Rhoda Broughton (1840–1920), writer whose lively early novels were considered scandalous.

p. 247, l. 15: 'Hale White': William Hale White (1831–1913), writer best known for *The Autobiography of Mark Rutherford* (1881).

## Alice Boughton

p. 251, l. 13: *'The Amazing Marriage'*: novel by George Meredith published in 1895.

p. 251, l. 23: 'Arthur Davies': American painter (1862–1928).

p. 252, l. 13: 'Daumier': Honoré Daumier (1808–79), French caricaturist and painter.

p. 252, l. 16: 'an article about him for Harper's': This piece was later included in HJ's collection of notes on painters, *Picture and Text* (1893).

## Sir Hugh Walpole

p. 261, l. 2: 'St. John Ervine': (1883–1971), a Belfast-born playwright and novelist.

p. 261, l. 12: 'Blake presences in *The Book of Job*': Blake illustrated *The Book of Job* between 1823 and 1826.

p. 262, l. 8: 'Colvin, Hewlitt': Sir Sidney Colvin (1845–1927), scholar and museum curator. HJ was friendly with Colvin and his wife – it was Lady Colvin who introduced HJ to Jocelyn Persse. Maurice Hewlett (misspelled Hewlitt here by Walpole) (1861–1923), novelist and poet.

p. 262, l. 26: 'John Silver': Long John Silver is the appealingly villainous pirate from R. L. Stevenson's *Treasure Island* (1883).

p. 262, l. 35: 'Robbie Ross ... Clutton Brock': Robert Baldwin Ross (1869–1918), a journalist best known as the loyal friend of Oscar Wilde; Sir Henry Maximilian Beerbohm (1872–1956), the famous caricaturist and writer; Arthur Clutton Brock (1868–1924), essayist and journalist.

p. 263, l. 4: 'Sturgis': Howard Sturgis (1855–1920), American novelist. He was upset when HJ, a friend of his, criticised his novel, *Belchamber* (1904).

p. 263, l. 35: 'Jocelyn Persse': (1873–1943), a handsome and amiable Irishman. HJ, who met Persse in 1903, loved him deeply.

p. 263, l. 35: 'Mrs Prothero': Frances Prothero and her husband George, a historian, became good friends of HJ after he moved to Rye.

p. 264, l. 17: 'Ethan Frome': published in 1911, *Ethan Frome* is a grimmer and more stark tale than most of Wharton's works.

p. 264, l. 22: 'E. M. Forster': Edward Morgan Forster (1879–1970), novelist, short story writer and essayist.

p. 265, ll. 34–5: 'a small privately-printed book': *Extracts from a Diary* was privately printed in 1934.

## Muriel Draper

p. 274, l. 12: 'The Irish angel': a maid.

p. 274, l. 28: 'buttons': This story recalls HJ's own childhood memories of being teased by Thackeray for wearing a jacket with very conspicuous buttons (see Introduction, p. xx).

p. 276, l. 22: 'Thibaud, Casals … Sczymanowski': Jacques Thibaud (1880–1953), French violinist; Pablo Casals (1876–1973), Spanish cellist; Arthur Rubinstein (1887–1982), Polish-born American pianist; Paul Kochanski (1887–1934), Polish violinist.

p. 278, l. 4: 'Bauer': Harold Bauer (1873–1951), pianist who originally trained as a violinist.

p. 278, l. 5: 'Mr. Edith': Draper is referring to the husband of an acquaintance called Edith whose name she has forgotten.

p. 278, ll. 7–8: 'one of the Goossens boys': a family of musicians of Belgian extraction. The horn player was probably Adolph.

p. 278, l. 9: 'Rubio': Augustin Rubio (1856–1940), cellist.

p. 278, l. 10: 'Watson': Victor Watson was a double bass player.

p. 279, l. 4: 'Mme. Suggia': Guilhermina Suggia (1888–1950), a Portuguese cellist with whom Casals had a liaison.

p. 279, l. 6: 'Susan Metcalf': an American singer. Metcalf and Casals separated in 1928.

p. 279, l. 14: 'Montague Vert Chester': an impresario.

p. 280, l. 5: 'Kien Lung': an eighteenth-century Emperor of China.

## Witter Bynner

p. 285, col. 1, l. 17: 'the Player's Club': founded in 1888 by the Shakespearean actor Edwin Booth and modeled on the Garrick Club.

p. 285, col. 1, l. 21: 'the Garrick Club': named after the actor David Garrick, this London club was founded in 1831.

p. 285, col.1, l. 36: 'the Bateman sisters': child actresses who performed in a number of Shakespeare productions.

p. 285, col. 2, l. 1: 'the Florences': Mr and Mrs William James Florence were a popular husband and wife acting partnership active in the mid-nineteenth century.

p. 285, col. 2, l. 3: 'Maggie Mitchell': (1832–1918), a successful comic actress.

p. 287, col. 1, l. 3: 'Henry Harland': (1861–1905), a novelist and the editor of the influential *Yellow Book*.

p. 287, col. 2, l. 29: 'Parsifal': an opera by Wagner, first performed in 1882.

**Preston Lockwood**

p. 290, col. 4, ll. 36–7: 'Derwent Wood's': (1871–1926), British sculptor.

p. 291, col. 1, l. 25: 'plasphemy': misprint for blasphemy.

p. 292 , ll. 34–5: 'They also serve who only stand and wait': the last line of Milton's poem 'On His Blindness'.

**Daily Telegraph**

p. 295, col. 1, l. 30: 'J. M. Whistler': James Abbott McNeill Whistler (1834–1903), an American born painter who, like HJ, spent most of his life in Britain.

p. 296, col. 1, l. 15: 'Hogarth': William Hogarth (1697–1764), painter and engraver noted for his satirical sequences such as *A Rake's Progress* (1735).

p. 296, col. 1, l. 21: 'Bailey Aldrich': Thomas Bailey Aldrich (1836–1907), an American poet and novelist.

p. 296, col. 2, l. 23: 'Rupert Brooke': a reference to Brooke's *Letters from America* (1916).

**The Times**

p. 299, col. 1, l. 9: 'John Glas': (1695–1773), Scottish Minister who founded the Glasite sect. The movement was developed in America by Robert Sandeman (1718–71).

p. 299, col. 2, l. 42: 'the gross rattle of the foreground': This expression is used by the narrator of HJ's tale 'The Beldonald Holbein' (1901).

**Daily Mail**

p. 301, col. 2, l. 8: 'Kipps': H. G. Wells's popular comic novel *Kipps* (1905) is the story of a young draper's assistant who receives an unexpected legacy.